A Life in Words

A LIFE IN WORDS

Paul Auster

conversations with

I. B. SIEGUMFELDT

Seven Stories Press
New York • Oakland

A Seven Stories Press First Edition

Seven Stories Press
140 Watts Street
New York, NY 10013
www.sevenstories.com

College professors and middle and high school teachers may order free examination copies of Seven Stories Press titles. To order, visit http://www.sevenstories.com/textbook or send a fax on school letterhead to (212) 226-1411.

Book design by Jon Gilbert

Library of Congress Cataloging-in-Publication Data

Names: Auster, Paul, 1947- author. | Siegumfeldt, I. B., author.
Title: A life in words : conversations with I. B. Siegumfeldt / Paul Auster.
Description: New York : Seven Stories Press, 2016. | Includes bibliographical
    references and index.
Identifiers: LCCN 2016012603 (print) | LCCN 2016026781 (ebook) | ISBN
    9781609807108 (paperback) | ISBN 9781609807115 (e-book)
Subjects: LCSH: Auster, Paul, 1947---Interviews. | Auster, Paul,
    1947---Criticism and interpretation. | Siegumfeldt, I. B.--Interviews. |
    Authors, American--20th century--Interviews. | BISAC: BIOGRAPHY &
    AUTOBIOGRAPHY / Literary. | LITERARY CRITICISM / Books & Reading. |
    LITERARY COLLECTIONS / American / General.
Classification: LCC PS3551.U77 Z46 2016 (print) | LCC PS3551.U77 (ebook) |
    DDC 818/.54 [B] --dc23
LC record available at https://lccn.loc.gov/2016012603

Printed in the United States

9 8 7 6 5 4 3 2 1

Transcription: Jesper Præst Nielsen

TABLE OF CONTENTS

PREFACE

"No one can say where a book comes from, least of all the person who writes it." This line was written twenty-five years ago and appeared in Paul Auster's seventh novel, *Leviathan*. He insists that it still holds true. But, as always with Auster, there is more than one truth. In this dialogue, we pursue the beginnings, the birth, and the life of Auster's novels and autobiographical works—books that have entranced and challenged millions of readers across the world in more than forty languages.

Auster is one of the most widely read contemporary writers. He first made his mark on the literary scene in the 1970s as a poet. In order to finance his writing, he worked as an essayist and a translator, but in 1979 he began to concentrate on narrative prose, and with the publication of the innovative memoir *The Invention of Solitude* and the ingenious novels of *The New York Trilogy* in the mid-eighties, a space on the international literary scene was irrevocably cleared for this master of stories and purveyor of the intricate workings of their telling. Then, in the 1990s, he explored a lifelong passion for film: he wrote and codirected two movies with Wayne Wang, *Smoke* and *Blue in the Face*, wrote and directed *Lulu on the Bridge*, and followed up with *The Inner Life of Martin Frost* in 2007.

Today, the body of his narrative prose includes sixteen novels (now seventeen, with the publication of *4 3 2 1*) and five autobiographical books. In one way or another, they all bear the imprint of these other artistic activities. Auster's poems have been described as "brittle as broken glass . . . [they] imbed themselves in the reader's flesh."* This penchant for transparency and brokenness runs as a lyrical subcur-

---

* Norman Finkelstein, "In the Realm of the Naked Eye: The Poetry of Paul Auster," in *Beyond the Red Notebook: Essays on Paul Auster*, ed. Dennis Barone (Philadelphia: University of Pennsylvania Press, 1995), 45.

rent through almost all his work. It has frequently set a certain tone and inspired an array of recurring themes, which we pursue in these conversations. Movies play an important role in Auster's plots, especially in *The Book of Illusions* and *Man in the Dark*, and different angles on objects and characters seen through the camera lens are folded into the writing. Translations are sometimes part of the texture of his novels, for instance, in *Invisible*—and the voice of the critic everywhere accompanies Auster's stories, commenting on the processes and mechanisms of writing.

More than forty scholarly books have been written about Auster's work. There are a handful of very fine studies among them, but others are saturated with attempts to squeeze this multiform body of writing into predefined categories. However, as our conversations show, every one of Auster's books is a journey down an unknown road for him—and for the reader. "The music of each book is different from the music of every other book," he says in our conversation on *Sunset Park*, and his principal concern, his constant struggle, is always to find the right way to tell a particular story. He is regularly on the brink of failure—or so he feels—and is truly humble in the face of his own doubts. "I'm really stumbling," he says in our conversation on *The Invention of Solitude*. "I'm really in the dark. I *don't know*." This is what reviewers and critics often fail to understand about Auster's work.

I first met Paul Auster when he kindly accepted my invitation to visit our PhD program, TRAMS, at the University of Copenhagen in May 2011. Later the same day, I interviewed Auster at the official ceremony when he received the university's honorary degree.* During the break, I talked to him about the need for a strong close reading of his work that is sensitive to the quality of the writing and faithful to the words on the page. A basis for further talks was evidently formed, for when, a few months later, I suggested that we undertake this project together, he agreed. "Maybe it's time to speak," he said, and we embarked on what was to become a grand three-year journey

---

* See webcast of the ceremony at http://hum.ku.dk/auster/.

through Auster's twenty-one narrative books, one by one, from a wide range of perspectives.

And so, for the first time, Auster enters into an extended dialogue about his work. Here, he provides background material, most of which is not publicly known, facts about how the stories took form, and discussions of key themes that run through the entire body of his work. We compare and contrast movements across more than thirty years of writing, and in the process, we arrive at new and often surprising insights that, one hopes, will spawn new avenues in future readings of Auster's books.

Auster had reservations about our project. He was reluctant to engage in intellectual discussions about writings that "come out of the unconscious rather than as the result of reflection" (conversation on *Moon Palace*). He was also uneasy about repeating information: "I've said this before. I can't remember where," he would sometimes remark. I was more concerned with questions of how to cover no fewer than nineteen books and two forthcoming manuscripts.[*] Especially if one is attempting to do this in collaboration with the writer: Paul Auster, known to be distrustful of reviewers and reserved with critics. A writer, moreover, who in one of our first discussions of the project remarks with some frustration: "A writer can't analyze his own work!" Would it be possible to bring together the author's inside point of view with the reader's outside perspective in a meaningful way?

The collaboration between author and critic is itself an interesting feature. Auster does not preside over his work as an omniscient originator or master of meaning. He is more interested in inquiry than in certainty and has no unequivocal truths to offer: In short, he was genuinely invested in the open exchange of our dialogues—and as his interlocutor I felt greatly privileged.

The book is divided into two parts.

---

[*] The conversations took place from November 2011 to November 2013. *Winter Journal* and *Report from the Interior* were discussed in their manuscript form.

PART ONE

As Auster explains in the prologue, it is important to him that a clear distinction be made between fiction and narratives that invoke his own remembered experiences. In part one the dialogue focuses on the texts that draw upon his life. Our talks about these five very dissimilar books provide much biographical information about the person "Paul Auster," but they cannot be used as keys to decipher the author "Paul Auster"—nor indeed his writings. As I see it, they add another, perhaps a more descriptive, layer to the body of his texts, subjective and molded by a memory that plays a central role in what Auster calls the "unbroken narrative within ourselves about who we are" (in the conversation on *The Invention of Solitude*). The author, here, is much like a character—no more "real," perhaps, no more extraordinary and possibly no more in command of the text than the imaginary narrators of his novels. And so, even if the five books in part one turn on memoir, it does not mean that they have primacy or authority over the fictional narratives. In fact, we could argue that the narration of self is inevitably as apocryphal as that of invented texts.

Placing the autobiographical books together in chronological order, as we have done here, allows us to look at the shifts and development over more than three decades of self-narration. *The Invention of Solitude* is the first extended narrative in Auster's transition from poetry to prose, with its description of his father, Samuel Auster, in "Portrait of an Invisible Man," paired with the strange ensemble of voices of poets and other artists who have had a formative effect on the autobiographical figure of A. in "The Book of Memory." *The Invention of Solitude* broke new ground on the literary scene and serves as a kind of gene pool of ideas on language, memory, representation, and the ongoing formation of the self for Auster's entire body of prose. The autobiographical element in *The Red Notebook* (1995) concerns not the writer as much as the nature of his writings. It serves as an ars poetica of storytelling without theory and relates a series of true tales about the kind of magic coincidence that informs what Auster calls "the mechanics of reality." An equally straightforward text, *Hand to*

Mouth (1997), focuses on the trials and tribulations of "the artist as a young man" struggling to keep his head above water and support his family. The two recent autobiographical books, *Winter Journal* (2012) and *Report from the Interior* (2013), take a different turn altogether. They set out to explore the history, in the former, of the things that have marked, altered, nourished, or sheltered the author's physical self, and, in the latter, the landmarks in the development of how he has understood the world around him. They are, Auster says, about "all the things that go into making a person" (in the conversation on *Winter Journal*). Both of these recent autobiographical books approach their subject through a consistent second-person perspective, which allows the author to look at himself from a point of view *in between* the closeness of the first person and the distance of the third person. It has the most unusual effect of giving the reader an impression of being taken into the narrator's confidence, of being almost directly addressed by the author—and then not.

PART TWO

The sixteen novels form a large organic body of fiction informed by Auster's explorations of the relationship between the world and the word, which often break with literary convention and scout out new paths of representation. Here, as elsewhere, his work is consistently determined by a loyalty to his material and a curiosity that often leads into unexplored territory, thus producing, in each instance, a different kind of story. At the same time, the texts intersect through recurring themes that run across the entire oeuvre. There is fable and myth, realism, comedy, metafiction, The books sometimes draw on elements from an array of modes and genres: memoir, fairy tale, dystopian writing, parallel or alternative history, the detective novel, trauma narrative, geronto literature, bildungsroman, poetry. Parts of novels are written as collages combining film script, newspaper clippings, interpretation or translation of texts by other writers, film analysis, stage directions, footnotes, lyrical monologues. The books often actively interact with one another through allusion, echoes, direct reference, and auto-intertextual characters, thus forming a dense web of entangled themes, places, movements, concerns, and unresolved problems.

Our conversations are structured around a set of eleven principal themes that inform the body of Auster's writing. The themes were carefully identified partly with the help of Auster's wife, the novelist and scholar Siri Hustvedt, pursued where relevant, and honed in the dialogue.

Language and the Body
The Word and the World
White Spaces
Ambiguity
Divestment
Enclosure
Abandoned Objects
Narrative Perspective
Male Pairs
America
Jewish Experience

An array of crucial but less prominent themes in the conversations include film, politics, baseball, the city, walking, silence, memory, and the gradual rounding of female characters.

This dialogue, with its abundance of new material, thematically and chronologically ordered, may spawn a series of new questions about Auster's work and about literature in general and the processes of writing and reading. Let me close this preface by thanking Paul Auster for his generosity and his patience with all my pertinent and impertinent questions. He listened to my assumptions and presumptions, my readings and misreadings of his work, sitting there in Brooklyn at the red table every morning at ten, prepared to enter the dialogue. For this I am truly grateful.

IBS, Copenhagen, November 2016

PROLOGUE
Clearing the Air

IBS: In your last novel, *Sunset Park*, one of your characters, Morris Heller, notes in his diary: "Writers should never talk to journalists. The interview is a debased literary form that serves no purpose except to simplify that which should never be simplified" (271). If you agree with Heller's remarks—and there's no reason to think that you don't—why would you agree to enter into a conversation that will, at least to some extent, take the form of an interview?

PA: Heller was referring to the short, superficial interviews writers get roped into doing to accommodate their publishers—with newspapers and magazines, with radio, television, and the Internet: the so-called popular media. These talks are inevitably connected to commerce, to the promotion of books. Thankfully, you aren't a journalist. You're a serious reader, a professor of literature, and when you proposed doing this project together, which you described as a "biography of my work," I was intrigued. Hesitant, too, of course, but intrigued.

IBS: Why hesitant?

PA: An inborn reticence, I suppose. Along with the fact that I don't feel qualified to talk about my own work. I'm utterly incapable of discussing it with any critical intelligence. People ask *Why*, and I can never answer them. *How* can also be very problematical.

IBS: And yet here you are, starting to talk to me.

PA: Yes, because you agreed to confine the conversations to *What*, *When*, and *Where*. I hope it will be possible to address those kinds of questions. And, in trying to answer them, maybe some good things will happen, maybe I'll discover some interesting things along the way.

IBS: You also said that you saw this project as an opportunity to "clear the air."

PA: For a couple of reasons. First, because I've stumbled across some remarkable misunderstandings of my books, errors so egregious that I feel they should be corrected. I'm not talking about matters of taste or interpretation, but simple facts. A fair amount of scholarly work has been published about my writing, about forty books or so along with a wagonload of articles. Some of these books are sent to me. I don't read them. I take a quick peek inside, then shut the book and put it on a shelf. Two or three years ago, however, I was taking my little peek at a book that had just arrived and fell upon the altogether baffling assertion that all my autobiographical works—*The Invention of Solitude*, *The Red Notebook*, and *Hand to Mouth**—were in fact works of fiction, made-up books, pseudo novels. I was astonished to read this—and saddened as well. So much spiritual labor went into exploring those remembered experiences, I worked so hard to be honest in what I wrote, and to see all that turned into some kind of clever, postmodern game perplexed me. How could anyone be so wrong? So I want to go on record, once and for all, and declare that my novels are fiction and my autobiographical writings are nonfiction. Just for starters.

IBS: And the other reason?

PA: To disentangle the twisted notions about my supposed influence on Siri's work.** Various misconceptions have been circulating for a long time—both in print and on the Internet—that I intro-

---

* This conversation took place in autumn 2011 when *Winter Journal* was still in manuscript form. *Report from the Interior* was not started until 2012.
** Siri Hustvedt, Auster's wife.

duced her to Freud and psychoanalysis, that I taught her everything she knows about Lacan, that I initiated her into the theories of Bakhtin, and so on. All of it is untrue. When Siri's first novel came out, there was even one journalist who told her—*to her face*—that she couldn't possibly have written the book and therefore it must have been written by me. It would be hard to come up with a nastier insult than that one. Did this man have such a prejudice against women that he simply couldn't believe that a beautiful woman could also be an intelligent person and a gifted novelist? These are the facts: I'm eight years older than Siri, and when we started living together in 1981, she was only twenty-six, a poet and a graduate student hard at work on her PhD in English, and because she didn't finish her degree until 1986, and because her first novel wasn't published until 1992, I was already a known quantity when she arrived on the scene. It was too much for some people—two novelists in one household!—and so the rumor started that I was running some kind of literary factory in Brooklyn. Utter nonsense. Siri has one of the best minds I've ever encountered. She is the intellectual in the family, not me, and everything I know about Lacan and Bakhtin, for example, I learned directly from her. In fact, I've read only one short essay by Lacan, the "Purloined Letter" piece in the *Yale French Studies* issue on poststructuralism—all the way back in 1966. As for Freud and psychoanalysis, the whole thing makes me laugh. Siri has been reading Freud attentively since she was fifteen, and in May of this year* she was invited to give the thirty-ninth annual Sigmund Freud Lecture at the Freud Foundation in Vienna. There has been only one person before her without a medical degree to be chosen, for goodness sake. Her book from 2009, *The Shaking Woman*, has made such a stir in the worlds of medicine, neuroscience, and psychiatry that the committee at the Freud Foundation was unanimous in wanting her for this year's talk.

---

* 2011.

IBS: Yes, I've heard her address a theater full of academics from different fields. She is extremely well read and very impressive. Clearing the air, is there anything else you'd like to add?

PA: No, I don't think so. I could go on, of course, but I've probably said enough.

IBS: Ready to start talking about your work?

PA: Yes, yes, fire away.

PART ONE
Autobiographical Writings

THE INVENTION OF SOLITUDE (1982)
"Everything Comes from Within and Moves Out"

The book he is writing has no meaning. (147)

IBS: *The Invention of Solitude* is a groundbreaking book that pushes straight through the boundaries of literary convention. You turn autobiographical material into two engaging narratives that explore ideas about memory, solitude, and ways of being in the world, which have been cornerstones in your work ever since. What prompted the writing of the first part, "Portrait of an Invisible Man"? Was it the death of your father?

PA: Yes, without question it was the death of my father, which, as you know, was unexpected and came as a shock to me. He was sixty-six or sixty-seven—I've never known exactly what year he was born—in any case, not an old man. He had been in good health all his life. He didn't drink, he didn't smoke. He played tennis every day. I always assumed he would live to be ninety and had given little or no thought to his potential death. Yet, there it was. It happened. And it caused a tremendous upheaval in my life. The frustration of having so much unfinished business with my father propelled me into wanting to write about him. Suddenly he was gone, suddenly I could no longer talk to him. All the questions I'd wanted to ask no longer could be asked. But you see, it's important to note that if he had died the year before, I might not have written "Portrait of an Invisible Man." At that time, I was still writing poetry, exclusively poetry, and had more or less given up the idea of writing prose. But then the poetry dried up, and I couldn't write anything. It was a miserable time for me. Then, as I've described in *Winter Journal*,* I went to that dance rehearsal, and something happened. A revela-

---

* This conversation took place in November 2011. *Winter Journal* came out in October 2012.

3

tion, a liberation, a fundamental something. I immediately plunged into writing *White Spaces*,* which I happened to finish the night my father died. I went to bed at two a.m., I remember, a Saturday night/Sunday morning, thinking how this piece, *White Spaces*, was the first step toward a new way of thinking about how to write. Then the phone rang early the next morning, just a few hours later. It was my uncle on the line telling me my father had died that night. That was the shock. Coinciding with the fact that I had returned to prose, that I felt it was *possible* for me to write in prose, finally, after so many years of struggling to write fiction, and then finally abandoning it.

IBS: What made it suddenly possible?

PA: The text I finished that night.

IBS: So, *White Spaces* marks a crucial transition in your career as a writer?

PA: It freed me from the constraints that had been blocking me for the past year or two. I had, in a sense, retaught myself how to write. I'd unlearned all the lessons of my education—which had been more of a burden than a help, I'm afraid.

IBS: Which education do you mean?

PA: I'm talking about my literary education. My studies at Columbia University and the intense scrutiny of texts you engage in as a student of literature. I'd come to such a point of self-consciousness that I somehow believed that every novel had to be completely worked out in advance, that every syllable had to give off some kind of philosophical or literary echo, that a novel was a great machine of thought and emotion that could be analyzed down to the phonemes in every sentence. It was too much. I hadn't realized that the unconscious

---

* Written in 1978–1979, published in 1980.

plays such a large part in the making of stories. I hadn't yet grasped the importance of spontaneity and sudden inspirations. It took me a very long time to learn that a lack of understanding about what you are doing can be just as useful as knowing what you are doing. *White Spaces*, however good or bad the piece might be, was an important step for me. I was ready to let my writing take new forms, and, in a sense, my father's death was the excuse to go ahead. "Portrait of an Invisible Man" was written feverishly. He died in mid-January 1979, and, I would say, by early February I had started writing the book. It's not a long text, and it took me only two months to finish it. Later, stupidly, I decided to expand it and write it in a more traditional way, but then I scrapped that longer version and went back to the original. It was clearly prompted by a combination of emotional distress, the need to say something about my father, and a very literal feeling that, if I didn't, he would vanish. At that moment, I was artistically ready to take it on. This is crucial.

IBS: What, then, motivated the second part, "The Book of Memory"?

PA: After I finished the first part, my life went through a number of other upheavals. My first marriage was essentially over by the end of 1978. Only six weeks later, my father died. Lydia* was very kind to me about it. We pulled together to get through that difficult period but stuck to the plan to separate, and by the spring I had moved into my grim little room on Varick Street in Manhattan. So much had happened to me in the intervening months that I wanted to write a chronicle of those disruptions. This then developed into "The Book of Memory."

IBS: "Portrait of an Invisible Man" and "The Book of Memory" are very different in terms of tone, style, structure, and perspective, but I think the contrasts only inform and enrich each of the texts. You told me earlier that originally you hadn't intended for them to be published together. What happened?

---

* Lydia Davis, Auster's wife from 1974 to 1979.

PA: I gave the first part to a poet friend of mine who had a minuscule publishing house. The plan was to put it out as a small book of about seventy-five or eighty pages. The problem was that he didn't have much money, and by the time he'd raised the funds to publish it, "The Book of Memory" was finished. Rather than produce two short books, it was financially sounder to do them both in a single volume. I then came up with the overall title, *The Invention of Solitude*. The book has a unity to it, even though it's two separate works, and, in retrospect, I'm glad it worked out that way. The two parts bounce off each other and seem to be stronger in tandem than they would have been alone.

I. "PORTRAIT OF AN INVISIBLE MAN":
THE SPECTRUM OF A HUMAN BEING

IBS: In "Portrait of an Invisible Man," you describe your father as fundamentally detached from the people closest to him. Paradoxically, it's precisely through this description that you bring into "presence" that which defined him most accurately, namely his absence.

PA: The strange thing about my father, as I say quite explicitly in the first half of the book, is that it was difficult for him to connect with the people he was most intimate with: his wife and his children. With other people it was different. For instance, if someone was stranded on a road in the middle of the night, that person would call my father because he knew he would come. He was also generous and sympathetic toward his poorer tenants and his nephew, my cousin, whom he took care of for many years. There was a lot of tenderness and a strong sense of responsibility in my father, even if it was difficult for him to express it to the people closest to him. Not so long ago, I received a letter from someone who had lived next door to him in the last years of his life. She wrote: "You have no idea how kind your father was to us when we moved in." She had one or two small children, and he would buy presents for them—snowsuits. I was very moved by this.

IBS: That's very strange.

PA: This was what I was trying to say in the book. *The mystifying forces of contradiction*: he was this, and he was that. You say one thing, and it's true, but the opposite is true as well. Human beings are imponderable, they can rarely be captured in words. If you open yourself up to all the different aspects of a person, you are usually left in a state of befuddlement.

IBS: There's a dynamic in this confusion, though, isn't there? I mean, isn't there an urge to try to piece the different aspects together?

PA: You make it sound as if I'd tried to create some kind of Frankenstein's monster [*laughs*]. No, I think the only metaphor I've used to talk about the range of selves within a single self is the idea of a *spectrum*. I believe that every human being is a spectrum. We live most of our lives in the middle, but there are moments when we fluctuate to the extremes, and we run that gamut from one shade of a color to another at different moments, depending on mood, age, and circumstance.

IBS: Yes, and the notion of a spectrum makes sense. Is there anything that holds the self together, do you think? A substratum of some sort?

PA: If there is, it would have to be self-consciousness.

IBS: I'm relieved you didn't say identity.

PA: Identity is what's in my passport. No, I don't even know what identity means in this context. I think a moment comes at around the age of about five or six when you have a thought and become capable of telling yourself, simultaneously, that you are thinking that thought. This doubling occurs when we begin to reflect on our own thinking. Once you can do that, you are able to tell the story of yourself to yourself. We all have a continuous, unbroken narrative within ourselves about who we are, and we go on telling it every day of our lives.

IBS: And it keeps changing.

PA: It changes, the story shifts. Of course, we're revising all the time. We tend, just as a matter of self-preservation, to leave out the worst. Oliver Sacks, the neurologist, worked with brain-damaged patients who had lost the ability to tell this story to themselves—Siri knows more about this than I do. The thread has been cut, and they don't have personalities anymore. They're no longer "selves" in the ordinary sense of the word. They're utterly fragmented beings. I think what pulls human beings together is this inner narrative. It's not "identity." I keep reading about the search for identity in my characters, but I have no idea what that means.

IBS: Yes, but there's almost always a search . . .

PA: But not for identity.

IBS: A search for understanding?

PA: Or just a way to live, a way of making life possible for oneself.

IBS: With the contradictions?

PA: Yes.

IBS: If the self is formed as a narrative, I suppose there's also an element of invention? We make up things to believe about ourselves.

PA: We do—and some of us are more deluded than others.

IBS: [*Laughs.*]

PA: Some people are able to tell a more or less truthful story about themselves. Others are fantasists. Their sense of who they are is so at odds with what the rest of the world feels about them that they become pathetic. You see it again and again in life: the aging woman who thinks she's still twenty years old and has no idea that she looks ridiculous in the eyes of others. Or the mediocre poet who thinks he's brilliant. It's painful to be with these people. Then, there's the other extreme, the people who diminish themselves in their own minds. They're often much greater people than they think they are, and, often, much admired by others. Still, they kill themselves inside. Almost by definition, the good are hard on themselves—and the less than good believe they're the best [*laughs*].

IBS: Could it be a kind of insecurity about himself that determined your father's reluctance to sign his name? It's a very striking scene in "Portrait of an Invisible Man":

> He could not simply put the pen against the paper and write [his signature]. As if unconsciously delaying the moment of truth, he would always make a slight, preliminary flourish, a circular movement an inch or two off the page, like a fly buzzing in the air and zeroing in on its spot, before he could get down to business. (30)

To me this is an image of someone so utterly detached from himself that it's disturbing even to commit to his own name.

PA: Actually, I find it rather humorous. There was a popular television show in America in the fifties called *The Honeymooners*, starring a comedian named Jackie Gleason and his sidekick, played by Art Carney, who would always loop his hand around in hilarious circles before he could write his signature. My father did something similar, though in a much more reduced way. I always found it endearing and strange.

IBS: I thought, perhaps, your description of this reluctance to commit his name to paper was another manifestation of the "invisibility" of the portraitee, you know, to link the title to the man, or vice versa, and—in more general terms—to provide a connection between name and character.

PA: Well, if there is such a connection, it's not one I consciously construct. Curiously, almost all the characters in my novels come to life with their names already attached to them. I can think of only one instance when I've changed the name of a protagonist. Jim Nashe, the hero of *The Music of Chance*, originally went by the old New England name of Coffin. I wrote the whole novel with Nashe as Coffin, then realized, when I was done, that even though I didn't intend it to be symbolic . . .

IBS: It would be read that way . . .

PA: It would be read that way, and so I decided to change it. That was the only time this happened. All my other characters have kept the names they were born with.

IBS: So, the connection between the characters' names and the role they play in the story is only rarely constructed? You're not flaunting the artificiality of the fiction and the fact that these characters are figments of your imagination?

PA: Every fictional character is a figment.

IBS: Exactly. Many readers, I imagine, will be wondering why you chose one name rather than another, especially when some of them appear so obviously to carry meaning.

PA: "No symbols where none intended," as Beckett wrote in *Watt*. I'm afraid it mostly comes out of the unconscious, out of the guts. The theater director Peter Brook once made a statement that impressed me enormously: "What I'm trying to do in my work," he said, "is to combine the closeness of the everyday with the distance of myth. Because, without the closeness, you can't be moved, and without the distance you can't be amazed." This is such a beautiful formulation. It's so succinct and to the point, and I suppose I respond to it because it expresses what I feel about art as well.

IBS: This duality plays very much into the relationship between the inner and outer dimensions of your portrait of the father, your father, in *The Invention of Solitude*, doesn't it?

PA: I hope so.

IBS: Toward the end of "Portrait of an Invisible Man" you say, "When I step into this silence, it will mean that my father has vanished forever" (65). Is this how it felt to you? I thought, perhaps, the purpose of writing about the dead was to keep them alive. Like memory, where, as you say, things happen for the second time. Is it that you can bring something back to life only in the process of writing about it? Then it vanishes?

PA: I didn't know what would happen, but I imagined it would be something like that. While I was working on the book, my father was very vivid to me, and the act of writing seemed to alleviate some of the shock and pain of his death. Yet, when the book was finished, it was as if I'd never written it. Everything was the same as before. Putting together the portrait didn't solve anything. Writing isn't therapy.

IBS: So it's the process of writing that matters, not the final result?

PA: Yes, because even as I was writing it, I kept trying to present all sides of my father simultaneously, and I was always heartened by the positive things I discovered about him. He did have very good qualities, after all, and I feel that if he'd grown up in different circumstances, his life would have turned out quite differently. He was deeply shaped by his environment. I mean, the immigrant story, the crazy mother, the murder of his father when he was a small boy, the constant dislocations of the family—it taught him to hide himself. So, one does feel sorry for him. I certainly do.

IBS: It must have been hard to be the son of somebody who kept himself so separate.

PA: I wrote that book more than half my life ago, and the fact is that I still think about my father all the time. As I wrote in *Winter Journal*, I also dream about him quite often. I have conversations with him in those dreams, and even if I can never remember what we talk about, the conversations are always friendly ones. I wish he'd lived long enough to see how well I've managed to take care of myself—after such a rocky start.

IBS: You'd have liked him to see your successes.

PA: Yes, of course.

IBS: What about your grandmother? You said she was crazy. She comes across as a very strong character with an iron grip on her four sons.

PA: She had four sons and a daughter. My aunt Esther, the oldest of the Auster children, was the mother of the nephew my father took under his wing. She had an unhappy life. Her mother, my grand-mother, was a ferocious woman.

IBS: Do you remember her?

PA: Vividly. According to family legend, she used to beat her sons over the head with a broom when she was angry at them.

IBS: Where was she from?

PA: Stanislaw, in what was then the Austro-Hungarian Empire. Galicia, which now finds itself in the western part of Ukraine, near Poland. I think she came to America when she was fourteen. She was an orphan. After she married my grandfather, they returned to Europe a number of times. The reality of immigration is much more complex than the myth. My uncle, the one just older than my father, was born in London, for example. When she was young, I believe my grandmother worked on the Lower East Side in a millinery factory—making hats. I don't know much about her family. Her name was Perlmutter, a common Jewish name. She was uneducated and never learned to speak English very well.

IBS: But she was not illiterate?

PA: No, she read the *Jewish Daily Forward* in Yiddish.

IBS: And spoke it, I assume?

PA: Yes. A funny thing happened a few years ago—a family thing. Siri and I went to the funeral of one of my first cousins. Another cousin was there, the oldest of the nine grandchildren, a woman whom I've always liked a lot, Jane Auster . . .

IBS: Jane Auster!

PA: Yes, my cousin Jane. Anyway, we were in the cemetery where most of my father's family is buried. We all walked over to our grand-mother's grave, and the outspoken, extremely humorous Jane looked down and said, "You know, I always hated you, Grandma. You were the worst person I've ever met. You were mean, and I was fright-ened of you. And on top of that, you were the worst cook in the world. You couldn't make a decent meal if your life depended on it." Everyone started laughing in a great rush of relief and amusement. No, she was ferocious, my grandmother. I was frightened of her, too. I didn't feel any connection to her at all.

IBS: Her sons were also afraid of her, weren't they?

PA: And devoted to her.

IBS: Out of fear?

PA: No, because of the murder. They pulled together.

IBS: So, they all knew about it?

PA: One of my uncles was a witness. My aunt Esther must have been about eighteen at the time. Yes, they knew, they all knew. They just didn't tell anybody. They held their collective breath and never divulged the secret. Until that fluky incident, which I describe in *The Invention of Solitude*, when my cousin (the one who died recently) happened to sit next to a man on an airplane who started talking about Kenosha, Wisconsin. That was how the story finally came out.

IBS: The portrait of your father is exceptionally vivid, I think, because you manage to make his "absence" so very "present," as it were. Even so, the "I" speaker—you—insists on the necessity of recognizing "right from the start, that the essence of this project is failure" (20). Why failure?

PA: Because I don't feel you can fully capture anyone. It's something you try to do, but, as we said earlier, you can never crack the mystery of a human being. In a sense, all writing is failure. You know that Beckett phrase—to cite Beckett once more—"Fail again, fail better." Fail better, yes, that's what you do. You keep going—and try to "fail better."

IBS: Can you explain that to me? Why is the success of a piece of writing conditional on failure?

PA: Because you can never achieve what you hope to achieve. You can come close sometimes and others may appreciate your work, but you, the author, will always feel you've failed. You know you've done your best, but your best isn't good enough. Maybe that's why you keep writing. So you can fail a little better the next time.

IBS: These reflections on the processes and mechanisms of writing you weave into the narrative are another reason why "Portrait of an Invisible Man" is so good, I think. The substratum of meta-commentary engages the reader in ways traditional autobiographical texts do not. For instance, here:

> I have a sense of trying to go somewhere, as if I knew what I wanted to say, but the farther I go the more certain I am that the path toward my object does not exist. I have to invent the road with each step, and this means that I can never be sure of where I am. A feeling of moving around in circles, of perpetual back-tracking, of going off in many directions at once. And even if I do manage to make some progress, I am not at all convinced that it will take me to where I think I am going. Just because you wander in the desert, it does not mean there is a promised land. (32)

PA: With this book, I was finding my path as I went along. And this is reflected in the work itself. I've always been interested in exposing the inner workings of what I'm doing—or trying to do—because the process of thinking seems to me just as interesting as the results of that thinking.

IBS: This is one of the reasons people say your work is postmodern.

PA: I don't understand that.

IBS: Because conventionally, a work of art will present itself as a complete entity informed by its own beauty and truth, which is passed on to a more or less passive recipient.

PA: And we hide all our doubts!

IBS: Yes, because everybody pretends the story is real: author as well as reader.

PA: Well, I guess I'm interested in *not* pretending. But again, "postmodern" is a term I don't understand.

IBS: It's just a label.

PA: Yes, but you know, there's an arrogance to all this labeling, a self-assurance that I find to be distasteful, if not dishonest. I try to be humble in the face of my own confusions, and I don't want to elevate my doubts to some status they don't deserve. I'm really stumbling. I'm really in the dark. I *don't know*. And if that—what I would call honesty—qualifies as postmodern, then okay, but it's not as if I ever wanted to write a book that sounded like John Barth or Robert Coover.

IBS: No, no, I'm not implying that at all. I understand what you are saying about honesty. It's the backbone of your work, and it's what makes it evocative and stimulating. There's that wonderful line in the passage we have just read: "Just because you wander in the desert, it does not mean there is a promised land." Is this a comment on the process of writing in general, or is it specific to the composition of this particular portrait?

PA: No, it's a general statement. It doesn't apply just to writing but to any kind of human endeavor. You grope toward something. Scientists, too—they "wander in the desert" looking for a solution to a scientific problem. It doesn't mean they're going to find it. You need to be a little lost sometimes.

IBS: A journey toward something, but you don't know where it's going to end?

PA: You have no idea.

IBS: And no guiding principles?

PA: No, no. No method.

IBS: Well, one doesn't get the impression that you were "wandering in the desert" when you wrote *The Invention of Solitude*. It's usually regarded as an innovative and elegant undermining of the conventions of biography and autobiography. Given what you have said about the motivation for the book, I don't suppose you deliberately set out to renovate literary form and genre?

PA: No, well, how shall I put it . . . *The Invention of Solitude* was the product of the breakthroughs I'd made in my own thinking about how to make art, how to make writing. I understood that everything comes from within and moves out. It's never the reverse. Form doesn't precede content. The material itself will find its own form as you're working through it. And so, I didn't arrive at a solution before I started, I simply found it as I was writing. It seemed necessary to do it that way. It wasn't a desire to be different so much as to find a way to tell what I had to tell. Then, if it came out sounding different from the conventions of the genre, so be it.

IBS: "Portrait of an Invisible Man" introduces the theme we have called "Abandoned Things" to signify the importance attached to the remains of a dead person, which is so prominent in many of your books:

> Things are inert: they have meaning only in function of the life that makes use of them . . . And yet they say something to us, standing there not as objects but as remnants of thought, of consciousness, emblems of the solitude in which a man comes to make decisions about himself. (10–11)

In the Country of Last Things is literally set among abandoned things; in *City of Glass*, Stillman collects and renames broken items found in the gutter; there are husbands obsessively sorting through their deceased wives' closets; a father playing with the toys of his dead sons . . .

PA: In *The Book of Illusions*, yes.

IBS: Everywhere! Things that are broken or no longer have owners.

PA: Disconnected, yes. Lost objects. Also in *Sunset Park*: Miles taking photographs of abandoned objects. Bing's Hospital for Broken Things. It's true. So this is something that keeps recurring. And?

IBS: And why this penchant for the vacated or masterless? Where does it come from?

PA: I'm not sure. I think it's visceral. Certainly in *Portrait* it was about a direct emotional experience. My father came from the generation of men who wore neckties, and apparently he kept every tie he ever owned. When he died, there must have been a hundred of them in his closet. You are confronted by these ties, which are, in a sense, a miniature history of his life. What will you do with them? You have to throw them out or give them to charity, but who wants a tie that was made in 1943? It was so poignant. That was the only time I cried. I didn't cry when I heard the news of my father's death, and I didn't cry at the funeral. Nothing. But I teared up when I was carrying the ties out to the truck to give them away. I was clutching his one hundred ties. They were all that was left of him. So, my interest in these abandoned things, as you call them, didn't come out of thoughts or ideas about objects, it was simply the experience of these things in my own life. Maybe that's the origin of the theory about objects in movies I developed later on in *Man in the Dark*. The great film-makers are able to invest objects with human emotion and tell stories through them.

IBS: You do that in your writing.

PA: Well, not as well as some people. In my films, I've never figured out how to do it.

IBS: Think of the moment in *The Book of Illusions* where David Zimmer is sorting out the baseball cards . . .

PA: And the toys and the Lego . . .

IBS: That's one of the most moving scenes in the book. You can almost see the boys playing on the floor, even if they're hardly described at all. You have achieved precisely that effect: abandoned objects bring their absent owners to life, if only momentarily.

PA: Only to reinforce their absence. That's why it becomes tragic or, if not tragic, poignant.

IBS: So, they become doubly absent in that way.

PA: Yes.

IBS: Photos are very important in this connection, aren't they, because they evoke the absent person in two-dimensional visual flashes. This brings us to the trick photo in "Portrait of an Invisible Man," which so effectively epitomizes the father's lack of engagement with the world that one thinks it must have been invented to perfect the portrait: the uncanny dearth of presence, the lack of communication.

> [I]t is as if he has come there only to invoke himself, to bring himself back from the dead, as if, by multiplying himself, he had inadvertently made himself disappear. There are five of him there, and yet the nature of the trick photography denies the possibility of eye contact among the various selves. Each one is condemned to go on staring into space,

as if under the gaze of the others, but seeing nothing, never able to see anything. It is a picture of death, a portrait of an invisible man. (31)

PA: Have you seen the picture? It's right here on the wall.

IBS: I wasn't sure it was a real photo.

PA: Let me show you. [*He stands up and points to a photograph on the wall.*] It's fascinating how deeply indifferent we are to the family pictures of other people. They don't tell us anything. We don't care. But when it's our own family, they're bathed in significance, aren't they? It's very private for each person.

IBS: Because of the memories attached to them.

PA: Yes, and also the evidence they give of the fact that indeed, yes, your father actually once was a baby.

II. "THE BOOK OF MEMORY": LANGUAGE AND THE BODY

IBS: Of course, these mechanisms of retrieval through objects, whether in the form of words, photos, or memory, inform part two of *The Invention of Solitude*. In a sense, "The Book of Memory" is a collection of vignettes held together by the opening and the closing paragraphs—which are identical.

PA: Except for the first sentence and the last word. The opening says:

He lays out a piece of blank paper on the table before him and writes these words with his pen. It was. It will never be again.

And the book ends with this:

He finds a fresh sheet of paper. He lays it out on the table before him and writes these words with his pen.It was. It will never be again. Remember.

IBS: Memory becomes the overriding principle here. The writer recollects as he paces up and down inside his solitary study. Could we say that, in a sense, he fills this bare room with his moving body, just as he fills the empty sheet with words: thought, emotion, images moving across the page? Just as in *White Spaces*, we are inside those square blank spaces that frame so much of your writing?

PA: I think that's true of this book and some other things I wrote later. Again, it came out unconsciously. I didn't have an overall plan for it. In fact, I didn't really know what I was doing. I tried to create a structure for the book, a musical rhythm for the little blocks of prose that kept doubling back on one another. Repeat, and then move forward, so that the reader would never forget that we're still in that moment. It was a difficult thing to do. I remember making a chart, which was later published somewhere.* There was a square with a room inside and little lines branching off into a kind of honeycomb of thoughts and ideas—a map of the book. I was already fairly deep into the writing when I sketched it, so it was part of the process rather than a preliminary plan, but it gave me a sense of where I was and how much more I had to do in order to cover everything I wanted to cover. As you can see, I was groping my way toward some kind of understanding. In a lot of the writing I have done since, the same dynamic is at work: enclosure and then wandering. Language, solitude, and movement are constantly referred to in this book. Being outside and moving through space, or being confined to a closed-in space. At the same time, there's a lot about sitting still inside a room and writing.

IBS: Or painting.

---

* Paul Auster and Michel Contat, "The Manuscript in the Book: Conversation," *Yale French Studies* 89 (1996): 160–187.

PA: Or painting. The writing or the painting takes the place of the movement through space. Then it becomes a mental journey.

IBS: So, you have inner movement, which is creative output, and outer movement, which is physical walking. In *White Spaces*, too, it's precisely that: enclosure, the movement of words and the movement of the body. Why is journey so important?

PA: I'm not sure I can explain it. Obviously, the act of writing forces you to sit still, but if you're spending every day of your life sitting in a room at a table with a piece of paper in front of you, it begins to affect you. You start to think about the environment and the machinery you use to explore the inner world and the outer world. It's the way the imagination can flourish—particularly under these very austere conditions: table, chair, page, pen, and a man or a woman sitting at that table.

IBS: One of the most prominent recurring themes in your work is no doubt language itself and its connection with the body. Here in "The Book of Memory," A. says:

> For no word can be written without first having been seen, and before it finds its way to the page it must first have been part of the body, a physical presence that one lives with in the same way one lives with one's heart, one's stomach, and one's brain. (138)

For me, these lines provide a link between *White Spaces* and *Winter Journal* . . .

PA: Maybe, maybe . . .

IBS: Because of your combination of linguistic and physical movement.

PA: Let's see, *White Spaces* was written in '78, *Winter Journal* in 2011, so there's a thirty-four-year gap between them. I'm writing about language and the body in both texts, even if the perspectives are different. And about winter. It's a big loop, isn't it? I never really thought about it. Then, toward the end of *Winter Journal*, I describe the origin of *White Spaces*. It's interesting. Maybe I should just quit now [*laughs*] because everything has come full circle.

IBS: [*Laughs*] Words, are they physical?

PA: Well, words are physical and then, of course, they're not. Physical just in the sense that you're writing them. That's a physical activity. You're scratching a sign onto a piece of paper, and there's the word. It's a physical object. Also, when we speak and articulate words with our voices, well, that's a physical activity, too. In this way, words have substance, even if they're abstractions. Signs.

IBS: Yes, of course you're right, there are different dimensions of language: abstract and concrete, meaning and form. Ideally, they should hang together or complement one another.

PA: Ideally, yes. But sometimes they're like the trick photo of my father: different aspects with no communication between them.

IBS: I was wondering whether your thoughts about different aspects of the self also played into the narrative perspective of *The Invention of Solitude*?

PA: I started "The Book of Memory" in the first person as a natural outcome of "Portrait of an Invisible Man." Then, after a while, I became dissatisfied with what I was doing. It felt wrong, and it took me a while to understand why. At some point in the middle of these confusions, I went to San Francisco to give a reading and stayed at a friend's house—Michael Palmer, the poet, the very, very good poet. I was down in the guest room of his house, tormenting myself: "What's

wrong with my book? Why don't I feel I'm doing it in the right way?"
That's when it suddenly came to me—I had to write about myself in
the third person. Once I did that, I was able to go full bore into the
project. It was an extremely complex book to write.

IBS: It's also a complex book to read. Especially the composition of
thirteen vignettes evoking famous writers and artists who were themselves working in solitary rooms, confined by choice or by force:
Anne Frank, Kierkegaard, Pascal, Hölderlin, Descartes, Leibniz, even
St. Augustine. How do they fit together?

PA: This is a book about a man alone in a room, namely myself.
What happens when you're alone is that you understand that you are
populated by others. You are inhabited by other people, and you exist
as an individual only because of your connection to others. I don't
just mean your family and friends. I also mean the people whose
work you have read. They are part of who you are. At a certain point,
I realized that this book about solitude had to be, in some sense,
a collective work. That's why I quote so freely from other writers,
because they're part of the inner conversations that are taking place
in the autobiographical figure of A. I'm talking to them, and they're
talking to me.

IBS: So there's an inner dialogue?

PA: It's a dialogue with other writers. They're all writers who've meant
a great deal to me. The ones I've thought about, thought with, and
argued with for many, many years.

IBS: Is this why A.

> imagines an immense Babel inside him. There is a text, and
> it translates itself into an infinite number of languages. Sen-
> tences spill out of him at the speed of thought, and each
> word comes from a different language, a thousand tongues

that clamor inside him at once, the din of it echoing through a maze of rooms, corridors, and stairways, hundreds of stories high. He repeats. In the space of memory, everything is both itself and something else. (136)

Is this a kind of exchange in and with "a thousand tongues" resounding through "a maze of rooms and stairways"? The ongoing narration of reality—and of our selves, which we talked about before? Processed through language, reiterated through memory?

PA: This is one of the essential passages in the book. When I say "immense Babel inside him," I mean a place in which every language exists: a "clamor" of languages. According to the biblical story, we have different languages because God created a confusion of tongues when man tried to usurp God by building the Tower of Babel. What I'm proposing in "The Book of Memory" is that we are intersubjective beings and that even the notion of solitude, the fact that I can tell myself that I am alone, means that I have learned language and can therefore think about my state of being alone. But I have acquired language through other people. No one learns to speak by himself. It's a group activity, and every child learns through verbal exchanges with other people. Therefore, even when you're alone, you're *not* alone. No one can be alone. The people who are locked up in closets, feral children who never have contact with human beings, do not develop. They become something less than human.

IBS: Is this because they have no contact with other people or because they have no language?

PA: It's both. They have no language because they have no contact.

IBS: This means you can develop a sense of self without language, as long as you have social interaction.

PA: Yes, definitely. You just can't think. I believe a dog has a sense of his own being. He can't tell himself, "I have a sense of my own being," but he feels alive in his own skin as a being separate from all other beings.

IBS: So, without language there's no real reflection?

PA: I don't think we would have the world without it. We wouldn't be able to distinguish between things. We wouldn't have tables and chairs, we would have a blur of objects.

IBS: That's true.

PA: It's interesting to look at people playing sports, a game of baseball, for example. A man picks up a ball and throws it, somebody swings, everyone starts running around, the crowd stands up and cheers. Until you learn the rules, the *words* of the rules, what you're looking at is chaos. Once you acquire the vocabulary to articulate what you're seeing, you begin to understand what's going on. The events are the same, but without language you can't understand them.

IBS: You often probe the arbitrary relationship between language and the individual's reality, and I was wondering whether, in your view, it's the writer, more than anyone else, who places himself in the blank space *in between* the word and the world and, from that vantage point, provides a perspective or a connection that carries meaning between the two. At the very beginning of "The Book of Memory," you write:

> Even as he stood in the present, he felt himself to be looking at it from the future, and this past-as-present was so antiquated that even the horrors of the day, which ordinarily would have filled him with outrage, seemed remote to him, as if the voice in the radio were reading from a chronicle of some lost civilization. Later, in a time of greater clarity, he would refer to this sensation as "nostalgia for the present." (76)

If we follow this and then read *White Spaces* again, I was wondering if this little chart might make sense:

WORLD		⇔	"I"	⇔	WORD
TIME	past	⇔	present	⇔	future
PLACE	room	⇔	body	⇔	page

You place your writing "I" in the middle, between the world and the word, as a kind of mediator or translator between the two. The "I" is here, right now, in his room writing, his body quietly seated before the page or pacing the floor. In terms of time, the "I" is located in the present, at times remembering a past that he is about to put into words, at times looking into the future with the hindsight of the past. You are saying something very much to this effect in *White Spaces* about the body situated in the present, mediating between the room and the page.

> I remain in the room in which I am writing this. I put one foot in front of the other. I put one word in front of the other, and for each step I take I add another word, as if for each word to be spoken there were another space to be crossed, a distance to be filled by my body as it moves through this space. (*Collected Poems*, 158)

PA: I think you're on to something here.

IBS: Well, if we follow your line of thinking, A. must situate himself in both the room and in language before he can achieve a sense of being in the world. He's right there, mind and body, between the concrete physical world and the abstract verbal realm of his reality. And he has set himself the task of mediating between the two, or to translate one into the other.

PA: I think you're right about this. In *Winter Journal* I actually say something quite similar:

> [B]ack and forth it went for the next hour, the dancers taking turns with the choreographer. Bodies in motion followed by words, beauty followed by meaningless noise, joy followed by boredom, and at a certain point something began to open up inside you. You found yourself falling through the rift between world and word. (33)

IBS: Falling!

PA: Falling.

> [T]he chasm that divides human life from our capacity to understand or express the truth of human life, and for reasons that still confound you, this sudden fall through empty, unbounded air filled you with a sensation of freedom and happiness, and by the time the performance was over, you were no longer blocked, no longer burdened by the doubts that had been weighing down on you for the past year. (*Winter Journal*, 223–224)

IBS: Well, I think there really does seem to be a consistent notion of this arbitrary relationship between the word, the world, and the writer from your very first piece of prose to your very latest.*

PA: I think so.

IBS: In *Winter Journal*, you inscribe a fall through the "rift between world and word." The rift is a kind of "white space," isn't it?

---

* Auster had just completed *Winter Journal* when this conversation took place. It was published almost a year later.

PA: Yes, and it was a happy fall. A feeling of exaltation. I've given a number of readings from *Winter Journal* now, and I've read the passage about the dance rehearsal several times. It was this woman, you see, the choreographer, unable to explain the beautiful performance she had created and which had so moved and excited me. She was not inarticulate. Far from it. It's just that her words had little bearing on what was happening on stage with the dancers. There it is: the enormous sense of relief I experienced when I finally understood that there's a rift between world and word. The word is approximate: it can't capture the world, but it's still the only tool we have. We're always going to fall short. Up to that point, as a poet and a writer, I thought I could achieve some kind of perfection. I put such pressure on myself, and the burden of it was so enormous that eventually it crushed me. I couldn't write for a while.

IBS: You needed Flaubert's *le mot juste*?

PA: I believed in *le mot juste* with all its burdens and philosophical ramifications. I think what freed me was the knowledge that I was always going to fail. There was a kind of release in that revelation. I was freer, I was freer. Of course, you do the best you can. You keep trying. Again: "Fail better." I think that was the visceral experience that allowed me to continue to write, indeed, to write all the prose books that have followed. Until then, I was blocked by the pressure I had put on myself.

IBS: In "Portrait of an Invisible Man," you mention a related rift:

> Never before have I been so aware of the rift between thinking and writing. For the past few days, in fact, I have begun to feel that the story I am trying to tell is somehow incompatible with language, that the degree to which it resists language is an exact measure of how closely I have come to saying something important, and that when the moment arrives for me to say the one truly important thing (assuming it exists), I will not be able to say it. (32)

PA: Here I'm talking about the sheer complexity of writing, the near-impossibility of expressing in words exactly the thought you have, the feeling you have. It really is difficult. Most human beings are not capable of doing it, few writers have the talent and skill to do it well. The understanding of failure, which we talked about earlier, and the struggle to achieve sufficient accuracy is part of it. The more challenging it is, the more important it becomes. The more difficult to express, the more essential it is to find the right words. It's easy to say, "I had a sandwich for lunch today." But to try to express something complex like "who was my father"—you can barely do it. When the stakes are low, nothing matters. When they're high, everything matters. And there's every chance you'll fall into the abyss.

IBS: What abyss is this?

PA: The abyss of not being able to express anything.

IBS: That's a "white space," isn't it? "Wordlessness." You say somewhere: "his mind flails in a wordless panic" (77).

PA: Wordlessness, yes.

> To be reduced to saying nothing. Or else, to say to himself: this is what haunts me. And then to realize, almost in the same breath, that this is what he haunts. (81)

IBS: Is there a double bind here? Seeking to fill the blank spaces: the naked room, the empty mind, the white page, and at the same time needing the "nothingness" that defines them? Is the hunger for fulfillment the underlying premise of writing?

PA: I think so.

IBS: Do you find these "white spaces" in language itself: things that can't be expressed in words? I'm thinking of the incompatibility of thoughts and emotions with language you mentioned earlier. It's not just one's own inability to express these things, it's also language itself that fails, isn't it?

PA: The thing is that reality is too complex, and language is always just an approximation of the real. Language is categories. This is the incompatibility Stillman (in *City of Glass*) obsesses about. This wooden artifact before us we call "a table," right? This is a unique table. It was custom made, it's red, no one else has this table. And so, to be absolutely accurate, you would have to name it: "red-table-number-one-that-exists-only-in-Brooklyn-New-York-in-the-house-of-Siri-and-Paul." That would be the word for this object. Just to say "table" doesn't do it. Even "red table" doesn't do it. So, extrapolate and think of all reality being like this. Everything is equally complex: "Red-table-number-one-that-exists-only-in-Brooklyn . . ." Once you get away from the general categories that help break down reality and allow us, in effect, to perceive it, you destroy language. Stillman's project would ultimately make words useless, meaningless—because every object would have to have its own impossibly complex name. You couldn't say "book." You would have to say "book-written-by-Paul-Auster-copy-number-7221-by-Faber-and-Faber-English-edition-bought-by-Gita-owned-only-by-her-creased-here-underlined-there . . ." That would be the word for this book, and it would be four pages long.

IBS: This is also a classical Jewish idea that the universe is precisely that one, infinite name for God.

PA: The infinite nothing, yes, but as far as language goes, saying that reality is incompatible with language means language as we know it. At the same time, every person is unique. To call my father a man, to call myself a man . . .

IBS: It's not enough.

PA: No, it's not enough. It's becoming more and more specific, but then the problem is—I have often thought about this—if you wanted to write a phenomenological novel about what it feels like to be sitting in this room right now talking with you, it would take a thousand pages even to tell the first second.

IBS: Yes, that's impossible. What is it, then, that you do when you capture something, as indeed you do, and make it come vividly to life on the page? Isn't it that you've found the right words to conjure up an image in the reader's mind?

PA: Yes, it's that. To capture something about the truth of the thing. I guess you come at it fitfully and sometimes at an oblique angle.

IBS: Many of your characters crave meaning, and I was wondering whether, in your view, meaning is to be found *in between* rather than *in* the things themselves?

> Like everyone else, he craves a meaning. Like everyone else, his life is so fragmented that each time he sees a connection between two fragments he is tempted to look for meaning in that connection. The connection exists. But to give it a meaning, to look beyond the bare fact of its existence, would be to build an imaginary world inside the real world, and he knows it would not stand. (147)

PA: People have often thought of me as obsessed with chance, but also with a kind of destiny or fate. What I am proposing is exactly the opposite. Look here:

> At his bravest moments, he embraces meaninglessness as the first principle, and then he understands that his obligation is to see what is in front of him (even though it is also inside him) and to say what he sees. He is in his room on Varick Street. His life has no meaning. The book he is writing has

no meaning. There is the world, and the things one encounters in the world, and to speak of them is to be in the world. A key breaks off in a lock, and something has happened. That is to say, a key has broken off in a lock. The same piano seems to exist in two different places. A young man, twenty years later, winds up living in the same room where his father faced the horror of solitude. A man encounters his old love on a street in a foreign city. It means only what it is. Nothing more, nothing less. Then he writes: to enter this room is to vanish in a place where past and present meet. And then he writes: as in the phrase: "he wrote The Book of Memory in this room." (147–148)

What we're talking about here is ambiguity. I guess what I'm trying to say is that sometimes life looks as though it were a novel, "an extension of the imaginary." Coincidences happen so unpredictably, they seem to be screaming in our face so loudly that we feel they must have a significance. Things occur in such strange ways that we want to assign some metaphysical meaning to them. Well, tempted as I am to want to believe this, what I'm saying in this passage is that I don't. How strange it is that reality should resemble fiction, but you can't interpret the two in the same way. You'd collapse into craziness if you started reading reality as if it were a novel. Later, as I continued to think about this, I came to call it "the mechanics of reality." Chance will create patterns. And those patterns will seem to have meaning, but they're arbitrary.

IBS: This notion of ambiguity is pivotal in a lot of your work. In fact, several of the themes we've discussed here in connection with *The Invention of Solitude* are really essential to the entire body of your writing, aren't they? From beginning to end.

PA: I've often felt that much of my work comes out of *The Invention of Solitude*. Or, at least that here I'm articulating the things I care about most; things I've gone on to embellish or change or develop in later works.

IBS: I sometimes think of *The Invention of Solitude* as a kind of toolbox or gene pool for your writing in general.

PA: Not all of it, but some things. Some of the essential things. You see, *The Invention of Solitude* was the condensation of many years of thinking about writing, the writing in my poems and in the prose I never published. It was all funneled into this book. It's my first prose book, even if it's not the first work of prose I wrote. Fortunately, as time has gone on, I've acquired new interests, found different things to think about. Otherwise, I would be running in place.

HAND TO MOUTH: A CHRONICLE
OF EARLY FAILURE. (1997)
"Permanently Penniless"

IBS: *Hand to Mouth* is essentially about tenacity, I think, but it opens with "failure" and "money trouble":

> In my late twenties and early thirties, I went through a period of several years when everything I touched turned to failure. My marriage ended in divorce, my work as a writer foundered, and I was overwhelmed by money problems. I'm not just talking about the occasional shortfall or some periodic belt tightenings—but a constant, grinding, almost suffocating lack of money that poisoned my soul and kept me in a state of never-ending panic. (3)

PA: Tenacity, yes, but money is the subject of the book. When you don't have money, all you think about is money. It's the curse of poverty. You're scheming, you're dreaming, you're planning, you're hoping, and you're counting how much you have and how much you need. The only good thing about having money is that it frees you to think about something other than money every waking minute of your life.

IBS: That's also what Nashe says in *The Music of Chance*: the inheritance set him free. In *Hand to Mouth* you describe how your parents always argued about money.

PA: My parents were polar opposites, and nowhere were their differences more pronounced than in their relationship to money. My father's family had been desperately poor, and he was so afraid of poverty that he couldn't spend money. My mother's family had been a little more comfortable, but not very, and she took pleasure in buying things. My father was tight-fisted; my mother was expansive and generous. That was one of the things that drove them apart. It all came to an end the moment my father said, "I don't want you to do the grocery shopping anymore. I'll do it." Back in those days, that was the same as kicking your wife out of her job.

IBS: Today it would just be a relief [*laughs*].

PA: Yes, but you know, in the world they lived in, running the household was the woman's responsibility, and my mother enjoyed it. Of course, arguments about money are never just about money. It's always about something else. How you deal with money is an expression of who you are. It's almost like handwriting analysis— or fingerprints. You see the parsimonious, skinflint misers and how deeply they mistrust the world, how afraid they are, compared to generous people, who seem to live for others as much as they live for themselves. Then there are the profligate ones who throw money away, like Willy,* for example. They don't understand that a certain prudence is required: not excessive and not elaborate prudence, but a measure of moderation is necessary. Money is a fascinating subject, an inexhaustible subject.

IBS: It is.

PA: Through my early adventures of trying to make a living, I ran into some colorful characters, and this book gave me the chance to write about some of them. I had been through some rough periods in my early adulthood, a desperate kind of poverty. Always on the brink of complete ruin. It went on for years after I left college. At one point, I considered writing a book called *Essay on Want*—as a parody of an eighteenth-century treatise. That's how *Hand to Mouth* began, but, rather than the treatise I first had in mind, it became an

---

* In *Timbuktu*.

autobiographical tale of my misadventures in the land of the dollar and the franc. That was it. But, as you say, the book is also about tenacity—or idiotic stubbornness.

IBS: And the fact that you refused to sell out.

PA: I didn't want to do the things I was supposed to do, and I think I was very stupid. In some way, *Hand to Mouth* is a "how-*not*-to" book.

IBS: Is it? I mean, I see it very much as a "portrait of the artist as a struggling young man."

PA: My father was a practical person with little or no poetry inside him. He simply couldn't fathom that he had produced a son who was a poet. It was so daunting, so difficult for him to take in. He gradually accepted it, but he disapproved till the end: "Fine, you want to write," he'd say, "that's a nice hobby, but you have to have a job." After I came back from Europe, he was beginning to get worried. He said, "Don't you think it would be a good idea if you went back to school and got a PhD? Then you can be a professor and write your books while earning a living."

IBS: At least he understood that much.

PA: Yes, he realized that I wasn't cut out to be a businessman. I said to him, "Yes, Dad, for once you're right." So, I called up my uncle Allen* and asked, "What's the best graduate program for literature?" "Princeton," he said. "Princeton would be the best place. I'll put you in touch with Robert Fagles." I sent my publications in advance— one book of poems, one book of poetry translations, and a number of critical essays—then went down to Princeton to meet with Fagles. He explained how many courses I would have to take and how many

---

* Allen Mandelbaum (1926–2011), translator, poet, and professor of Humanities at Wake Forest University.

years the program would last. I listened and nodded. It sounded dreadful to me, actually, but I thought I'd just have to get through it. Then, very surprisingly, Fagles paused for a long moment and said that he didn't think I should enroll in the program. "You're a fine poet," he said, "a fine writer. Don't bury yourself in a university the way I have. I've earned a living, but a part of me regrets it. Don't do it." A great burden was lifted from my shoulders. Free again—to struggle and starve—but free. There's a footnote to this story: My meeting with Fagles took place in 1974. In 1986, I was hired to teach writing classes at Princeton. Fagles then became my colleague, and we saw each other every week. He would always joke about that first conversation: "I gave you some good advice, didn't I?" [*Laughs*] Wonderful Bob Fagles.

IBS: So, this explains why in *Hand to Mouth* you write:

> Just on principle, it felt wrong to me for a writer to hide
> out in a university, to surround himself with too many like-
> minded people, to get too comfortable. (5)

I was wondering about that.

PA: Yes, but you're a scholar. It's different for me: I'm a poet and a novelist. I don't think universities are good places for creative artists. I have nothing against universities. God knows I loved being a student, and in the end, I did wind up teaching at Princeton for five years anyway.

IBS: Because you needed the money?

PA: We needed the money. It lasted from 1986 to 1990. I taught creative writing. It's a subject I've never studied myself and an activity I had very mixed feelings about. The one possible benefit, as I saw it, was that the effort involved in trying to write something would teach the students how difficult it is to do it well and therefore enhance their appreciation of good writing. I also taught translation. That was more interesting, and I enjoyed it a great deal, but I'm glad I don't have to do it anymore.

IBS: So, you decided against an academic career and worked as a translator, right?

PA: By then, I was married to Lydia Davis, and the idea was to make our living as translators.

IBS: Your father didn't help you?

PA: No, he didn't help. Every once in a while he would give me a little money, but no, I was basically on my own. My mother didn't help, either. She and her husband weren't in a position to help. Lydia and I started translating books, but we couldn't earn enough to live on. We were constantly in danger of collapse. Still, we stuck with it. Every now and again I would get rescued by a grant. Twice I got four or five thousand dollars from the Ingram Merrill Foundation. Back then it was almost a fortune. Two people could get by—minimally— on about eight or nine thousand dollars a year, so it was really a huge help. Twice I got grants from the National Endowment for the Arts. Ten thousand dollars the first time, I think, and twenty thousand the second time. These kept us afloat, but we still did a lot of translations. They were usually quite bad books, and we had to work on tight deadlines. I was ready to prostitute myself in any number of ways. It was demoralizing.

IBS: Among the failures, there was one big success: the birth of your son, Daniel.

PA: It was a great moment in my life. At the same time, it put more pressure on me than ever before. That's when I stepped up my efforts to get a full-time job. But with no luck. Magazine jobs, teaching jobs, newspaper jobs—I was turned down everywhere. It was grinding, difficult, and dispiriting. There I was with a small child and a marriage falling to pieces in large part because we were permanently penniless. I went a year without writing. I couldn't do it anymore. The only writing project I managed was that pseudonymous detective novel. But that was only to make money—which didn't happen.

IBS: *Squeeze Play?*

PA: *Squeeze Play*, yes. The resurrection took place after going to the dance rehearsal I write about in *Winter Journal*. Then, suddenly and unexpectedly, my father died, and I inherited some money. Not a lot of money, but more than I'd ever seen in my life. That gave me a little breathing room, and I started writing *The Invention of Solitude*. My life turned. I was emboldened to go back and try to write fiction. As you know, there are about seven hundred pages' worth of material written during those early years described in *Hand to Mouth*: novels that were never finished, aborted projects. *Hand to Mouth* is about those years of struggle.

IBS: While *Hand to Mouth* is very much about the difficulties of making a living as a young writer, it's also about your travels, your adventures, and we get a strong sense of your curiosity about the world:

> What I wanted were new experiences. I wanted to go out into the world and test myself, to move from this to that, to explore as much as I could. (5)

Can we read it as a *Bildungs* narrative?

PA: I understood that I didn't want to follow the path preordained for me by my middle-class background. I wanted to jump off that road and explore other worlds. Most of my experiences came through blue-collar jobs and encounters with people very different from myself, people who hadn't gone to college, people who didn't read books, people in low-paying jobs. I got to know them well. The most interesting job I had was on the oil tanker. That was a big adventure, and I'm glad I did it. I learned so many things by getting off the main road and *thrashing out into the woods.*

> It's not that I wanted to make a career of it, but those little excursions into the backwaters and shit holes of the world never failed to produce an interesting discovery, to further my education in ways I hadn't expected. Casey and Teddy are a perfect example. I was nineteen years old when I met them, and the things they did that summer are still feeding my imagination today. (29)

Later, I took on many different kinds of freelance white-collar work. Translating, ghostwriting, giving private English lessons, translating the North Vietnamese constitution (!), working for a film producer. Not to mention nighttime telephone receptionist for the *New York Times* office in Paris.

IBS: In *Hand to Mouth* you describe how you grew up with contradiction as a constant tension at the core of your family. You describe it in terms of

> [t]wo styles, two worldviews, two moral philosophies were in eternal conflict with each other, and in the end it broke their marriage apart. (7)

Do you think that background of ambiguity has found its way into your writing?

PA: It's possible.

IBS: You were marked by the contradictions, weren't you?

> I believed in myself and yet had no confidence in myself. I

was bold and timid, light-footed and clumsy, single-minded and impulsive—a walking, breathing monument to the spirit of contradiction. My life had only just begun, and already I was moving in two directions at once. I didn't know it yet, but in order for me to get anywhere, I was going to have to work twice as hard as anyone else. (19)

PA: Yes, I was affected by my parents' bad marriage when I was a boy, there's no question about it. I knew that home wasn't a place of refuge for me in the way it can be for many people, and so I made an effort to succeed at school and in sports. I was a good student, I was one of the best athletes, I was popular. The other kids looked up to me. I was one of those winning young boys who managed to do most things well. In the passage you quote here, I'm talking about my adolescence, when I was beginning to observe myself and to form ideas about how I wanted to interact with the world. After adolescence, I became horrendously shy. I had trouble speaking if there were more than three or four people in the room. Actually, I think teaching at Princeton and having to talk in front of the students was an enormous help. Now, I can get up and give speeches in front of hundreds if not thousands of people and feel quite comfortable with it. When I was eighteen, I couldn't. In *Hand to Mouth*, I talk about my time in Dublin, a pivotal moment in my life. I was two weeks on my own there, and I only talked to one or two people. Completely alone, wandering around the streets every day. As I say in the book, it was as if I had gone down into some deep place inside myself and was finally beginning to discover who I was. I was a little nuts, I think. A very strange boy. I didn't even go into a pub. Why?

IBS: You were shy?

PA: So shy I couldn't do it.

IBS: You couldn't bear having to talk to anyone.

PA: But I liked talking to people. One-on-one was fine. I think it was the crisis of adolescence, the tremendous tumult of it, the physical developments we all go through, but also intellectual, moral, political changes, waking up to the sterility of middle-class American life, understanding how unfair America was in so many ways to so many people. You can't imagine the anger I began to feel. It made me very rigid for a while: the passions of youth, the inward move into anger and silence. Eventually, I outgrew it. To some degree.

IBS: It looks as if you did [*laughs*]. When did it become clear to you that you were going to be a writer?

PA: I was determined to be a writer even earlier, from the time I was about sixteen or seventeen. When I finally came home from Paris, I was already twenty-seven and had written quite a lot. There was no turning back: this was going to be my life. There was nothing else I could do, nothing else I wanted to do, and the only question now was how to go on doing it.

THE RED NOTEBOOK. (2002)
Ars Poetica

IBS: *The Red Notebook* is a collection of stories about strange real events that have happened either to you or to people you know. In which way is this little book of anecdotes an ars poetica?

PA: The style of these little stories is modeled on the joke—the simplest form of storytelling. Bare-bones sentences building up to a punch line. Very concise, very precise, not one word wasted, quick and efficient in the way a good joke is quick and efficient. At the same time, I was trying, in an indirect way, to use these stories to present my view of what we spoke about earlier: the "mechanics of reality." There's no theology involved in this. There's not even much philosophy. It's simply an observation of how strangely events intersect in the world. Such things don't happen every minute, but they happen with astonishing frequency.

IBS: This penchant for magical occurrences would seem to be a red thread that runs through these anecdotes and indeed a few of your other writings, most notably *The Music of Chance.*

PA: Of course, I'm attuned to these things, and the more they happen, the more alert I become to them. At the same time, the book is the result of a basic impulse to share these fascinating little anecdotes with other people.

IBS: There's a contrast embedded in the stories, isn't there, between the content, which is extraordinary, and the narration, which is simple. As you say, there's not a single word too many. Story number nine in the American edition is a good example:

> C.'s life had now become two lives. There was Version A and
> Version B, and both of them were his story. He had lived
> them both in equal measure, two truths that canceled each
> other out, and all along, without even knowing it, he had
> been stranded in the middle. (43)

This story turns on contradiction and your attentiveness to ambiguity. As often before in your work, it leaves everything "stranded in
the middle" between two truths.

PA: Two truths that are equal and opposite, yes.

IBS: Your interest in the nature of memory is vividly captured in the
story about how, as a young boy, you saved the little girl slipping on
the ice in her mother's high heels.

> I realized then that she hadn't known the car was moving.
> She hadn't even known that she was in danger. The whole
> incident had taken place in a flash: ten seconds of her life, an
> interval of no account, and none of it had left the slightest
> mark on her. For me, on the other hand, those seconds had
> been a defining experience, a singular event in my internal
> history. (45)

PA: After the book was published, I gave a reading at the University
of Pennsylvania and a young man, a student, came up to me and
said, "I'm the son of that woman. The girl you pulled out from under
the car is my mother." A beautiful moment—but I must admit that
it made me feel old [*laughs*].

IBS: It tells us something about the "mechanisms of memory,"
doesn't it? You remember this as an act of heroism, whereas she has
suppressed it completely. Or maybe, as you say, she wasn't even aware
that she was in danger.

PA: No, she wasn't aware of it. We don't remember most of the things that happen to us. Much of our life just vanishes.

IBS: So what is it that makes some memories stay with us and not others?

PA: Siri has done vast amounts of work on neuroscience and questions of memory. What she tells me, and what I'm convinced is true, is that emotion consolidates memory. If it's just an ordinary occurrence in an everyday movement of your life, you're not going to remember it. You don't recall what you ate for dinner on April ninth thirty-six years ago. But if on that April ninth thirty-six years ago, your parents had a tremendous argument in front of you, or someone died, or you broke your arm, you might have a clear memory of what you ate that night. It's possible. There must be something sufficiently powerful to make a deep impression on you. Then again, there are things I remember that seem entirely insignificant, and yet, there they are. Little scenes without much emotion to them that come back for no apparent reason. For example, a memory from about twenty years ago, when my good friends from Paris, Jacques Dupin, the poet, and his wife, Christine, were visiting New York. We spent a whole day together, and at one point we were in Chinatown standing on a street corner discussing where we wanted to go for dinner. I'm back at that corner frequently, just standing there with them, talking to my two friends. Why? I don't know. I have no idea.

IBS: Our senses take us back to such moments.

PA: Smell, more than anything else for sure.

IBS: Sound, music, colors . . . they transport you straight into the past. Of course, it's all connected to emotion, as you say.

PA: In *The Red Notebook*, I'm also interested in exploring things that don't happen, that almost happened but didn't. That's why, in some sense, the most important story in the first sequence is the one about my father falling off a roof and *not* dying. In *Sunset Park*, Renzo, the novelist, tells Morris that he's thinking of writing a book about "the things that don't happen." It's a fascinating subject. For instance, how many times have two countries been on the verge of war and somehow managed *not* to go to war? In retrospect, historical events seem to be inevitable—but they're not. It's an endlessly debatable topic. Do individuals count in history, or is it some invisible social force that causes things to happen? These are fascinating questions. They apply both to the small lives of individuals and to large historical events.

IBS: This is relevant also to *The Red Notebook*, isn't it: the individual, little story, the example, and then the general, big story.

PA: True enough. In the second sequence, "Why Write?," which is all about children, there's the story of that horrific experience I went through at the age of fourteen, when I was right next to a boy who was electrocuted by lightning and killed on the spot. It's one of the most important things that has ever happened to me—perhaps the most important. It absolutely informs the way I think about the world. The arbitrary nature of things—one minute you're alive, the next minute you're dead. The pure randomness of it all. I never thought, in those early hours after it happened, "If it had been four seconds later, I would have been killed and he would be alive." We were crawling under a barbed wire fence single file, and he was right in front of me. The bolt of lightning hit the fence and electrocuted him. I didn't even know he was dead. I pulled him into the meadow after I had crawled through. I went on rubbing his hands for close to an hour as the rain poured down on us and the storm continued.

IBS: It must have been a shock to realize he was dead.

PA: I had never seen a dead person. His lips were turning blue, he was utterly still, but it never occurred to me that he wasn't alive.

IBS: How did you react when you finally realized that he was gone?

PA: It wasn't until a couple of hours later that we were all told that Ralph was dead. We were stunned. We were all stunned. I think this is important because I've had a very lucky life in so many ways. I haven't gone hungry. No matter how impoverished I've been at times, I've always had a roof over my head. But more significantly, I've never lived through a war or an occupation by a foreign army. I've never been thrust into the kind of daily violence that corrupts your soul and destroys the very fabric of your being. But this day, it was like being in a war. It was just as if a comrade in the trenches had been shot.

IBS: So you've had a taste of disaster.

PA: I've had a taste of it. That's right. There were, of course, some near-death experiences, I suppose, that could be mentioned in this connection. Most particularly the car crash in 2002, which I describe at great length in *Winter Journal*. I think that's probably the closest I've come to dying, except for the lightning storm in 1961.

IBS: It puts things into perspective.

PA: Well, I don't know if it puts things into perspective. It creates a new perspective. I'm interested in this question of accidents. That's why the third section in *The Red Notebook* is called "Accident Report." We have the word "accident," which means "an unexpected thing that happens, usually with harmful results." In another context, a philosophical context, "the accidental" refers to that which is not necessary. So every accident is something that doesn't necessarily have to happen. It happens because of a confluence of circumstances. The slightest lapse of attention, the smallest distraction, and your life can be changed forever. An English friend of mine pulled into a gas station. He got out of the car, slipped on a puddle of oil, and broke his leg in several places. He's going to suffer from that broken leg for the rest of his life. Just because he stepped on that bit of oil. Accidents can irrevocably affect your health, your well-being, even your sanity. One random movement, one split second—it can kill you. This interests me a great deal.

IBS: I was wondering about the chapter headings in *The Red Notebook*. "Accident Report," I suppose, is self-explanatory, but what about "Why Write?" Why use a question as your title when you make no apparent attempt to provide an answer?

PA: It's a bit of a joke. The last story, if you remember, is the one about Willie Mays. You won't have any idea who he is, but Willie Mays was the single greatest baseball player of my lifetime, probably the greatest player who has ever lived. He was in the early days of his career when I was a little boy—and obsessed with baseball. He became an exalted, heroic figure for me, and the tragedy of *not* having a pencil when I met him and asked for his autograph had an effect on my young life. The whimsical conclusion is this:

> After that night, I started carrying a pencil with me wherever I went. It became a habit of mine never to leave the house without making sure I had a pencil in my pocket. It's not that I had any particular plans for that pencil, but I didn't want to be unprepared. I had been caught empty-handed once, and I wasn't about to let it happen again.
>
> If nothing else, the years have taught me this: if there's a pencil in your pocket, there's a good chance that one day you'll be tempted to start using it.
>
> As I like to tell my children, that's how I became a writer. (78)

[*Laughs.*]

IBS: Ah yes, of course [*laughs*].

PA: There's a coda to the Willie Mays story. Initiated by the American writer Amy Tan, who happens to be (how strange!) the subject of the first story in "Accident Report." I met her in the nineties through our mutual friend, Wayne Wang. I don't know her well, but a number of years ago, in January 2007, Siri and I went to a writers festival in Key West, Florida. Amy was there. I hadn't seen her in years, and I realized that I had never given her the book that contains the story about her. All our books were for sale at the auditorium where we were doing our talks and readings, so I bought a copy of *The Red Notebook* and gave it to her. She read it on the plane ride home, and she was very touched that I had put her in the book. She also read the Willie Mays story, and, as it turns out, Amy has some good friends who live next door to Willie Mays in the Bay Area, in a town outside San Francisco. As soon as she got home, she called her friends and said, "Go and buy Paul's book. Then knock on Willie's door and go in and read him the story."

IBS: And they did?

PA: They did. And Willie just sat there.

IBS: That's incredible.

PA: Yes. He had tears in his eyes and kept shaking his head, again and again, shaking his head and saying, "Fifty-two years, fifty-two years, fifty-two years." Then he took out a baseball and signed it for me. On my sixtieth birthday, Amy presented me with this ball. On my sixtieth birthday I got the signature I had wanted fifty-two years earlier. Of course, it was no longer important to me, but I was moved by the gesture. The story finally had an ending. Strange. So very strange.

IBS: In the story of the impostor who wrote letters in your name you conclude:

Perhaps it is a way to remind myself that I know nothing and that the world I live in will go on escaping me forever. (37)

That's a fairly accurate summary of this little book, isn't it?

PA: Yes, because there are no conclusions to be drawn. Things happen, and we don't know why they happen. They don't seem to make any sense. Hence the title of the last section, "It Don't Mean a Thing."

WINTER JOURNAL. (2012)
Memory and the Body

Winter solstice: the darkest time of the year. No sooner has he woken up in the morning than he feels the day beginning to slip away from him. There is no light to sink his teeth into, no sense of time unfolding. Rather, a feeling of doors being shut, of locks being turned. It is a hermetic season, a long moment of inwardness. The outer world, the tangible world of materials and bodies, has come to seem no more than an emanation of his mind. He feels himself sliding through events, hovering like a ghost around his own presence, as if he were living somewhere to the side of himself—not really here, but not anywhere else either. A feeling of having been locked up, and at the same time of being able to walk through walls. He notes somewhere in the margins of a thought: a darkness in the bones; make a note of this. (The Invention of Solitude, 78)

IBS: The first time I came to talk with you,* you gave me a manuscript version of *Winter Journal*. I was very excited and sat in a bar half the night reading it. I didn't have the confidence to say so at the time, but it kept reminding me of *The Invention of Solitude*. It has to do with tone and this slightly peculiar perspective on oneself. Am I completely off the mark here?

PA: I don't see it, really. But that's just my opinion.

IBS: The first page of *Winter Journal* is very striking because of the many contrasts and shifts. You open with the second-person perspective and use the present tense throughout, whether you're six years old, ten years old, or an adult. In the second paragraph there's the

_____

* In November 2011.

cold floor, it's winter, the trees are white. Then, in the next paragraph, you're ten, it's midsummer, it's warm, you mention the trees in the backyard again, and you're sweating . . .

PA: And in between, I'm about to turn sixty-four.

> Speak now before it's too late, and then hope to go on speaking until there's nothing more to be said. Time is running out, after all. Perhaps it is just as well to put aside your stories for now and try to examine what it has felt like to live inside this body from the first day you can remember being alive until this one. A catalogue of sensory data. What one might call a *phenomenology of breathing*. (1)

There are several things we should discuss here. One of them is the second-person perspective, or the choice to write in that way.

IBS: Yes, there's quite a lot to say about that. I don't think I've ever seen an autobiographical work written in the second person.

PA: Nor have I. Of course, there are novels written in the second person.

IBS: That's true, and you've used it in your own fiction: in part of *Sunset Park* Morris Heller writes his journal in the second person.

PA: In *Invisible*,* too, there's one part narrated in the second person. But in neither case a whole book. In *Winter Journal*, as in the sequel, *Report from the Interior*, we're in the second person throughout.

IBS: Yes, the two are closely linked partly through this strangely angled autobiographical perspective, right?

---

* See conversations on *Sunset Park* and *Invisible*.

PA: It's important to stress that I don't find my life to be exceptional in any way and that this is not an autobiography. It's a book composed of autobiographical fragments shaped like a piece of music. It's a poem rather than a narrative. One would normally write something like this from a first-person point of view. Had I done that, my own story would have been in central focus, and that's not what I wanted to do. The third person was another option, but it seemed too distant for this particular book, which focuses on the body. Then there was the second person. The more I thought about it, the more I realized that its effect would be to open up a little space between myself and myself in which I could engage in a kind of intimate dialogue with myself. I wanted to look at myself from a distance—but only a small one, and the distance of the third person would have been too big. At the same time, I wanted to implicate the reader. In many ways, the book is an invitation to the reader to explore his or her own memories, to think about his or her own life. I hope it can serve as a sounding board for people to remember the kinds of things I'm remembering about myself in the book. We all have the memories of our bodies. We've all been sick, we've all hurt ourselves, we've all felt joy, we've all tasted food we like. Everyone recalls these experiences. It's part of being human. Time is a strange factor here, and by using the same tense through all the chronological shifts, I tried to produce a kind of simultaneity for the experiences I write about: the six-year-old boy is the same person, finally, as the sixty-four-year-old man.

IBS: That makes sense, and it explains the seamlessness of the shifts. Even if there's a time difference of sixty years, it's just a split second.

PA: I wrote this book in a kind of trance, and it came to me in the order you see in the final version. I didn't map it out. I made a little list of some of the things I wanted to examine, but the order never changed. It was there from the beginning. The music was in my head, and I just transcribed it, so to speak. I've rarely felt so integrated with what I was writing. I've rarely had to struggle less with my material.

Sometimes you're digging through rocks to get to where you have to go, other times it's as if you're swimming. There's a little phrase from the American painter Philip Guston that has always meant a lot to me: "Years and years of struggle for a few moments of grace." This book was like that for me. It was written in just three or four months.

IBS: In the paragraph you quoted a moment ago, there's a pronounced urgency: "Speak now before it's too late." Why is that?

PA: Because I'm getting old, and I don't know how much time I have left. If I'd put this off for a couple of years, maybe I wouldn't have been around to do it. It's very strange to become as old as I am now.

IBS: Old?

PA: I was turning sixty-four when I wrote this. Now I'm sixty-six.

IBS: Well, that *is* old [*laughs*].

PA: I'm officially a senior citizen now. Ay-ay-ay.

IBS: You also urge the addressee—"you"—to "put aside your stories for now and try to examine what it has felt like to live inside this body." Is *Winter Journal* entirely autobiographical, or are there elements of autofiction? Is there anything invented, anything *deliberately* invented?

PA: No, not at all. In the five autobiographical works I've written so far, the effort in every case has been to be as accurate as possible, not to cheat. I think cheating would vitiate the whole project, make it meaningless. It's as if you make a pact with the reader and say, "I'm telling you the truth as I remember it. I know there are probably inaccuracies in here, but they're not intentional." I couldn't proceed in any other way. A long time ago,* we were talking about memoirs and how it's impossible to recall conversations from fifty years ago accurately. When people claim to remember exactly what was said, they're merely using the conventions of popular fiction to embroider their lives. I find those works dishonest. It's really a moral problem, isn't it; if you lie and insist you're telling the truth.

IBS: [*Laughs*] You provide several lists of detailed autobiographical information here in *Winter Journal*: your favorite foods, schools, places you've traveled to, the scars on your body, and roughly fifty pages on the twenty-one places where you've lived during your life. Interestingly, you combine the factual data with sensuous impressions in almost equal measure. Why give this rich information in the form of lists rather than weave it into the prose?

PA: I think there's a kind of lyrical force to these lists that harmonizes with the tone I wanted to create with the prose. It's essentially a book about the body, but not one hundred percent. This inventory of dwelling places is justified because those are the places that have sheltered my body from the elements. So there's a reason to include it. The same goes for the sections about my mother, because it was in her body that my body began, and so, it seemed right and proper to talk about her. The passages about her are at the very center, right in the middle of the book.

IBS: Yes, *The Invention of Solitude* focused on your father, but here in *Winter Journal* you give us a vivid portrait of your mother:

> There were three of her, three separate women who seemed unconnected to one another, and as you grew older and began to look at her differently, to see her as someone who was not just your mother, you never knew which mask she

---

* In the conversation on *The Invention of Solitude* in November 2011. This conversation took place in May 2013.

would be wearing on a given day. At one end, there was the diva . . . In the middle, which was far and away the largest space she occupied, there was a solid and responsible being . . . At the other end, the extreme end of who she was, there was the frightened and debilitated neurotic. (140–141)

PA: Earlier, we talked about spectrum in a personality. My mother had a wide spectrum, and it was unclear which part of her was going to manifest itself at any given moment. It took me a long time—nine years after her death—to be able to write about her. Interestingly, I wrote about my father immediately after he died. I think the difference is that I had a more complex and troubled relationship with my father. With my mother there were none of those problems. She adored me from the minute I was born, and she always wanted the best for me. She was kind and generous. Very generous. My mother's life, in effect, turned out to be a sad life. She was someone, it seemed to me, in spite of her neuroses and problems, who was born to be happy. She was always optimistic, never depressed. Her life took some crazy turns, and she suffered because of them.

IBS: It makes perfect sense to write about your mother and indeed to list homes and other key elements to do with the history of your body, but there's data here about things that would not seem to be of equal importance, for instance, your favorite foods. I was wondering, why give this particular information rather than other things to do with the body like, say, your favorite garments or dances, performances, beautiful poems that have affected your body? Are there any criteria for the selection of these facts?

PA: No, these are the things that occurred to me as I was working on the project, things that seemed significant. This book is about what it feels like to sit in a chair or walk on grass. That's the kind of thing I wanted to talk about. Very basic things. This is what I remember. That's all.

IBS: In *The Invention of Solitude* you say, "Memory: the space in which a thing happens for the second time" (83). Here, in *Winter Journal*, you use the present tense throughout the book as if all these things are indeed "happening for the second time": happening as *you* write and again, I suppose, as *we* read.

PA: Yes, events recur—if only in the mind. But I never thought about *The Invention of Solitude* while I was writing this book. I don't go back and read my own work.

IBS: We keep coming back to *The Invention of Solitude*. Somehow it echoes through many of your books, doesn't it?

PA: Well, as we said earlier, I do feel that it's a primary source, the foundation of much of my later work. Writing down memories seems to make the events happen again. It also triggers discoveries. There's something about the act of holding a pen in your hand, or, I guess, putting your fingers on a keyboard, and getting into the zone of language, that generates more language, that generates thoughts, sensations, memories, and ideas that can only occur while you're writing. Without the pen in my hand, I don't have the same thoughts. Curious.

IBS: So, it's a physical thing?

PA: Definitely.

IBS: *Winter Journal* highlights the physical dimension of life and makes tangible things that we normally consider to be immaterial. For instance, the list of your twenty-one homes is not just a list of facts: for each place you knit factual data together with memory, and memory, here, is triggered almost exclusively either by emotion (love, failure, loss, frustration, anxiety, and a rare triumph) or by the senses (sight, touch, and pain).

PA: Well put. Straight to the point.

IBS: [*Laughs*] This identification of factual with sensory data, I think, is what makes *Winter Journal* such a wonderful book to read.

PA: As we know, place and memory are linked. Most memory systems use spatial representation. Cicero's, Bruno's, nearly all of them. I wasn't interested in dredging up *everything* in *Winter Journal*, only the things that sprang to mind first because, somehow, as you say, the emotion is going to dominate.

IBS: How did you do it? Did you sit down, pen in hand, and say, "Okay, I want to project my mind into this flat where I used to live. Here is the room, this is the space, this is what it looked like, and then we'll see what happens."

PA: That's right. "Then we'll see what happens." I never knew what I was going to find. That's what made this such an interesting book to write. And also why I called it a journal—and not a chronicle or a history.

IBS: What makes it interesting, I think, is this marriage between place, emotion, and sensory data. As elsewhere in your writing, rooms offer protection and you place your body, often in motion, inside these spaces:

> Your body in small rooms and large rooms, your body walking up and down stairs, your body swimming in ponds, lakes, rivers, and oceans, your body traipsing across muddy fields, your body lying in the tall grass of empty meadows, your body walking along city streets, your body laboring up hills and mountains . . .
> Enclosures, habitations, the small rooms and large rooms that have sheltered your body from the open air. (224–225)

PA: That's right. This is the body in motion. Then we come to rest inside the habitations, the enclosures. I've written very little while sitting outdoors. Some writers prefer that, sitting outside with their notebook or typewriter. Many people write in outdoor cafés or at the beach; on the porch of their house or in the garden. I've never done that. I sometimes jot things down on the subway or even walking down the street. Not often, but it does happen. In general, however, I've always done my writing indoors . . .

IBS: Have you thought about why that is? Do you need to have a roof over your head, four walls, to contain something?

PA: Probably, yes, I think so. It's as if the room is a body, and the body inside the room is the brain. A curious kind of doubling effect.

IBS: The intimate connection between writing and physical movement is prominent in *Winter Journal* also:

> In order to do what you do, you need to walk. Walking is what brings the words to you, what allows you to hear the rhythms of the words as you write them in your head. One foot forward, and then the other foot forward, the double drumbeat of your heart. Two eyes, two ears, two arms, two legs, two feet. This, and then that. That, and then this. Writing begins in the body, it is the music of the body, and even if the words have meaning, can sometimes have meaning, the music of the words is where the meanings begin. You sit at your desk in order to write down the words, but in your head you are still walking, and what you hear is the rhythm of your heart, the beating of your heart. (224–225)

PA: There is a rhythm in walking, a binary rhythm, as with so many things that pertain to the human body: two eyes, two hands, two legs, two feet, and the heartbeat, which is a kind of *thump-thump,*

thump-thump. Walking seems to create a rhythm that is conducive to the production of language, especially, of course, poetry. In "Conversation about Dante," Mandelstam argues that Dante's poetry mimes the rhythms of the human gait and then he asks this beautiful question: "I wonder how many pairs of sandals Dante wore out while writing *The Divine Comedy*." Only a poet could have come up with that question. So much is churning inside me while I write that I find it difficult to sit still for long. I get up and pace around the room a lot, and just that, the act of moving around, the act of walking, seems to generate the next gust of words. Writing is an intensely physical activity for me; not only am I holding the pen or typing on the typewriter, which are material objects, I'm also moving around, as if building up momentum for the next round with the pen or typewriter.

IBS: Not unlike the Peripatetics,* I assume.

PA: When I first learned about them as a student, I thought, "This makes sense to me." But then, the real words can only come from the act of pressing the pen against the page. It's not as though I'm thinking of words when I walk around. I'm just thinking of what I'm doing, seeing pictures in my head.

IBS: So you're not formulating sentences?

PA: No, I'm dreaming with my eyes open. Somehow, as I move around the room, it's easier for these things to come to me than when I'm sitting down. I don't know why.

IBS: It makes sense. So that's why you always say that "writing begins in the body." It is the "music of the body" that produces meaning for you?

---

* Followers of Aristotle who would walk as they discussed philosophy.

PA: Yes.

IBS: And then you sit down to write. This is precisely what you describe in *White Spaces* and *The Invention of Solitude*.

PA: It's interesting how *White Spaces* keeps coming back in these conversations. Eight little pages. However minor or unimportant those pages are, they were a new beginning for me.

IBS: It's a piece only a few people have read. Remember when I asked you to read it in Copenhagen in 2011? Most of the people in the audience didn't know it, even if they were readers of your work. Now it has come back into focus in more ways than one.

PA: Bizarre.

IBS: From these memories of the body you went on to focusing on the mind?

PA: Well, it's a little more complex than that . . .

REPORT FROM THE INTERIOR.* (2013)
Becoming Human

PA: *Winter Journal* and *Report from the Interior* are a pair, a diptych. After finishing *Winter Journal*, I realized there were other things I wanted to explore—but from another point of view. If *Winter Journal* is essentially a book about the physical self, this one is more about inner life, inner development, thought, morality, aesthetics, politics, religion. All the things that go into making a person. That was my object, I think. At the same time, I'm not a dualist, and it would be wrong to say one is the "body book" and the other is the "mind book." The perspective shifts, that's all. *Report from the Interior* is probably the strangest book I've ever written.

IBS: Thematically, *Report from the Interior* revolves around peak moments of realization, and, as I see it, it's very much your own personal history of epistemology in words and images. You point out that this is

> not because you find yourself a rare or exceptional object of study, but precisely because you don't, because you think of yourself as anyone, as everyone. (4)

I thought it's precisely on this point that your autobiographical writing differs most distinctly from the traditions of the genre: you seek to describe—not the extraordinary, not the exceptional—but rather that which is ordinary, or simply human. For me, this is the principal appeal of *Winter Journal* and *Report from the Interior*.

PA: As I said earlier, I hope they can serve as an invitation for readers to unlock their own memories.

---

* This conversation took place in May 2013 on the basis of a manuscript version that did not include the "Album" of pictures. The book was published six months later.

IBS: In the opening paragraph you contemplate the difficulties of giving an accurate account of your mind "as you remember it from your childhood."

PA: Yes, it was more difficult to write *Report from the Interior* than *Winter Journal.*

IBS: It must have been, and you did anticipate major difficulties, as I recall it.

PA: The first part is about a hundred pages long, and it goes up only to the age of twelve. The problem was that there was a lot of material that seemed important but which I'd mostly forgotten. I needed to concentrate on the things I remembered well in order to discuss them in enough detail. So many other things have vanished. I have no access to them. The first passages focus on the animistic thinking of early childhood. Oddly enough, I can still remember some of those thoughts. Hence, the opening words of the book:

> In the beginning, everything was alive. The smallest objects were endowed with beating hearts, and even the clouds had names. Scissors could walk, telephones and teapots were first cousins, eyes and eyeglasses were brothers. The face of the clock was a human face, each pea in your bowl had a different personality, and the grille on the front of your parents' car was a grinning mouth with many teeth. Pens were airships. Coins were flying saucers. The branches of trees were arms. Stones could think, and God was everywhere. (3)

Then there's a leap into the next phase—of being six years old—when memories start to coalesce. Until then, I think we're largely fragmentary beings, but a moment of self-awareness comes, self-consciousness, of being able to say to yourself: "I'm thinking the thought that I'm thinking." This kind of reflection is very different from just thinking. Once you have the ability to look at yourself from the outside, memories become continuous and the narrative self begins. As time goes on, you lose much of it. Here, I try to bring up early school experiences of learning how to read and write. I found that some of my most vivid memories were of the foolish and ridiculous things I did, such as imitating the boy who didn't separate his *W*'s. I don't recall what it was like to do *A* and *B* and *C* and *D*, but I have a lucid memory of *W*. So I put it in the book. After this, I move into my first reading experiences and mention the books I liked. This is also the time in which moral development begins: analyzing moments of bad behavior—taking apart the radio, trying to chop down the tree. Then, there's the sense of being an American, the discovery that I was Jewish, beginning to think for myself, saying, "Well, actually, if America is such a wonderful country, what about the Indians? What about the slaves?" Then, I'm moving toward the brink of adolescence. That awful time of being eleven and twelve, when you become obsessed with being part of the gang. We outgrow that, of course, or most of us do, but it's a bad time. Then the exploration of hero worship, which is something fundamental to childhood, especially to boys. That was when the preoccupation with sports started for me. It was central to my whole existence back then. This was also the time when I became interested in films, and here I briefly discuss *War of the Worlds*. As I say, it was a kind of theological jolt because suddenly the all-powerful God was shown to have no power. That was a revelation, a mighty and enduring experience.

IBS: So, there was religion in your life then?

PA: Not really. As I say in the book, my parents were not religious, but they sent me to Hebrew school when I was nine because that was the thing to do. It was no fun being chained to another desk three times a week, but I don't regret it. It was another formative experience.

IBS: *Report from the Interior* revolves around these peak moments of realization and describes how you acquire knowledge about yourself and the world. In this process of exploring what you call "the internal geography of your boyhood," you discover that your parents had no idea what they were doing, that the fortress most couples try to build for their children was no more than a tumbledown shack, and therefore you felt exposed to the elements, unprotected, vulnerable—which meant that in order to survive it was essential that you toughen up and figure out a way to fend for yourself. (46)

That's essential, too, isn't it? You "felt unprotected, vulnerable" and had to rely on yourself.

PA: There was something deeply vacant about our family life—to a shocking degree, actually. There were exceptions, of course. Good moments. It wasn't all bleak, but mostly it was. I had to find a life for myself outside the family—in school, with my friends. That was the road to survival. I couldn't let myself be crushed by the miseries of home—no, I had to find another way.

IBS: You say that there was a need to retreat from all this unhappiness, and solitude became your home base as well as your starting point.

PA: It's in those states of boredom and loneliness that you think about things. You lapse into dreamy, wistful speculations about the world, ideas come to you that wouldn't come to you in any other way. Even though you're feeling unhappy, these moments of emptiness can be very productive.

IBS: Revisiting such painful places can be difficult, and I was wondering whether writing this book brought a measure of clarity. Did it heal old wounds? Was there a therapeutic effect to the process?

PA: As I said earlier in connection with *The Invention of Solitude*, while you're writing, it seems to have a cleansing effect. Once you finish, however, nothing has changed. These memories are not deeply painful. When my friend's grandfather kicked me out of their house in anger, I was upset, but looking back on it now, I understand exactly what happened. I was shaken at the time, but it doesn't disturb me now.

IBS: They're not traumas.

PA: No, and even the last passage in the first part, where I'm breaking down in front of my English teacher in the seventh grade when he falsely accuses me of lying . . .

IBS: That's horrible. We've all been through something like that.

PA: Horrible, yes, because we all have an idea about justice, and to tell the truth and not be believed is about the worst injustice there is.

IBS: Those things you remember very vividly.

PA: Yes, because the injustice of it still rankles.

IBS: [*Laughs*] Yes, it does, even in the reading it's upsetting.

PA: Yes, the smell of that man's handkerchief . . . it's still disturbing.

IBS: [*Laughs*] Really?

PA: Yes [*laughs*].

IBS: It *was* terribly unfair. Is he still alive?

PA: I have no idea. This was 1959, for God's sake.

IBS: Well, if he's still alive, perhaps he'll write back to you and apologize. Then, as with the story of Willie Mays in *The Red Notebook*, the circle will be completed.

PA: I can tell you another thing about this teacher: he was a great believer in the virtues of public speaking, so we were often assigned to write speeches and deliver them to the class. His evaluation of me was: "You have a terrible voice, never speak in public."

IBS: [*Laughs*] You had your own radio program, didn't you?

PA: Yes. My voice was changing then, and I must have been a little squeaky. But you know, even now, every time I go on the radio I think about that teacher telling me, "You shouldn't be doing this." I also record all my own work for audiobooks. I enjoy reading aloud, really enjoy it. But every time I do one of those recordings I think about that teacher.

IBS: [*Laughs*] That's terrible.

PA: Anyway, these seem to be fundamental stories. Stories we all have. Memory consolidated by emotion, as we said in connection with *Winter Journal*. That's essentially the first part of *Report from the Interior*.

IBS: In part one, "Report from the Interior," you briefly describe your first appearance as a writer when reading your own work out loud in primary school. After that, in "Two Blows to the Head," you give massive attention to two films: *The Incredible Shrinking Man*, which you saw at the age of ten, and *I Am a Fugitive from a Chain Gang*, at fourteen. You devote twenty or thirty manuscript pages to each of these films. I realize that they truly gave you a "blow to the head," but I'm thinking there must have been other things, books, for instance, that influenced your mind just as much.

PA: The thing is, I didn't read many good books when I was young. Literature came later for me. When I was small, I read stupid sports novels, stories about baseball players and watered-down biographies of famous people. I didn't read anything truly memorable until I was around fourteen. Films had a bigger impact on me than books at the time. They changed me. I was absolutely overwhelmed by *The Incredible Shrinking Man* when I was ten. And the fact is, I've always been terribly interested in movies.

IBS: Even at that age?

PA: My appetite for films has been undiminished since childhood. I seriously thought about becoming a filmmaker when I was twenty. During my time as a student in Paris, I wrote a screenplay and was considering going to film school, shifting into film and not becoming a writer. As I said to you the other day, I was very shy then, and I couldn't talk in front of people. How would I be able to direct a movie if I couldn't speak? So I gave up the idea.

IBS: Part three, "Time Capsule," opens a door to an interesting time when you were in your early twenties at the university, traveling, experimenting with your writing. It's also the time in which you wrote hundreds of pages of fiction, some of which ultimately went into the three novels *City of Glass*, *In the Country of Last Things*, and *Moon Palace*.

PA: The early incarnations and rough drafts of things I later rewrote and published. All those manuscripts are sitting in the Berg Collection at the New York Public Library now—at least the ones that weren't lost.

IBS: You say that, however much you tried, you were incapable of writing a novel when you were twenty. You were too young.

PA: There are exceptions, of course, but very few people can do it at that age. Since writing a novel is such a long process, you have to have grown into your own way of writing. You must have your own style, your own approach to things, and it takes a long time to acquire that. Many young people can write short stories. I wrote them when I was a teenager, but then I began thinking about longer forms. It was too soon, and I wasn't ready.

IBS: The fragments or anecdotes, as you sometimes call them, in *The Red Notebook*, they're not short stories?

PA: Well, they're stories, and they're short [*laughs*].

IBS: Sure [*laughs*]. What's the story behind the letters to your ex-wife, Lydia Davis?

PA: Not long after I started writing *Report from the Interior*, Lydia contacted me. She was planning to sell her papers to a library, and it turned out that she had saved most of the letters I had written to her. The letters themselves, the physical letters, belonged to her, but the words belonged to me. That's the law. No one can publish anything from those letters without my permission, but she has the right to sell the physical objects. So, she wanted me to go through them and see if I wanted anything sealed off. Incredibly enough, there were five hundred pages.

IBS: Oh dear!

PA: "Oh dear" is right. I read through my own letters and felt I was encountering a stranger, a boy I only vaguely knew and had completely lost sight of.

IBS: It was fortunate that she kept them.

PA: It's astonishing that she kept them. Anyway, I decided to use extracts from the letters written between the ages of nineteen and twenty-two in this book. Most of those early letters were dashed off very quickly, they tend to be rather sloppily written, in fact. Even so, there are some flashes of not altogether horrible writing.

IBS: I think so, too. Some of it is very interesting to read.

PA: A portrait of a young man in a time of turmoil—and also of a young person trying to become a writer. Nearly all the personal stuff is left out. Who cares about the romantic dramas of my late boyhood? I don't even care about them myself anymore. What matters is that it was the late 1960s, and every second it seemed as if the world was about to blow up.

IBS: There's Columbia, too, and the student uprising. This is historical material. I was wondering why you decided to report it through fragments extracted from letters written to your girlfriend at the time rather than as an eyewitness account? I mean, this is important stuff.

PA: Because there are so many books written about it already.

IBS: In "Time Capsule" we also get a glimpse of the ideas that had a formative effect on you. You were interested in philosophy and you come back to this paradox: "The world is in my head. My body is in the world" (192).* Here, you conclude that Merleau-Ponty influenced you more than any other philosopher with his "vision of the embodied self." Why is that? It affected you then, but can you see the effects of it in your writing later on? Does it play into your notion of the interconnection of language and body?

PA: Merleau-Ponty was the one philosopher I read who seemed to integrate mind and body at the profoundest levels, the one philosopher who was not a dualist. So it felt truer to me, more valid and more connected to the way I thought about reality. We gravitate toward the things that seem right to us. I read a lot of philosophy: Kierkegaard, Sartre, Hume, Berkeley, Kant, Descartes, Pascal, Marx, Schopenhauer, Wittgenstein, and all the pre-Socratics. I was obsessed

---

* "Report from the Interior" (unpublished manuscript), 154. It first appears in "Notes from a Composition Book" (1967) in *Collected Poems*, 203.

with Heraclitus. When I think about it now, it's astonishing how much I read. I was eating books. Every day. I devoured them. I don't read that much anymore. I can't.

IBS: Surely, reading all that classical philosophy and existentialism and what came after must have influenced your thinking in some ways.

PA: Definitely, but I can't tell you exactly how.

IBS: What about the paradox: "The world is in my head. My body is in the world"?

PA: I was just twenty years old when I wrote that—all the way back in 1967—but I think I explain it in *Report from the Interior*:

> You still stand by that paradox, which was an attempt to capture the strange doubleness of being alive, the inexorable union of inner and outer that accompanies each beat of a person's heart from birth until death. (192)

That's it. We perceive the world. The world is our idea. We can only see the world to the extent that we can perceive it. In other words, the world is somehow a construction of our imagination, but at the same time, we're concrete beings who occupy space. We have bodies, and we're in the world that we perceive. So it's a paradox. I think those two sentences capture the essence of what I've been trying to do all my life.

IBS: Part four, "Album," is not just a pictorial accompaniment to your memories, is it? I mean, it opens to an alternative world where images from films, cartoons, and historical scenes were as real to you as people of flesh and blood. This is where cartoon figures like Farmer Gray and Felix the Cat truly exist. You describe the early realization that

The real is so defiantly at odds with the imagined, you can't help feeling that a nasty trick has been played on you. (9)

In several of your novels, characters, narrators, even the author (whoever he is), cross effortlessly between different worlds, and I was wondering whether this disappointment might have prompted some of your shifts between the "real" and the "imagined" inside the fiction?

PA: In the case of the cartoons, I imagined the world as one thing, but then I saw that it was something else. I couldn't absorb it. It was an infinitely receding reality. TV, I knew, was not real. It was just images of something familiar and real. For me cartoons were the same. I just couldn't understand that cartoons were images of images rather than images of things. You saw a human being on TV, and you knew there was a human being in the studio. Ergo, if you saw a cartoon, the cartoon character had to be in the studio as well.

IBS: You weave your considerations about writing into the book itself and lay bare these thoughts about how to begin to revisit the terrain of your childhood mind:

Dig up the old stories, scratch around for whatever you can find, then hold up the shards to the light and have a look at them. Do that. Try to do that. (5)

PA: I didn't really know what I was getting myself into, and I felt that this debate with myself about what I was proposing to do was a natural part of the book.

IBS: Here it means, of course, that you have, side by side, the perspective of the mature author, the adult mind of Paul Auster, accompanying that of the very young boy. There's a lot of humor in that relation.

PA: Yes, all the funny misconceptions of childhood:

> Until you were five or six, perhaps even seven, you thought
> the words *human being* were pronounced *human bean*. You
> found it mystifying that humanity should be represented
> by such a small, common vegetable, but somehow, twisting
> around your thoughts to accommodate this misunder-
> standing, you decided that the very smallness of the bean was
> what made it significant, that we all start out in our mother's
> womb no larger than a bean, and therefore the bean was the
> truest, most powerful symbol of life itself. (11–12)

[*Laughs*] You twist around the things you don't understand in order
to make sense of them. Errors compounding errors.

IBS: Later, in the letters, you reflect on the role of the artist in the
world:

> Once I thought that art should be . . . divorced from
> society . . . Once I wished to live with my back turned to the
> world. I see now that this is impossible. Society, too, must
> be faced—not in the purity of contemplation, but with the
> intention of acting. But action, when generated from an
> ethic, often frightens people . . . because it does not seem
> to have a one-to-one correspondence to its intention. (250)

PA: I was struggling to resolve the conflict between politics and
art, trying to figure out how to justify being an artist at a moment
when it seemed imperative to act. There were two examples on my
horizon: socialist realism in the Soviet Union, which was bankrupt,
and the Surrealists in France, who had tried to combine avant-garde
literature with political activism. Clearly, I was interested in the Surrealists. In fact, the first book I ever published was *A Little Anthology
of Surrealist Poems*, translations of Breton, Éluard, Artaud, and half a
dozen other poets.

IBS: On the following page you also talk about social revolution:

> The social revolution must be accompanied by a metaphysical revolution. Men's minds must be liberated along with their physical existences—if not, any freedom obtained will be false & fleeting. Weapons for achieving & maintaining freedom must be created. This means a courageous stare into the unknown—the transformation of life . . . ART MUST POUND SAVAGELY ON THE DOORS OF ETERNITY . . . (250)

Was this a kind of manifesto?

PA: [*Laughs*] I don't know what I was talking about.

IBS: "Doors of eternity"! Not reality, but eternity?

PA: I have no idea.

IBS: But you put it in, anyway.

PA: Yes, because I was so emphatic, so emphatic that I wrote it in capital letters. I kept it in, but I don't understand it.

IBS: "This means a courageous stare into the unknown—the transformation of life." This is big stuff.

PA: Big stuff, oh yes. I was a very young man thinking very big thoughts.

IBS: You were also thinking about religion, weren't you?

> God was the commander of the celestial mind police, the unseen, all-powerful one who could invade your head and listen to your thoughts, who could hear you talking to yourself and translate the silence into words. (12)

PA: I didn't explore this business as fully as I might have. I just didn't want to. It made me weary just to think about it. But you're right, after being thrust into Hebrew school and having gone through my bar mitzvah, I did start to take an interest in Judaism around the time I was thirteen. I wasn't sure if I believed in God. I wasn't even sure whether religion was important. I was filled with all the questions young people ask. I actually continued after my bar mitzvah for about a year and even switched synagogues because I wanted something more serious. The rabbi there was a terrific man, Theodore Friedman. We had one-on-one conversations every week for about eight months. He would give me things to read and we discussed them. I was so lucky to have such an intelligent man to listen to me and talk things out with. I was probably about fourteen when I came to the conclusion that it wasn't for me. I couldn't believe in God, I didn't want to practice any religion. Friedman was a good enough person to wish me well—and to let me go without an argument.

IBS: Here, I thought, perhaps we also find part of the reason why you often downplay the fact that, actually, you do have a kind of Jewish background. Your parents, you say,

> were simply Americans who happened to be Jews, thoroughly assimilated after the struggles of their own immigrant parents, and therefore in your mind the notion of Judaism was above all associated with foreignness. (68)

We see this Jewish "foreignness" reflected, for instance, in *Timbuktu*, don't we? You continue,

> Jews were invisible, they had no part to play in American life, and they never appeared as heroes in books or films or television shows. (70)

PA: That's true.

IBS: Even so, you were exposed to a measure of anti-Semitism.

> [T]o be a Jew was to be different from everyone else, to stand
> apart, to be looked upon as an outsider. And you, who until
> then had seen yourself as thoroughly American, as American
> as any Mayflower blue blood, now understood that there
> were those who felt you didn't belong, that even in the place
> you called home, you were not fully at home. (72)

PA: When I was young, anti-Semitism was still rampant in America.
Less so today, but it's still with us. It will always be with us.

IBS: You also say that being Jewish had little to do with religion and
came to signify

> a history of struggle and exclusion that culminated in the
> disasters of World War II, and that history was all that con-
> cerned you. (73–74)

Is that how you still feel about being Jewish? Is that what defines it
for you?

PA: Yes, pretty much. I feel connected to the history but also to many
of the ideas. Let's not sell it short, after all. Much of Jewish thought
is thoroughly revolutionary. The idea of the Sabbath, for example.
The Sabbath was for slaves as well as for free people, the first instance
in human history when the high and the low were looked upon as
equals. And if there was such a thing as justice, it had to be justice
for all people. Think of the Book of Jonah, the only prophetic book
written in the third person, that little comic tale, which is read on the
darkest day of the Jewish calendar, Yom Kippur. Why this particular
book? It's because the message of Jonah is that you can't have justice
for just one people and not for all. It's an overwhelming idea. In
Christianity, it seems to me, if you're going to be a good and serious
Christian, you have to turn yourself into a saint. The golden rule: do

unto others as you would have them do unto you. Do you know how hard it is to live like that? The Jewish idea is the opposite: don't do unto others what you don't want them to do unto you. This strikes me as a much more plausible way to negotiate your way through the world than demanding near perfection.

IBS: In *Report from the Interior*, you talk about watching these "clusters of old Jews huddling in the darkness around 'Old Country' singers," and it "filled you with dumb despair." You say it was like

> stepping among corpses, dead things, which I had known only from hearsay, now confronted for the first time. (258)

Yesterday, you told me it was the first time you saw those Ashkenazis. I was wondering why you associated them with something of the past only, an ominous past of "corpses" and "dead things"? It's because of World War II, isn't it?

PA: That and the oppression of the Jews, yes. I had grown up in a different kind of Jewish world, a suburban Jewish world, and I had never encountered these people. So it was a bit surprising. All this came back to me when I reread those old letters—written by a young man I can barely recognize anymore.

IBS: There is a line in a letter you wrote while in Paris in August 1967 that I think is pivotal in your work even today:

> I have been writing. It makes me feel human. (207)

Becoming human is your gloss on Pinocchio, isn't it? It's a recurring notion in your work, and you've talked about becoming or remaining human in different contexts a few times in the course of these conversations, for instance, in connection with *In the Country of Last Things* you said that "the essence of the book is about how to remain human."

PA: But that's what all writing is about: how to find your own humanity and your connection to other human beings. I realize I've been writing seriously for fifty years now. It's been a long journey. I'm much happier and feel more integrated when I'm working, when I'm writing, when I'm involved in a project. It's not that writing is easy; it can be agonizingly difficult, but even the struggle is good. I sometimes ask myself, "Why do I do this? What's the point of writing books, of spending my life in this way?" The only justification I've ever been able to come up with, the only thing that makes some sense to me, is that in order to write you have to give everything you have. It's a total effort, and you have to expose yourself completely, you have to give and give and give. And you must put in a maximum effort every day. I think there are very few jobs in the world that ask so much of you. You can slide through in just about any other profession. You can rely on habits, you can be lazy, you can have days when you don't need to make a maximum effort, whether you're a lawyer or a doctor or a garbageman or a plumber. So, when I get up from my desk at the end of a day of work, even if I've accomplished nothing, even if I've crossed out every line I've written, I can at least get up and say, "I gave it everything I had. I'm exhausted, and I did the best I could." Somehow, living at that level of intensity makes you feel human in a way that most other jobs don't allow for.

PART TWO
NOVELS

THE NEW YORK TRILOGY. (1985–6)
"Learning to Live with Ambiguity"

And whatever the man called each living creature,
that was its name. (Gen. 2:19)

IBS: *The New York Trilogy* is probably your most widely read book, principally, I think, because it breaks new ground through the unique combination of exploration, captivating story, and reflection that characterizes much of your work. The reader is at once drawn into the world of detection and obsessive surveillance only to find him- or herself thoroughly taken in by the existential and literary mysteries you put before us in the three short novels—*City of Glass*, *Ghosts*, and *The Locked Room*—that form the Trilogy. Jan Kjærstad is quite right to describe it as a "crystal that refracts light into colors that have rarely been seen before."* What prompted these strange stories?

PA: They come out of material I'd been thinking about and working on for many years. In *The Red Notebook*, I describe the phone call I received from the person who wanted to talk to the Pinkerton Agency. It triggered the first novel, *City of Glass*. The idea of a wrong number intrigued me and, because it happened to concern a detective agency, it somehow seemed inevitable that my story should have a detective element to it. It's not in any way a crucial part of the story, and it was always irritating to me to hear these books described as detective novels. They're not that in the least.

IBS: No, not at all. Even if the protagonist in each of the stories at some point devotes himself to an investigation, the element of detection here concerns linguistic and existential issues rather than

---

* See back cover of the Penguin edition.

criminal ones. Did you deliberately set out to experiment with the detective genre or was it simply useful to you as a form?

PA: It was useful to me in the same way old musical hall routines and vaudeville were useful to Beckett in writing *Waiting for Godot*. Or the way romances were useful to Cervantes in writing *Don Quixote*. You could also say *Crime and Punishment* is a detective story, I suppose. Many novelists have used crime fiction forms to write about other things. I'm hardly the first to do this. So, I didn't feel I was setting out to explode anything. I was just curious.

IBS: I thought perhaps you wanted to cast writing here as a kind of detection?

PA: I just wanted to remain loyal to the inspiration prompted by that phone call. It was a challenge I set for myself. There are sources of much greater importance to this book. At a strictly intellectual level, one of them derives from my intense reading of John Milton when I was an undergraduate. I had a brilliant professor, Edward Tayler, who taught the famous Milton course at Columbia. It completely altered my way of thinking about literature. I was young and impressionable: a sophomore completely immersed in the reflections on language that come out of Milton. They informed my ideas of the New Babel and triggered the mad theories I ascribe to Henry Dark in *City of Glass*. At the personal level, *City of Glass* is also a kind of shadow autobiography or biography. I imagined, in an exaggerated way, what might have happened to me if I hadn't met Siri. In some sense, it's an homage to her. I truly felt she saved my life when I met her.

IBS: Without her you would have been Quinn?

PA: Maybe, maybe. Other crucial sources of inspiration were the wild child stories, which opened on to all the questions about language that have always interested me. I wrote a great deal about these linguistic issues when I was younger. They were integrated into an earlier project that was somehow a combination of *Moon Palace* and *City of Glass*—one enormous work, far too big for me to handle. Many of the ideas in *City in Glass* come out of those embryonic writings, for instance, forming letters with the steps of a person walking through a city and the conversation about Don Quixote with the "Auster" character. It's a completely mad reading of *Don Quixote*, by the way, and I have to insist that I was making fun of myself. Almost everything "Auster" says is the opposite of what I believe.

IBS: I can see that [*laughs*]. He's also described as an unreliable person and unpleasant.

PA: Well, not so unpleasant . . .

IBS: He "behaved badly throughout."*

PA: Yes, yes [*laughs*].

IBS: There's a moment toward the end of *The Locked Room* where the narrator suddenly injects this somewhat astonishing declaration:

> These three stories are finally the same story, but each one represents a different stage in my awareness of what it is about. (346)

Did you plan for them to mirror one another from the beginning?

PA: No. This is how it started: as I was working on *City of Glass* in 1981, I realized that I'd written something similar about five years earlier in a play entitled *Blackouts*,** and I revisited the play to see if it

---

* See the final paragraph of the novel.
** A play printed in the hardcover edition of *Hand to Mouth*.

could be reconfigured as a piece of narrative prose. So, I went back, adapted ideas from the older material and, indeed, *Blackouts* became the origin of *Ghosts*. Once I was writing the second volume, I knew there had to be a third. And so, it became a trilogy.

IBS: You say the three novels are different dimensions of the same story.

PA: The issue that runs through all of them is ambiguity. Ambiguity and uncertainty. If I had to boil it down to one phrase, it's this: "learning to live with ambiguity." This is the essence of *The New York Trilogy*. That explains why, at the very end, the narrator of *The Locked Room* throws away Fanshawe's manuscript.

IBS: Because it marks yet another dead end for him?

> All the words were familiar to me, and yet they seemed to have been put together strangely, as though their final pur-pose was to cancel each other out. Each sentence erased the sentence before it, each paragraph made the next paragraph impossible. (370)

PA: It's about uncertainty, and the fact that there are no eternal givens in the world. Somehow, we have to make room for the things we don't understand. We have to live with obscurity. I'm not talking about a passive, quietistic acceptance of things, but rather the realiza-tion that there are things we're not going to know.

IBS: That's very interesting, "learning to live with ambiguity."

PA: Perhaps.

IBS: I suppose it plays into the narrator's considerations here:

> I have been struggling to say goodbye to something for a

long time now, and this struggle is all that really matters. The story is not in the words; it's in the struggle. (346)

I took this struggle to be about writing.

PA: It *is* about writing, but at the same time it's about accommodating the unknown.

IBS: Saying goodbye to the absolutes?

PA: I believe so, yes.

IBS: Well, if this book is where some of your major realizations concerning knowledge and truth were consolidated, might we not see *The New York Trilogy* as one of your most important books, if not *the* most important? The reviewers and critics do.

PA: I don't know. I think there's a tendency among the journalists to regard the work that puts you in the public eye for the first time as your best work. Take Lou Reed.* He can't stand "Walk on the Wild Side." This song is so famous, it's followed him around all his life, and he'll always be best known for having done that. Similarly, no matter how many movies he made afterward, Godard will always be best known for *Breathless*. It's true for novelists; it's true for poets. Even so, I don't think in terms of "best" or "worst." Making art isn't like competing in the Olympics, after all.

IBS: I'm not suggesting *The New York Trilogy* is your best book but that, generally speaking, it may be your most important work.

PA: Most important in the sense that it's the most read and most studied of my books, perhaps.

---

* Auster made two films with Lou Reed, *Blue in the Face* and *Lulu on the Bridge*.

IBS: Why do you think that is?

PA: I don't know, I don't know. It seemed to have struck a lot of people as innovative.

IBS: It *is* innovative. Very much so, and, for one reason or another, what's new about it concurs with the ideas that emerged in French theory and hit the literary scene round about the time you published *The New York Trilogy*.

PA: As you know, I was not involved with any of this.

IBS: I know. It's just a strange coincidence.

PA: I have a feeling that, as the years go by and as French theory diminishes in importance, people will stop reading my books in that way. At least I hope they will.

IBS: Perhaps. Still, I think some of your early work will go down in history as quintessentially postmodern. I know you're not happy about being placed in this category.

PA: *The New York Trilogy* is always going to be attached to my name, no matter where I go, no matter how many other things I write. There's nothing I can do about it.

IBS: Is it necessarily a bad thing? Does it irritate you?

PA: The fact is that I don't even know if I think *The New York Trilogy* is very good. To me, it seems rather crude. I think I've become a better writer. These are youthful texts that mark the end of a certain phase of my life.

IBS: Even so, you experimented with literary convention, opened new possibilities in fiction, explored ideas. These early books, especially *The New York Trilogy*, raised very important questions about truth, about language, about being in the world. They prompt reflection about issues that were absolutely pivotal in contemporary literary theory.

PA: I'm not going to pretend they're not philosophical books.

IBS: More so than *The Invention of Solitude*, I think, even if it also invites a great deal of reflection.

PA: In the second part of *The Invention of Solitude*, I explore many of the same questions, but more from a historical perspective than from a purely philosophical one.

IBS: Both *The Invention of Solitude* and *The New York Trilogy* have captivated audiences all over the world. My students absolutely love them. I taught them again (probably for the tenth time) last week and after the lecture one of my students came up to me and asked me to give you this letter. It says that your work has changed his life and now he wants to become a writer!

PA: [*Laughs*] I pity him.

IBS: It has that effect. He was overwhelmed. He could hardly breathe, and he had to stay behind to talk about his experience.

PA: Is he a graduate or undergraduate student?

IBS: Well, they're in their fourth or fifth year. Just before they finish their MA. I've had several students with similar reactions over the years.

PA: Well, I'm happy.

IBS: I think it has to do with your special combination of enchanting storytelling and intellectual challenge: it opens up new ways of thinking about how we try to make sense of the world. It addresses issues we all grapple with, perhaps especially when we're young. One of the most striking features, not just in your early work, is the fact that your questions only ever open to more questions. Answers are rarely provided. You are so interested in the processes and mechanisms of writing that you lay them bare and weave your thoughts about them into the stories themselves.

PA: I've been reflecting on these questions all my life.

IBS: Surely, all writers do that.

PA: Most writers are perfectly satisfied with traditional literary models and happy to produce works they feel are beautiful and true and good. I've always wanted to write what to me is beautiful, true, and good, but I'm also interested in inventing new ways to tell stories. I wanted to turn everything inside out. I suppose it's a tremendously ambitious stance: not to be satisfied with conventions, to play with them sometimes, then to expose traditional norms and stretch them beyond their limits.

IBS: With a view to laying them bare or just to see what happens when you probe?

PA: I want to turn things inside out. Like an architect building a house with all the plumbing and wiring exposed. I'm fascinated by the artificiality of literature. We all know it's a book: when we open it, we all know that it's not the real world. It's something else. It's an invention. I think that's why I found it so interesting to put my own name in the first volume of the Trilogy. The name is printed on the cover and then, well, wouldn't it be curious to have the same name also inside the book—and then see what happens? I was playing with the split between what I call the "writing self" and the "biographical self." Here I am, I'm still sitting at the red table with you, I take out the garbage, I pay my taxes, I do everything everybody else does. That's me. At the same time, there's the writer who's living in another world altogether. I somehow wanted to connect those two worlds.

I. *CITY OF GLASS*: THE NAME AND THE NAMED

IBS: Then who is the writer of *City of Glass*?

PA: It's a third person. It's not Quinn, it's not Auster. It's another character who is nameless.

IBS: Is he identical to the "I" introduced at the very end of the story?

> I returned home from my trip to Africa in February, just hours before a snowstorm began to fall on New York. I called my friend Auster that evening, and he urged me to come over to see him as soon as I could. (157)

PA: Suddenly, there's an "I." Suddenly, the whole thing is shaken up, right at the end, and we can't be sure about anything. He has just arrived from Africa. I've never been to Africa, but in my mind, it was always the mystery continent, the unknown place—"darkest Africa" [*laughs*].

IBS: I see, so he remains unnamed, unknown—ambiguous, as you said earlier. I was wondering about this in connection with Stillman's insistence that names are synonymous with the bearer. As we gather from the three introduction scenes in chapter nine, Stillman registers only a name, not a person's appearance, and so, when Quinn introduces himself as Henry Dark—Stillman's pseudonym—Stillman simply accepts Quinn as his own invention without batting an eyelid. Even more astonishingly, it never occurs to him that something is amiss when Quinn introduces himself by the name of Stillman's own son:

> Oh. You mean my son. Yes, that's possible. You look just like him. Of course, Peter is blond and you are dark. Not Henry Dark, but dark of hair. People change, don't they? One minute we're one thing, and then another another. (101)

For Stillman, the name invokes the essence of the person bearing it. The two are identical.

PA: The same goes for name and object. Part of him can't recognize that Quinn isn't his son, part of him is just pretending.

IBS: The linguistic theory he has developed dictates that he must accept Quinn as who he says he is, despite the fact that he has introduced himself three days in a row each time under a different name without changing his appearance.

PA: Yes, but Stillman is mad. He's lost in his own thoughts, and he can't be understood in any rational way.

IBS: I know, but readers are detectives too, and we think about all these details and try to make sense of the mysteries. The thing is that Stillman's ideas about the transparency between word and object actually correspond to what you're doing in the book. That is, up until the whole thing is obscured by the disappearance of basically all the central characters. So even if he's mad, or if you think of him as mad, some of his ideas are congruent with the nature of the fictional world you have constructed for him.

PA: For me, the important thing here is that Stillman's project will finally destroy language. He doesn't realize it, but, essentially, what his ideas are leading to is this: everything would have to have a different name. We talked about this the other day—in connection with the red table.

IBS: You've also filmed this idea in *Smoke*, haven't you? The tobacconist takes a photo every morning at the same time from the very same angle. Even so, the pictures are never identical.

PA: Yes, it's the same idea, you're right.

IBS: Also in *Moon Palace*, when Marco is wheeling Effing around in the streets and is required to describe the nuances in a brick wall.* No two bricks are the same.

PA: Exactly.

IBS: This is where Marco realizes that language is inadequate:

> I was piling too many words on top of each other, and rather than reveal the thing before us, they were in fact obscuring it, burying it under an avalanche of subtleties and geometric abstractions. (*Moon Palace*, 123)

PA: I'm interested in things that butt up against the limits of language. As you can see in "Notes from a Composition Book," I was grappling with questions about language, reality, literature, and the world when I was just twenty.

> The eye sees the world in a flux. The word is an attempt to arrest the flow, to stabilize it. And yet we persist in trying to translate experience into language. Hence poetry, hence the utterances of daily life. This is the faith that prevents universal despair—and also causes it. (*Collected Poems*, 204)

When I started writing novels, there seemed no point in writing them unless I took a different approach.

---

* See discussion of *Moon Palace*.

IBS: It seems to me that you weren't really looking for answers. It was the process that mattered.

PA: Because I knew to begin with that we can never arrive at any stable truth. There *is* no one answer. Once you think you have one, that's the moment when you begin to drown. This is the problem of epistemology, isn't it? There's a bit of dialogue in *Smoke* that captures it in a humorous spirit. Let's see where it is, yes, scene 55—it's when Auggie is talking to Jimmy, his mentally retarded assistant, and the scene begins with this:

> If it happens, it happens. If it doesn't, it doesn't. Do you understand what I'm saying? You never know what's going to happen next, and the moment you think you know, that's the moment you don't know a goddamn thing. That's what we call a paradox. Are you following me?

Jimmy then replies,

> Sure, Auggie, I follow. When you don't know nothing, it's like paradise. I know what that is. It's after you're dead and you go up to heaven and sit with the angels. (*Collected Screenplays*, 109–110)

IBS: [*Laughs*] Could we say that *City of Glass* is principally about the ambiguity of language?

PA: No doubt, the central questions in the book, even the action, revolve around it.

IBS: Peter Stillman Jr., here, is one of the most astonishing examples of a character who embodies language:

> The body acted almost exactly as the voice had: machine-like, fitful, alternating between slow and rapid gestures, rigid

and yet expressive, as if the operation were out of control, not quite corresponding to the will that lay behind it. (17)

There's complete correlation between physical movement and speech here—both as broken as Peter's mind.

PA: Speech is a physical activity. Mental as well, of course—how else could I summon up the words I want to say?—but as I speak, my mouth is moving, my tongue is moving, my lungs are involved. It's happening in the body. The words are going out into space, hitting your eardrum, you're hearing them. It's physical.

IBS: Sure, but here you have a person moving in perfect accordance with the cadence of his own speech. That's taking it a step further, I would have thought.

> It seemed to Quinn that Stillman's body had not been used for a long time and that all its functions had been relearned, so that motion had become a conscious process, each movement broken down into its component submovements, with the result that all flow and spontaneity had been lost. It was like watching a marionette trying to walk without strings. (17)

The mastery of language and the mastery of bodily movement are finally the same. Stillman Jr. has had to learn both very late in childhood.

PA: Not only has Peter been physically abused, he's been deprived of language. He's doubly damaged.

IBS: As I read it, he embodies the transparency his father was trying to reinscribe in the modern world. Hence the title: *City of* Glass, right? In a sense, he's fixed between the pre- and postlapsarian worlds, stuck between the Adamic principle and the confusion of tongues in

Babel. He *is* what he *says* at any given time, and the grammar of his sentences determines his movements. At the same time, he utterly fails to communicate.

PA: Because he has a tenuous hold on language.

IBS: Yes, speech is nothing but sound to him. His grasp of the semantic side of language is less than firm, isn't it? There are signifiers but no signifieds. He doesn't understand the meaning of words.

> This is what is called speaking. I believe that is the term. When words come out, fly into the air, live for a moment, and die. Strange, is it not? I myself have no opinion. No and no again. (19)

Even if, in appearance, he's transparent, pale, dressed in white, innocent, and would therefore seem to embody the language of Eden, the speech he produces is radically postlapsarian: one word cancels out the one before it and there's no stability of meaning whatsoever. As he says to Quinn:

> What are these words coming from his mouth? I will tell you. Or else I will not tell you. Yes and no. (18)

Or is he just mad? His father's experiment gone awfully wrong?

PA: Yes, he has failed. At the same time, Stillman Jr. is an ambiguous character: his connection with language has been damaged but not completely destroyed. He can speak, and he can reflect on his own utterances: "This is what is called speaking."

IBS: He sort of stands back from language and looks at it from a different perspective from the rest of us, I think.

PA: He likes to flaunt common expressions such as "You bet your bottom dollar." He's picked up these phrases, but he doesn't understand their idiomatic meanings.

IBS: He defamiliarizes them, doesn't he? He dislocates them from their normal context.

PA: That's right.

IBS: This is one of the tremendous appeals of this book: the way you play with the relationship between language and meaning, explode truisms, turn everything inside out, as you said. I was stunned when I first read *The New York Trilogy*. It still amazes every new generation of students and other readers.

PA: I know you insist on a theoretical reading, and the correspondence between language and movement is obviously there in the text, but I have to let you know that the monologue by Peter Stillman is one of the rare times when the first draft was the finished draft for me. I didn't revise a word. It came out in exactly the way it is in the book. I simply got into it—I was *him*. For the hours and minutes it took to write that passage, I was Peter Stillman.

IBS: That's very strange. I'm wondering about sources of inspiration here. You mentioned Milton earlier, and I know you've read extensively about biblical notions of language: the Adamic principle, the Tower of Babel, the Fall of Man, the Fall of Language.

PA: They were crucial. Especially the idea of Adam naming all the plants and animals and objects in the world. This is the human enterprise, this is what God gives man as his central task: name the world!

IBS: And what does Adam do: he names the essence.

PA: And so, words and things were the same, interconnected, as Stillman says. After the Fall, they were severed from one another.

They become arbitrary signs and no longer express the essence. It's a fable explaining something about human life.

IBS: Which is what religion does, I suppose.

PA: Or tries to. We mustn't lose sight of the emotional content of the book. It's not just a philosophical puzzle. There's a real story here, and Quinn is a real character: a man with a body and a life. The question of the child in *City of Glass* is essential, and the loss of Quinn's son resonates throughout the story. We must also think about the role of the city in all of this, too. It's no accident that during the long passage when Quinn is walking around New York and sits down to record his observations, he's mostly writing about the broken, down-and-out people on the streets. He's sitting in front of the United Nations, which, in several ways, is the modern Babel—in New York City. I didn't make a big point of it, but the location was deliberately chosen to forge that link.

IBS: You are right, we must talk about Quinn. One of the most striking features of this character is his ardent devotion to the case and to walking. He walks tirelessly, without direction or purpose. Is he a flâneur, a peripatetic?

> By wandering aimlessly, all places became equal, and it no longer mattered where he was. On his best walks, he was able to feel that he was nowhere. And this, finally, was all he ever asked of things: to be nowhere. (4)

PA: I think the aimlessness of it is what attracts him. He doesn't want to have a fixed destination. He's a man in pain, a man with sorrow in his heart. He's disconnected from life because of his losses. I think these walks are ways to forget. They're an escape from himself. Wandering brings him a kind of peace. He's doing it to keep himself going. Some people drink, some people take drugs—Quinn walks.

IBS: Some people write.

PA: Yes, some people write.

IBS: So, walking here isn't an appropriation of urban space? It's not a way of taking in the city as when Auggie in *Smoke* takes that same photo every morning of his little corner?

PA: His little corner of the city, yes. These things are related to each another.

IBS: Auggie's photos would also appear to be pointless.

PA: They're arbitrary. They document whatever is happening at exactly seven a.m. every morning—click. That's it. It's one way of organizing reality for yourself. We all have to bring order to the chaos of our daily lives, we all have to figure out a way to keep ourselves from going mad.

IBS: Then, what about Stillman Sr.'s walks? They take the physical shape of letters, which spell four words that are key to the story:

> Quinn then copied out the letters in order: OWEROFBAB. After fiddling with them for a quarter of an hour, switching them around, pulling them apart, rearranging the sequence, he returned to the original order and wrote them out in the following manner: OWER OF BAB. The solution seemed so grotesque that his nerve almost failed him. Making due allowances for the fact that he had missed the first four days and that Stillman had not yet finished, the answer seemed inescapable: THE TOWER OF BABEL. (85)

This is mind-boggling! I was completely stunned the first few times I read it. Is it really happening, I mean in the reality of the narrative, or is Quinn merely interpreting or imagining this crucial connection between walks and words?

PA: Whether Stillman is doing it on purpose or whether it's purely random—who knows? As the author, I can't give you an answer. Maybe yes, maybe no. The point is that Quinn attaches meaning to Stillman's cryptic routes through the city. That's the important thing here. He's getting sucked up into something that might not be real.

IBS: So, he finds meaning in it, and whether it's real or not doesn't really matter?

PA: Not for us, but it matters for him. It begins to push him over the edge.

IBS: [*Laughs*] Yes, it does.

PA: There's the other curious thing that happens to Quinn, probably the most enigmatic occurrence in the book: toward the end when Quinn is alone in the room, someone slips in trays of food for him. We never know who does that.

IBS: Do you know?

PA: Yes, the author is feeding him.

IBS: That *is* strange.

PA: Perhaps. To me it seems perfectly normal that an author should want to feed one of his beloved characters.

IBS: So, once again, you have the author crossing the ontological barrier between the three-dimensional world and the two-dimensional. You can't do that.

PA: I know, I know [*laughs*]. But I did it anyway.

IBS: So, the "nowhere" Quinn finds is not just a kind of equilibrium?

It's also a space where he's at peace—and indeed safe if the author, his maker, is looking after him: "Quinn was nowhere now. He had nothing, he knew nothing, he knew that he knew nothing." (124)

PA: It's a kind of exorcism. An emptying out. He had set up a life for himself that allowed him to be no one. He writes under a pseudonym, his central character is a detective, Max Work, he has an agent he's never met in person. In more senses than one, he's been able to erase himself. Even so, he's not passive. He goes to the opera in the winter, he goes to baseball games in the summer, he takes his walks and he writes his books. And he reads. He reads a lot.

IBS: What happens to him in the end?

> Quinn no longer had any interest in himself. He wrote about the stars, the earth, his hopes for mankind. He felt that his words had been severed from him, that now they were part of the world at large, as real and specific as a stone, or a lake, or a flower. They no longer had anything to do with him. (156)

Then he disappears, naked in that sterile room. Even if there's an author who feeds him, Quinn disappears. Where to? Into language? Flesh become words? Or back to some prelapsarian beginning?

PA: As I see it, he evaporates out of the story. So, whatever happens to Quinn, he's in the next phase of his life. He's out of the story now. As the narrator says at the end, "And wherever he may have disappeared to, I wish him luck." I wish him luck, too.

IBS: But it's not quite the end of Quinn, is it?

PA: No, Quinn pops up again in *The Locked Room*—if it's the same Quinn—and Anna finds the passport of a man named Quinn in *In the Country of Last Things*, and Dan Quinn, a university professor, turns out to be Walt's nephew in *Mr. Vertigo*, and then, in *Travels in the Scriptorium*, Quinn reappears as Mr. Blank's lawyer. But we can't be certain if all these Quinns are the same person. Perhaps. And then again, perhaps not. It could be another Quinn. It probably is another Quinn.

IBS: Perhaps not?

PA: Perhaps.

II. *GHOSTS*: A FABLE OF REPRESENTATION

IBS: At first, we think *Ghosts* is a perfectly straightforward detective novel: Blue is hired by White to watch and report on Black. Then, suddenly, the tables are turned and we don't know what to believe anymore. Nor does the protagonist:

> Blue no longer knows what to think. It seems perfectly plausible to him that he is also being watched, observed by another in the same way that he has been observing Black. If that is the case, then he has never been free. (200)

What kind of a story is *Ghosts*?

PA: *Ghosts* is a more direct engagement with the detective novel than either of the other two parts of the Trilogy. As I said earlier, it derives from the play, *Blackouts*. It's the first book I wrote in the present tense, and it's the first time I left out quotation marks to indicate direct speech. The narrative voice in the beginning is first-person plural, "we," but then, for the most part, the story is told in the third person. It has an altogether different tone from anything I've ever written before or since. There's a comic feel to the narration, to the whole tone, in fact. Blue is a kind of ridiculous character, but, at the same time, everything is described in a deadly serious way.

IBS: The fact that you've named each character after a color adds to the sense of artificiality?

PA: I wanted to create a fable-like effect and emphasized this by giving untraditional names to the characters. It could have been X, Y, and Z, but I decided on colors: Green, White, Black, Brown, Blue. They're all real names, but artificially grouped like this, we see them as colors, and they cease to refer to human beings but become indications of something else. We can read this as a comment on the defeat of Stillman's theory, and the questions of language raised in *City of Glass* are opened again here in *Ghosts*. I've always been fascinated by the question of color, philosophically, visually, emotionally. Words cannot convey color. I cannot describe to a blind person what red is. Color must be experienced. You only know what red is when you see it. In the same way, you only know a human being by interacting with that person. It's a kind of tautology, but that's what motivated me to use those strange names.

IBS: So, could we say that these color names explain the title? They indicate that the individual character is unimportant; he's merely a form with no real substance: a ghost.

PA: Perhaps, but we must also take into account the real ghosts in the story: Lincoln, Thoreau, Whitman—and all the famous dead people who walked down Orange Street in Brooklyn. They're all ghosts. So, in a sense, are writers:

> Writing is a solitary business. It takes over your life. In some sense, a writer has no life of his own. Even when he's there, he's not really there.
>   Another ghost.
>   Exactly. (209)

This is one of the keys to the story.

IBS: This is where Blue has become desperate to leave his solitary room and to be taken off the case. In fact, he wants out of the story.

> [T]his book offers him nothing. There is no story, no plot, no action—nothing but a man sitting alone in a room and writing a book. That's all there is, Blue realizes, and he no longer wants any part of it. But how to get out? How to get out of the room that is the book that will go on being written for as long as he stays in the room? (202)

PA: Blue is stuck, a prisoner of the case he's been hired to work on. So, how to get out? He can only get out by breaking into the room opposite, smashing things, shaking it all up. It becomes extremely violent at the end.

IBS: Yes, it does. You said earlier that this is a book about reading a book, but it's also a story about writing, isn't it?

PA: Yes, of course. You're reading a book about a man writing a book, which creates the impression of what it means to read a book. There's hardly any action in *Ghosts*. The narrative is propelled by myriad digressions—for instance, the reference to *Walden* and the story about Whitman's brain, which is a true story, as are all the stories about the Brooklyn Bridge.

IBS: They have a strong effect on the reading. All these surprises, we don't see them coming, and you offer no explanations.

PA: No, because in fables you don't explain. People just are, and they act. Think of *Mr. Vertigo*. There's no explanation about Master Yehudi. Other books of mine, the so-called more realistic ones, go into great detail about who the characters are, their motives, their pasts, the places they come from. In *Ghosts*, I didn't want to give away too much. Blue is everyman, he's any man. Black hires Blue to watch him, as if driven to live out the Berkeleyan principle, "to be is to be perceived."

He needs a witness to confirm his existence in the world. The pivotal moment is when Blue steals Black's papers and discovers that

> they are nothing more than his own reports. There they are, one after the other, the weekly accounts, all spelled out in black and white, meaning nothing, as far from the truth of the case as silence would have been. (224)

IBS: And so, we realize, it's the surveillee, Black himself, who has ordered the surveillance. Black is also White, isn't he?

PA: It's one person. He comes in disguises. Later, he also wears a mask at the post office.

IBS: Oh yes, postbox no. 1001, alluding, I assume, to Scheherazade's fables in *Arabian Nights*. This is where the boundary between factual reports and fiction becomes completely blurred.

III. *THE LOCKED ROOM*: THE SELF-DESTRUCTIVE TEXT

IBS: *The Locked Room* tells the wonderful story of an asymmetrical male relationship in which the nameless protagonist is drawn into an intricate web of loyalties and obsession spun by his childhood friend, Fanshawe. The story both opens and ends with the uncanny proximity of Fanshawe. In this way, I think, he is a "ghost."

> For if I could convince myself that I was looking for him, then it necessarily followed that he was somewhere else— somewhere beyond me, beyond the limits of my life. But I had been wrong. Fanshawe was exactly where I was, and he had been there since the beginning. (344)

Fanshawe regularly places himself in these confined empty spaces: the cardboard box, the grave, the locked room.

> Fanshawe alone in that room, condemned to a mythical solitude—living perhaps, breathing perhaps, dreaming God knows what. This room, I now discovered, was located inside my skull. (345)

The impact of that realization is so strong that the narrator loses track of himself.

PA: Precisely because he has imagined Fanshawe so vividly. This is the essence: "Fanshawe was exactly where I was." This is the obsession. It makes perfect sense to me.

IBS: Each of the protagonists of the books in *The New York Trilogy* has a similar obsession with another man, which prompts the grinding surveillance, the intense observation of the other, the endless scrutiny of clues.

PA: They're all trying to find themselves by interacting with another person.

IBS: Are there any autobiographical elements in this story?

PA: Yes, there are quite a number, in fact. In this book, more than with any of the other novels I've written, I took things from my own life and used them. It's not something I normally do. You will see as we go along that in most of my books I've used little bits and pieces from my life, but never in such a concentrated way as here. There's no particular reason for it; it's just material that was close to me and that I found interesting. For instance, the narrator and Fanshawe come from a town very much like the one I grew up in in New Jersey. I worked on an oil tanker and lived in Paris—just as Fanshawe does. I was a field worker for the 1970 census, and the old composer Fanshawe gives the refrigerator to, Ivan Wyshnegradsky, was a real person. Ivan was my friend. He was a quarter-tone composer; he owned one of three quarter-tone pianos in the world. (I have to say, just in parentheses, that when I was in Toronto last week, I found a recording of Ivan's quarter-tone pieces for piano. I was thrilled, positively overjoyed.) And the incident in the graveyard the day Fanshawe's father dies is something that happened to a friend of mine. He was sixteen, he lived in Chicago, his father was dying. He went down into an empty grave, the snow was falling in his face. When he went back home afterward, he learned his father had died that day. He told it to me so vividly, I remember every detail. What else? I have a feeling I'm forgetting things. Ah yes, Norwegian Christmas, that's from my own experience, too. At the same time, everything is make-believe. It's a novel. There was no Fanshawe in my life.

IBS: Well, there was Hawthorne's *Fanshawe*.*

PA: Yes, but that's a book. I don't know if you've ever read it. It's not very good.

IBS: I haven't, but I know the story of how Hawthorne tried to burn every copy that was printed.

PA: The point here is that the moment you use autobiographical material in a novel, it becomes fiction. So it doesn't really matter where it comes from.

IBS: The narrator finds Fanshawe's writing utterly enigmatic:

> He had answered the question by asking another question, and therefore everything remained open, unfinished, to be started again. I lost my way after the first word, and from then on I could only grope ahead, faltering in the darkness, blinded by the book that had been written for me. And yet, underneath this confusion, I felt there was something too willed, something too perfect, as though in the end the only

---

* Nathaniel Hawthorne, *Fanshawe*, published anonymously in 1828.

thing he had really wanted was to fail—even to the point of failing himself. (370)

PA: I imagined Fanshawe's book as something Blanchot might have written, but even more difficult and obscure, the kind of writing that cancels itself out, almost with every sentence, every thought, so that, ultimately, it's confusing. It seems to have a beautiful, coherent surface, but as you penetrate the text, it starts to make no sense at all.

IBS: A kind of obscurity integral to clarity?

PA: A self-destructive text.

IBS: Fanshawe self-destructs in much the same way as his writing. Is the text correlated with its author?

PA: His writing is an embodiment of who he is.

IBS: Toward the end of *The Locked Room* you say:

> The entire story comes down to what happened at the end, and without that end inside me now, I could not have started this book . . . I have been struggling to say goodbye to something for a long time now, and this struggle is all that really matters. The story is not in the words; it's in the struggle. (346)

Who is speaking here?

PA: The narrator of the third book. He's the author of all three stories. The first two are metaphorical enactments of what he'd been living through, and now he's able to tell his own story straight.

IBS: So he's the "I" who crops up toward the end of *City of Glass*?

PA: No, not necessarily, because it's a fiction. The first two novels are fictions, and the third is supposed to be "reality." The truth in the fiction.

IBS: This paradoxical relation between "truth" and "fiction" is prominent in each of the novels in the Trilogy. At the beginning of this conversation, you said that all three stories illustrate the passage toward "learning to live with ambiguity." It seems to me that this process is determined by a form of self-effacement in relation to language and being and that, in a sense, all three stories turn on precisely this erasure. At the risk of repeating myself, if we go back to the description of Fanshawe's writing in *The Locked Room*, the narrator says:

> All the words were familiar to me, and yet they seemed to have been put together strangely, as though their final purpose was to cancel each other out. I can think of no other way to express it. Each sentence erased the sentence before it, each paragraph made the next paragraph impossible. (370)

This lucidly describes the peculiar way in which Peter Stillman speaks in *City of Glass*:

> My name is Peter Stillman. Perhaps you have heard of me, but more than likely not. No matter. That is not my real name. My real name I cannot remember. Excuse me. (18)

And indeed, as we said earlier, the way he walks:

> The body acted almost exactly as the voice had: machine-like, fitful, alternating between slow and rapid gestures, rigid and yet expressive, as if the operation were out of control, not quite corresponding to the will that lay behind it. (17)

Similarly, in *Ghosts*, Blue is disturbed by the ephemerality of meaning in language:

It's as though his words, instead of drawing out the facts and making them sit palpably in the world, have induced them to disappear. (175)

PA: That's an interesting point. I think I said something to that effect in *The Invention of Solitude*:

The rampant, totally mystifying force of contradiction. I understand now that each fact is nullified by the next fact, that each thought engenders an equal and opposite thought. (*The Invention of Solitude*, 61)

IBS: Yes, one thing cancels out the next: "My name is Peter Stillman; yes, no; it is and it isn't."

PA: And Fanshawe, who has been canceling himself out, writes a book that nullifies itself. Right. As for Blue, nothing makes sense to him anymore, he's completely lost. The more he writes, the less he understands.

IBS: This movement of self-erasure, or nullification, is key in all three stories, isn't it?

PA: Yes. They're all going over similar ground, but in different ways, each one in a different tone of voice. They belong together. It's a group. That's why it's a trilogy [*laughs*].

IN THE COUNTRY OF LAST THINGS. (1987)
Ephemerality

IBS: The interplay of hope and despair is extraordinary in this dystopian tale set in an apocalyptic yet strangely familiar urban environment. In many respects, *In the Country of Last Things* is a bleak story, but your heroine, Anna Blume, brings to it an undercurrent of optimism through her integrity, stamina, and humanity. What inspired the construction of this uncanny place?

PA: It was inspired by New York City. I started thinking about this story in 1969, during my one postgraduate year at Columbia. At that moment, New York was in a state of near disintegration: crime was rampant, there was menace in the streets, and the infrastructure was collapsing. It culminated in the financial default of the city in the early seventies. It was hard not to feel, right along your skin, how desperate the place had become.

IBS: So it's really a political book rather than an existential dystopia?

PA: Difficult to say, since the book evolved over many years. I heard Anna Blume's voice, and at first I made her the narrator of the story. Then I started having second thoughts about writing from a female point of view and switched to a male narrator. Then, for a long while, I actually gave up on the whole thing because I wasn't sure how to make the story work. Later on, every now and then, Anna's voice would come back to me and I'd write a little bit, but then she would disappear and I couldn't go any further. This went on for years. It wasn't until I was working on *The New York Trilogy* (I think I was between *Ghosts* and *The Locked Room*) that she came back to me in a big flood. I wrote the first forty pages or so, but I was still uncertain about it. I showed those pages to Siri and said, "This isn't very good,

113

is it? I don't have to write this book, do I?" She read it and said, "No, it's very good, I love it, I think it's the best thing you've ever done. You have to finish the book for me." That's why the book is dedicated to her. So, once I'd finished *The New York Trilogy*, I went back to Anna and continued. Before that, however, I did something I've never done before or since: I published a fragment of the novel before it was finished—while I was working on the last volume of the Trilogy.* I did that so I would feel committed to finishing the project—a secret promise to go back to it.

IBS: So, parts of the book are inspired by historical sources, but a great deal is clearly invented.

PA: Oh yes, but not all of it. For example, the garbage collection system was inspired by an article I read about Cairo [Egypt] where the work of trash removal was apparently farmed out to brokers. So that was based on fact. As were several other things inspired by events from World War II. For instance, from reading Harrison Salisbury's book** about the siege of Leningrad, *The 900 Days*, I learned about the human slaughterhouses that sprang up around the city—nightmare places in which people killed other human beings in order to sell their bodies as food. They would lure their victims in with the promise of a pair of shoes. That's what happens to Anna in a pivotal scene in the book. I took it directly from historical sources. Fantastical as the book might seem, it has struck a chord with people living in places that have gone through profound upheavals. I've been moved, at times even overwhelmed, by their strong, passionate responses to the book. For example, when I met the Argentinian woman who translated it into Spanish, she said, "What you're writing about feels like our day-to-day reality in Argentina." Later, there was the Sarajevo story. Do you know about this?

---

* "In the Country of Last Things," the first pages of the later to be completed novel, came out in the *Paris Review*, no. 96 (Summer 1985).
** *The 900 Days: The Siege of Leningrad*, 1969.

IBS: No.

PA: During the siege in Sarajevo, a journalist from somewhere in the West gave his copy of *In the Country of Last Things* to a local theater director named Haris Pašović. Haris thought, "Why do I want to read a book written by an American ten years ago?" But then, living as he did in a cold, bare room with no heat or electricity, that is, alone at night with nothing better to do, he started reading it. For him, too, it was a book about the day-to-day reality of what was happening in Sarajevo during the siege. He became so enthusiastic that he decided to adapt it as a play and have it performed right there and then—in Sarajevo, smack in the middle of the fighting and bloodshed. They did a Bosnian version but also an English version. He managed to get Vanessa Redgrave involved, and she went over to perform in the play. I was going to go as well, but when I was about to leave, all the airports were shut down and I couldn't get through. I don't know how he organized it, but when the war was over, Haris got support from Peter Brook, the director of the Bouffes du Nord in Paris. His company gave Pašović's group a grant to tour Europe with the play. I met up with them in Berlin. It was sometime in the mid-1990s. There were about twenty-five people in the company, ranging in age from seventeen to seventy-five. What was so remarkable and moving to me was that they had all memorized the book: *they could all recite every word of the book by heart*! I've never seen anything like it. An extraordinary experience.

IBS: Given these responses, the city in *In the Country of Last Things* takes on almost universal significance, doesn't it? Were you thinking of this when you decided to leave it unnamed?

PA: I didn't name it because it was inspired by several different places, and I wanted to create the impression that it could have been any-where. Crumbling New York City from the late sixties—the Warsaw Ghetto from World War II, somewhere in South America from any moment in the twentieth century—first world, third world, second world. It comprises elements from so many different cities, I wouldn't have known what language to use if I'd chosen to give it a name. Americans read this book and think it's fantasy, but you know, for people in these less fortunate places, it's not. There are fantastical elements to it, but it's about the real world.

IBS: I must admit I took it to be a fable about existential problems.

PA: Well, it's that, too. I think the essence of the book is about how to remain human in a world that's falling apart.

IBS: Anna Blume certainly doesn't lose her moral compass.

PA: That's why I think of her as a heroic character. She's probably the character I care about most from all of my novels. That's why she keeps coming back.

IBS: In *Travels in the Scriptorium*?

PA: Yes, she returns there, but also in *Moon Palace*. She's the person Zimmer is desperately waiting to hear from.

IBS: So you haven't been able to let go of her?

PA: Not really, no. That's the funny thing about invented characters: they become real.

IBS: Might we consider Anna the most important of your female characters?

PA: I'm not sure about that. She's the only central female protagonist, but in other books, especially later books, there are quite a few important female characters: *Sunset Park*, *Invisible*, *Man in the Dark*, *The Brooklyn Follies*, *Leviathan*.

IBS: Women become rounder and more prominent in your later work, don't they?

PA: Perhaps.

IBS: Have you wanted to take up the female perspective again?

PA: Yes, definitely.

IBS: You said you found it difficult.

PA: It's difficult, but then, once you get going, it's not as hard as you think. Writing novels is like falling under a spell. You become the characters—whether it's an old person or a young person, a woman or a man. If you're able to go down deep enough into that subconscious spot where you are completely open, then you can do it. Think of how many men have written brilliantly from a feminine point of view.

IBS: Absolutely, and vice versa. That's why one is wondering why, in your writing, Anna is the only truly rounded female character in the first half of . . .

PA: Of my literary output? Yes. Well, stories take hold of you, you go with them; you're sucked up into them, and two or three years go by, and then something else takes hold of you. There's no master plan in this. It's mostly about what grabs you at any given moment. As you know, it takes a lot of time and effort to write a novel. You have to be completely involved. You can't do it halfheartedly. And so, whatever it is that's pulling you, whatever it is that seems most urgent—that's what you go with. And no other female protagonist has called out to me as loudly as Anna Blume did. Not yet, in any case, although women characters seem to have become more and more dominant in my novels.

IBS: The story is set in the country of "last things," and it's very much a book about ephemerality. Nothing lasts here for very long. There are several reports on how language is deliberately used as an instrument to change reality:

> For the best results, you must allow your mind to leap into the words coming from the mouths of others. If the words can consume you, you will be able to forget your present hunger and enter what people call the "arena of the sustaining nimbus." There are even those who say there is nutritional value in these food talks—given the proper concentration and an equal desire to believe in the words among those taking part. (9–10)

Words describing culinary pleasure can fill your belly here. That's extraordinary.

PA: When the desired object is absent, conjuring it up in your mind doesn't help much, but these people can't stop themselves from doing it anyway. They're desperate. So, they invent these activities to satisfy their needs. Those needs aren't fulfilled, but it's a distraction.

IBS: Elsewhere thoughts can be constitutive of reality:

> There is a small minority, for example, that believes that bad weather comes from bad thoughts. (26)

That's really funny.

PA: Yes, there's a perverse edge of humor to all this. In catastrophic times, when it looks as if the world is about to end, the crazies come out in force: new religions are invented, strange sects, bizarre philosophies, desperate attempts to deal with the intolerable. A basic human response. End-of-the-world madness.

IBS: Even in the most wretched circumstances, your central characters here find the energy to continue writing. Sam, for instance, has
devoted everything to his grand narrative:

> The book is the only thing that keeps me going. It prevents
> me from thinking about myself and getting sucked up into
> my own life. If I ever stopped working on it, I'd be lost. I
> don't think I'd make it through another day. (104)

PA: Sam is a journalist. That's his job. He was sent there to report on
the collapse of the city, and he wants to give a full-scale picture of
what has been happening. It becomes his cause.

IBS: It's almost as if dedication to writing is a form of survival here.

PA: Yes, and a distraction, too. By focusing on his project, he has something to keep him going, which helps ward off permanent despair.

IBS: The Jews in the library also persist with their studies, and it
seems that their devotion to the book is proportional with the hardship of living.

PA: Yes, but the Jews are always studying [*laughs*].

IBS: [*Laughs*] Then, suddenly, they're gone from the library. People,
objects, words cease to exist all the time here:

> It's not just that things vanish—but once they vanish, the
> memory of them vanishes as well. Dark areas form in the
> brain, and unless you make a constant effort to summon
> up the things that are gone, they will quickly be lost to you
> forever. (87)

Are you saying that when a thing disappears, its name in language is
also lost?

PA: It's not just that physical objects are vanishing, but the words for those things evaporate as well, and once we don't have the words anymore, the things can never be brought back—or even imagined. They're gone.

IBS: Is Anna's project, then, similar to Stillman Sr.'s or to the son's in "Portrait of an Invisible Man"? They all seek to keep alive what is lost or broken by speaking or writing about it?

PA: The books were all in my head at the same time, so there are bound to be some echoes from one to the other—especially about the relationship between language and reality.

> Entire categories of objects disappear—flowerpots, for example, or cigarette filters, or rubber bands—and for a time you will be able to recognize those words even if you cannot recall what they mean. But then, little by little, the words become only sounds, a random collection of glottals and fricatives, a storm of whirling phonemes, and finally the whole thing collapses into gibberish. (89)

IBS: This means that you have the name but not the object it refers to.

PA: First the object goes, then the name goes, and finally the memory of it.

IBS: And not the other way around?

PA: No.

> In effect, each person is speaking his own private language, and as the instances of shared understanding diminish, it becomes increasingly difficult to communicate with anyone. (89)

IBS: This is the story of the Tower of Babel again.

PA: It sounds like it, doesn't it?

IBS: *In the Country of Last Things* is often described as a dystopia, a place in constant disintegration. I was wondering, is there a connection between the crumbling of space, the collapse of social structure, and the fragmentation of the self here?

PA: I never thought of it in those terms, but yes. In fact, what's going on here, in this city right now,* illustrates precisely that. As the days go by, the people out there in Rockaway become more and more desperate, more and more angry—and every day the veneer of civility wears a little thinner. It's only been a week. Imagine if they had lived in that chaos for a year. Circumstances can change you utterly. Siri's mother tells a story about the German occupation of Norway in World War II. She was friendly with an obsessively clean middle-class girl. She was so clean that she took two or three showers a day and changed her underwear just as often. She had the misfortune to fall in love with a German soldier who died on the Russian front, and for a while she had to go to Germany to look after her mother-in-law—in a city under constant bombardment. They were destitute: wretched, dirty, hungry, living out of garbage cans. After the war, after having gone through all that, she came back to Norway and immediately began taking three showers a day again and changing her underwear just as often [*laughs*]. We adjust to circumstances. You see this same mechanism in the residents of Woburn House in the novel: once conditions improve a little, they start complaining. It's not that they're ungrateful. They just want more. All of us always want more.

IBS: That's the uplifting dimension of *In the Country of Last Things*,

---

* This conversation took place six days after superstorm Sandy hit the East Coast in November 2012. Rockaway is on the Queens shore, which was badly damaged. Many people still had no roof over their heads a week after the disaster.

Woburn House. The perfect place for Anna, among people just like herself, who want to help. They don't lose their humanity—on the contrary!

PA: Victoria is another exceptional person, almost a visionary. Then you have Boris, a schemer, an operator, but also someone with a moral commitment to helping the doctor's daughter. He's one of the few people left in the city with a sense of humor and a taste for adventure. A survivor. He can cope with situations that would crush other people. A man clever enough to outsmart the system, whatever the system might be. There *are* people like this. And there are also people like Ferdinand—bitter, angry, and abusive.

IBS: Where do these nasty old men come from? Ferdinand reminds me of Effing;* he even talks a bit like Effing.

PA: Not really. But what the two of them share is an immense talent for ranting. Ferdinand is a shattered human being. He's lost his masculinity, and he's grown to hate his wife.

IBS: Even if she does everything she can for him.

PA: Especially because she does everything she can for him.

IBS: Does she kill him?

PA: Yes, she kills him. If you read the passage closely, I think it's clear. I didn't want to say it outright, but I think Anna understands that Isabel has killed him because of his attack on her. That's the last straw: Isabel can't take it anymore.

IBS: In fact, death is one of the few things they still have some control over in *In the Country of Last Things*:

---

* In *Moon Palace*.

I sometimes think that death is the one thing we have any feeling for. It is our art form, the only way we can express ourselves.

Still, there are those of us who manage to live. For death, too, has become a source of life. (13)

Death as an art form *and* a source of life? That's an interesting idea.

PA: She's talking about the Leapers. They're trying to make death as beautiful as possible.

IBS: So, orchestrating their own death adds a quality to their miserable existence?

PA: It's the ultimate aesthetic experience.

IBS: Yes, I was wondering about that because there's so much death in this book and very few births.

PA: There are no births.

IBS: There's a miscarriage. It's one of the most harrowing moments in the novel. It struck me that, in your writing in general, there are very few births.

PA: That's an interesting point. Well, let's see: in *The Locked Room* there are the births of the little boys.

IBS: It's such a small part. It happens, but you don't really describe it.

PA: In *Moon Palace* there's an abortion . . . In *The Book of Illusions*, of course, Zimmer has two boys. In *Leviathan*, Sachs and Fanny can't have children, but then, Aaron has a son and a daughter. In *Oracle Night*, Grace is pregnant, but, of course, she loses the baby. In *Man in the Dark*, there's a crucial passage in which Brill tells Katya that it was her birth that brought him back together with his wife, remember? He said, "You're responsible, your birth did it."

IBS: But she's grown up when he tells her that. There's a child in *The Brooklyn Follies*, of course. She plays a prominent role.

PA: Yes, definitely.

IBS: And in *Mr. Vertigo*, the protagonist is a child through much of the novel. So, there are children in your novels, but more often than not they have been lost, either through abortion or in some tragedy. Isn't that true? And we hardly ever—if at all—hear about them being born.

PA: It's strange that you mention it, because in fact it's something I've been fiddling with lately. I don't know if it will come to anything, but I've written a long passage about a father writing to his daughter on the day she's born and describing her birth in great detail. It's in a notebook, not yet typed up. Who knows what will happen to it, but getting back to *In the Country of Last Things*, what I was trying to evoke was a world in which no children could be born anymore—not as an individual problem but as a societal problem. In *The Last Kings of Thule*, a book written by the French anthropologist Jean Malaurie, he explains how babies cease to be born among the Eskimos during times of famine. Then, in times of plenty, children begin to be born again. Interesting, no?

IBS: Yes, it is. There's definitely an almost apocalyptic sense in *In the Country of Last Things* of the world coming to an end. The rabbi has an interesting perspective on this:

> Every Jew, he said, believes that he belongs to the last generation of Jews. We are always at the end, always standing on the brink of the last moment, and why should we expect things to be any different now? (112)

This is very central to Jewish self-understanding, isn't it?

PA: This is a world in which everyone might be part of the last generation. It's just that the Jews have a deeper understanding of what this means.

IBS: So, every generation, in a sense, believes itself to be the last? This plays into the ending of the novel, I think. We don't know whether they managed to escape the city.

PA: They do get out. Even if we don't know what happens to Anna exactly, we know that the letter reaches the person she sends it to. That's the optimistic conclusion to the book: that somehow or other this notebook made it—one assumes—to Zimmer.

IBS: Yes, but we're not sure, are we?

PA: From *Moon Palace* we know that Zimmer is waiting for a letter from Anna, and the opening pages of *In the Country of Last Things* imply that someone has received a letter. "These are the last things, she wrote." The person writing the word "she" has read the letter, but whether that person is Zimmer or someone else is not clear.

> That is how it works in the city. Every time you think you know the answer to a question, you discover that the question makes no sense. (85)

MOON PALACE. (1989)

"The Song Is in the Step"

IBS: *Moon Palace* takes us on an epic journey through the inner and outer landscapes of young Marco Fogg. He nearly perishes in Central Park, he loses the woman he loves, he walks across America—and becomes a man. In the process, he discovers both his father and grandfather: Solomon Barber, the obese history professor who never recovered from his love for Marco's mother, and the rambunctious old man in the wheelchair, Thomas Effing, whose turbulent life is told in the biography Marco is hired to write. It's quite a tour de force combining elements from the bildungsroman, the American road novel, metafiction, and the frontier novel in one dense and complex book. It's your first extended work of narrative fiction, isn't it?

PA: The longest up to that point, in any case. I finished writing it in 1987, but the earliest versions of the book go back to 1968, with dozens of false starts and new beginnings over the next year or two. All the early versions must be in the library.* As I said earlier, *Moon Palace* and *City of Glass* were originally the same book. When I finally sat down and wrote *City of Glass* as it is now, I plundered material from the old manuscript. The same was true of the final version of *Moon Palace.*

IBS: Even so, they're very different in almost every respect.

PA: Each one evolved into its own narrative, and everything changed. *Moon Palace* is a circular book—three interconnecting stories about three generations of men.

IBS: Three generations making the same mistakes, as you've said

---

* The Berg Collection of English and American Literature, New York Public Library.

somewhere. Three lonely men searching for a place to belong, mostly within themselves. They've all suffered losses, and they're all orphaned. There's a desire for origins here, isn't there, a need to emerge from something that has formed you?

PA: Everyone wants to know who his parents are.

IBS: Are there any autobiographical elements in the book?

PA: I know the book sounds autobiographical, but it's not. Almost nothing comes from my own life. Just a few incidental details, and even those are utterly transformed. The books Uncle Victor gives to Marco . . .

IBS: The 1,492 books.

PA: That clearly refers to the books my uncle left behind in our house. You know that story. When he went to live in Italy, his library was stored in our attic and then, one day, my mother and I took the books downstairs and put them on shelves. Suddenly, I had a library! My parents didn't read, but I did, by then I had become a passionate reader, and it was a tremendous resource to have those books in the house. Curiously, when I wrote about the books in *Moon Palace*, I wasn't thinking about my uncle at all. It only occurred to me later that that in fact had been the inspiration for the episode. Another thing, a very small thing, comes from a friend of mine, a painter, someone I met on a ship going to Europe in 1965. As an opponent of the Vietnam War, he starved himself so he would flunk his draft physical. He lost tremendous amounts of weight. He told me later that when he went to the draft board, he was so skeletal that the doctor asked him, "Young man, have you had breakfast this morning?" My friend replied, "Doctor, do I look like someone who could go without breakfast?" [*laughs*]. I use that line in *Moon Palace*. It comes directly from my friend. After college, he went to live on the Navajo reservation that spreads across the Arizona-Utah border—in a town called Ojeto, which means "moon-over-the-water." When I started writing *Moon Palace*, I wanted to go out West; I needed to explore, to feel the landscape. My friend went with me, and we spent about ten days wandering around that territory together. We visited Mr. and Mrs. Smith, who are described in the book. I just lifted them from life. She was Kit Carson's granddaughter or great-granddaughter, and Smith was a fascinating character. He looked to me like the prototypical westerner and talked with a western accent—a little like an old Gary Cooper. It turned out he'd grown up in the same New Jersey town where I grew up and that we'd gone to the same high school. Later, he became a hoofer on Broadway. I was astonished. Imagine that, the old man of the West had been a Broadway dancer! He had completely reinvented his life. My friend and I also went to Lake Powell, rented a motorboat, and cruised around on the water. In the novel, of course, all of Effing's paintings are submerged under that lake.

IBS: Wow, that's quite a story.

PA: Another autobiographical fact, which you probably remember from *Hand to Mouth*, concerns the novelist H. L. Humes, Doc Humes (one of the founders of *Paris Review*), who wound up staying at my apartment when I was a student. He was the mad writer who gave away money. That was the inspiration for what Effing does in the novel. I had actually witnessed Doc do this, handing out money to strangers in the street. You can imagine the astonishment! Especially the bums. Getting a fifty-dollar bill in 1969 would be like getting five hundred dollars today.

IBS: You saw him do it?

PA: He'd burst into a coffee shop, slap down fifty-dollar bills in front of everyone sitting at the counter, and shout, "Spread a little sunshine, spread a little sunshine!"

IBS: That's unbelievable.

PA: No one does these things. There's a good documentary about Doc Humes made by his daughter.* I make an appearance in the film and talk about those excursions with Doc.

IBS: We get a very vivid impression of the 1960s in the novel: the moon landing, the Vietnam War, student life, glimpses of the city . . .

PA: The historical background, the real stuff embedded in the make-believe.

IBS: What about Uncle Victor's tweed suit?

> It functioned as a protective membrane, a second skin that shielded me from the blows of life. Looking back on it now, I realize what a curious figure I must have cut: gaunt, disheveled, intense, a young man clearly out of step with the rest of the world. But the fact was that I had no desire to fit in. (15)

PA: That's another autobiographical thing [*laughs*]. When I went to Europe at eighteen, I bought myself a tweed suit in Dublin. It was the first time I'd bought a suit: a beautiful, thick Irish tweed, greenish with brown and dull-red flecks. I loved that suit so much that I wore it every day when I was a freshman at Columbia, and by the second year it had completely worn out. The seat of the pants had holes in it, the whole thing disintegrated. That's the origin of the suit in the novel.

IBS: What about the moon? Did the moon landing make a big impression on you?

---

* Immy Humes's documentary, *Doc*, won the International Literary Film Festival award in 2011 for a documentary film about literature.

PA: It started with Kennedy's speech. He announced that we were going to send a man to the moon. I was about to turn thirteen then, and so I grew up with the expectation that Americans would travel to outer space.

IBS: The next frontier?

PA: That's right. The next place for America to go.

IBS: The moon symbolizes just about everything in the novel. In an interview you said:

> The moon is many things all at once, a touchstone. It's the moon as myth, as "radiant Diana, image of all that is dark within us"; the imagination, love, madness. At the same time, it's the moon as object, as celestial body, as lifeless stone hovering in the sky. But it's also the longing for what is not, the unattainable, the human desire for transcendence. And yet it's history as well, particularly American history . . . But the moon is also repetition, the cyclical nature of human experience. (*Collected Prose*, 566)

PA: The novel tries to embrace all that.

IBS: It's many very different meanings to attach to one object.

PA: Yes, but you see, once you start thinking about something, you begin to make connections. I've described this associative mechanism as a kind of pinball machine, where one thing touches on another and then another and another, and soon you have an enormous system of interrelated references.

IBS: China is a prominent feature in this web of associations.

PA: I stayed in Chinatown for about two or three weeks in the late 1960s. What a strange place to live back then. Nobody spoke English. It was like being in another country. I tried to express that in the book as well. Also—and this is very interesting to me—the only man-made structure on earth that can be seen from space is the Great Wall of China. Or so I've read somewhere. I hope it's true.

IBS: When Marco is delirious with hunger and loneliness, China, America, and the moon become intimately connected through his one view onto the outside world: the neon sign of the Chinese restaurant from which the novel takes its title:

> I can't be sure of any of it, but the fact was that the words *Moon Palace* began to haunt my mind with all the mystery and fascination of an oracle. Everything was mixed up in it at once: Uncle Victor and China, rocket ships and music, Marco Polo and the American West. (32)

PA: This is Marco's inner experience of it.

IBS: Yes, there's an interesting relationship between inner and outer worlds in *Moon Palace*. Marco's room is very much the "site of inwardness" you describe in *The Invention of Solitude* and indeed the scene of radical divestment:

> The room was a machine that measured my condition: how much of me remained, how much of me was no longer there. I was both perpetrator and witness, both actor and audience in a theatre of one. I could follow the progress of my own dismemberment. Piece by piece, I could watch myself disappear. (24)

PA: The inherited books stand in for Marco here, and they're gradually sold off. That was an inspired piece of business, I must say, turning boxes of books into furniture.

IBS: It's wonderful! He's putting the Western canon to very good use.

PA:

> Think of the satisfaction . . . of crawling into bed knowing
> that your dreams are about to take place on top of nine-
> teenth-century American literature. Imagine the pleasure of
> sitting down to a meal with the entire Renaissance lurking
> below your food. (2)

It's supposed to be funny.

IBS: [*Laughs*] It is. Why is Marco unable to leave that room? Why
doesn't he just go out and get himself a job? Why does he have to fall
apart like this?

PA: Because it's an experiment. He's pushing himself beyond the
limits of the rational. "I would turn my life into a work of art," he
explains,

> sacrificing myself to such exquisite paradoxes that every
> breath I took would teach me how to savor my own doom.
> The signs pointed to total eclipse, and grope as I did for
> another reading, the image of that darkness gradually lured
> me in, seduced me with the simplicity of its design. (21)

Of course, there are many options open to him: scholarships, loans
he could have taken to avoid disaster. He refuses to be helped. Marco
is not a typical boy of the 1960s. He stands apart from everything—a
complete eccentric. He's not taking drugs, he's not in the rock and
roll world, he's not plotting a revolution. He's obsessively pursuing
his own inner path, which is a strange and twisted one. He refuses.
It's an existential position, a categorical no to the world as it is.

IBS: As with Bartleby, he "prefers not to."

PA: Exactly. He's rebellious, but in an inward way, and to such a degree that he almost winds up killing himself. Then he's rescued by the two people who love him most, Zimmer and Kitty. As you said the other day, love is the only thing that can catch you from falling, and once he's been caught, he becomes more responsible. That's the crucial next step in Marco's development. The madness that initially took hold of him was a manifestation of grief. He's entirely alone after Uncle Victor dies. Victor was his whole family.

IBS: It's that harrowing solitude again, isn't it? Being orphaned.

PA: It's simply too much for him.

IBS: For Marco, solitude is destructive. For Effing, however, seclusion is constitutive. He finds his true artistic perspective in a doubly isolated place: the hermit's cage at the bottom of a blind canyon.

> He had worked steadily for the past seven months at being alone, struggling to build his solitude into something substantial, an absolute stronghold to delimit the boundaries of his life, but now that someone had been with him in the cave, he understood how artificial his situation was. (176)

PA: Solitude *is* restorative.

IBS: It's interesting that we have grandson and grandfather both isolating themselves in order to either prove or achieve something. Effing produces the best paintings he has ever made. Of course, they are all lost under Lake Powell. No one will ever lay eyes on these fabulous works of art. Even so, he creates something new and wonderful in his solitary space. Marco, by contrast, disintegrates.

PA: Which means that their stories are actually different, doesn't it? Then there's Marco's father. To me, the descriptions of Barber are among the most tender passages in the book. His unrequited love for Marco's mother, Emily, the disgrace at the college, running off to Cleveland. We assume that Victor, who was working with the Cleveland Orchestra at the time, possibly saw Barber in that restaurant—devouring his food in a gluttonous frenzy to ease his pain.

IBS: Yes, that's another stark contrast in the book: the son starves himself while the father tries to eat himself to death—more or less for the same reason.

PA: Yes, there are all sorts of extremes in this book.

IBS: Barber feels imprisoned inside his own frame:

> His body was a dungeon, and he had been condemned to serve out the rest of his days in it, a forgotten prisoner with no recourse to appeals, no hope for a reduced sentence, no chance for a swift and merciful execution. (240)

So, we might say that all three generations are radically reclusive figures, each in his own way confined to a physical space: the son falls apart in his little airless room opposite the "Moon Palace"; the father is miserably alone trapped inside an obese body, the grandfather hides in the hermit's cave. Then, Barber falls into an empty grave.

PA: Yeah, what a book [*laughs*].

IBS: Over the years, you've placed several characters in graves and other types of underground seclusion: Walt in *Mr. Vertigo*, Owen Brick in *Man in the Dark*, Nick Bowen in *Oracle Night*.*

PA: That's true, and as we said the other day, there's that moment in *The Locked Room* when the protagonist watches Fanshawe climb down into the open grave with the snow falling on top of him.

---

* See conversation on *Oracle Night*.

IBS: *Moon Palace* and *Mr. Vertigo* are sometimes referred to as your "frontier novels."

PA: "Frontier novels." I like that [*laughs*].

IBS: If we stay with this metaphor, could we say that Marco probes the contours of his own inner territories, just as he discovers America on his trek across the country? Many frontiers are crossed in these processes: the West, space, manhood, fatherhood, love, sex.

PA: Yes, all those things.

IBS: The Western literary canon is also a discovery for Marco as he reads through Uncle Victor's library:

> It was almost like following the route of an explorer from long ago, duplicating his steps as he thrashed into virgin territory, moving westward with the sun, pursuing the light until it was finally extinguished. (22)

Is reading a journey? Educationally, aesthetically, ethically?

PA: Reading is certainly a discovery. Not least for Marco. In connection with Victor's books, it also becomes a process of mourning:

> As far as I was concerned, each book was equal to every other book, each sentence was composed of exactly the right number of words, and each word stood exactly where it had to be. That was how I chose to mourn my Uncle Victor. One by one, I would open every box, and one by one I would read every book. That was the task I set for myself, and I stuck with it to the bitter end. (21)

IBS: He doesn't reflect on what he's reading at all.

PA: No, he's doing this as a kind of mad homage to his uncle. He wants to read the words his uncle read, every one of the words in every one of the books. It's an emotional experience rather than an intellectual one. It's a ritual he establishes for himself. It's his form of secular prayer.

IBS: He's intensely self-absorbed at this stage:

> I could no longer see things for what they were: Objects became thoughts, and every thought was part of the drama being played out inside me. (54)

This is when the line between Marco's inner and outer worlds is seriously destabilized. We're not always sure which is more concrete.

PA: The boundary is blurred for him.

IBS: The balance is restored later, isn't it, after the Central Park experience when he nearly perishes but is "rescued by love."

PA: This is when he begins to form a more solid self. I always thought of this book as a coming of age story—David Copperfield in twentieth-century clothing. Where the book ends is the beginning of his adult life. Now, he's ready to be in the world. I don't think anyone can fully grow up until he's experienced the loss of a person he loves. You can't really become human until your heart has been broken. And Marco's heart *is* broken, but he's building himself up again—partly by way of his journey across the West to California, where he finds meaning in the mere fact of walking.

IBS: Could we say that the rough experience of traversing one's country on foot is instrumental in the forming of the individual self here? I think we realize this when Marco, completely absorbed in Blakelock's painting, *Moonlight*, understands that "you cannot live without establishing an equilibrium between the inner and outer" (58).

PA: The Blakelock painting is central to the book. Again, it brings together all these themes: the Indians, the West, the moon, madness, the search for understanding—all of it. In the end, the book is an echo chamber.

IBS: Perhaps that's why our discussion today keeps flying off in several directions at once [*laughs*]. More than with any of the other books.

PA: You're probably right.

IBS: Was there a plan?

PA: With all my books, I start with an idea about the story, often a vague idea, and then I inch my way forward—guided by intuition and gut feeling. This book, however, needed a plan. It was all in my head—never written down—but I knew what the progression was going to be. Otherwise, I wouldn't have been able to do it. The crucial thing for any narrative is to present the information in the right order. Here all the elements are linked, and so it became imperative to think about sequence. I wanted to tell the entire story in the first paragraph and then have the rest of the book unpack those opening lines:

> Little by little, I saw my money dwindle to zero; I lost my apartment; I wound up living in the streets. If not for a girl named Kitty Wu, I probably would have starved to death . . . From then on, strange things happened to me. I took the job with the old man in the wheelchair. I found out who my father was. I walked across the desert from Utah to California. That was a long time ago, of course, but I remember those days well, I remember them as the beginning of my life. (1)

Then comes the story.

IBS: As you said earlier, the story is mostly about Marco's development. There are these wonderful instructive moments, for instance, when wheeling Effing around in the streets becomes

> a process of training myself how to look at the world as if I were discovering it for the first time. What do you see? And if you see, how do you put it into words? The world enters us through our eyes, but we cannot make sense of it until it descends into our mouths. (122)

PA: It's a little parable about how to write.

IBS: Yes, and again here, we see the intimate connection between walking and naming objects. Somehow, Marco's steps pace his translation of the world into words for the allegedly blind man to "see."

PA: In one of my earliest poems, the last line reads, "The song is in the step."* It means that the rhythm of walking creates the rhythm of language. I go back to it in *Winter Journal*.

IBS: I think you return to this idea a few times: *White Spaces*, "The Book of Memory," *City of Glass* . . .

PA: Always from a slightly different angle. My feeling is that the rhythm in the language of a book also creates meaning.

IBS: You're saying that the rhythm in the sentences is not just aesthetic and meaning-making, it's also physical?

PA: But it can't be articulated. It's part of the experience of reading, which is a physical experience as well as a mental and an emotional one. I would argue that the reader responds physically to what's on the page: You hear the words in your mind, meanings are produced,

---

* "Spokes," no. 9, *Poetry* (March 1972); *Collected Poems*, 2004.

images are formed. They're generated by the words that go into your head. Then, something starts happening to you.

IBS: What, then, about silences and gaps? Both Effing and Marco learn to embrace blanks, each in his own way and with very different outcomes. Marco discovers that

> the more air I left around a thing, the happier the results, for that allowed Effing to do the crucial work on his own: to construct an image on the basis of a few hints, to feel his own mind traveling toward the thing I was describing for him. (123)

This is important, isn't it, because it allows the reader to become actively involved in the process of creation.

PA: It's something I discovered myself. The more I wrote, the more I understood that what you leave out is just as important as what you put in. In my experience as a reader, I've always found it most pleasurable when the author writes in such a way that I become fully engaged. In other words, not everything should be told. There must be room for the reader to fill in the blanks. It's more stimulating. In this way, the book is a collaboration between the writer and the reader, and, in a sense, every book is a different book for every person who reads it. You bring your own past, your own character, your own story to whatever text you read. There are writers who overwhelm you with too many words. There's not enough space. They don't let you in.

IBS: This is the valuable lesson of representation Marco learns as he struggles to describe everyday things to Effing, isn't it? One of your best critics argues that Marco "learns to exult in gaps" and that it's precisely in the spaces between word and object that we have "chances of innovation."* Could it be that what you leave out is in fact the principal source of significance, because it activates the reader's imagination and spawns meaningful images?

PA: I would say that the blanks and the words are equally important in this process. You need one to offset the other. They interact. The most important question in writing is: "What comes next?" I write one sentence; what will the next one be? How big a leap can I make? If you go too far, the text becomes incomprehensible. Flaubert does this extremely well, particularly in his late work, for example, *Bouvard et Pécuchet*. There are massive spaces between the sentences. It's exciting because as a reader you must learn to jump—you're leaping when you read Flaubert. As a writer, it's thrilling to do something like this: "Gita put down her pen and stared at the table. Five years later, when she was in Vienna . . ." [*Laughs*] It's a jolt, isn't it? You mustn't overdo it. Then it becomes a gimmick, and it's tedious. But if you find the right way to pull it off, it can be electrifying.

IBS: So, the reader is invited to leap with you across these blanks, and meaning is produced in mid-air?

PA: There's no question about it. As a writer, I want to efface myself and become invisible. As I've said in the past, my ideal would be to write a book so transparent that the reader would forget that the medium is language and take in the narrative as pure experience.

IBS: This is how Effing works, isn't it?

> The true purpose of art was not to create beautiful objects, he discovered. It was a method of understanding, a way of penetrating the world and finding one's place in it, and whatever aesthetic qualities an individual canvas might have

---

* Steven Weisenburger, "Inside *Moon Palace*," in *Beyond the Red Notebook: Essays on Paul Auster*, ed. Dennis Barone (Philadelphia: University of Pennsylvania Press, 1995) 141.

were almost an incidental by-product of the effort to engage oneself in this struggle to enter the thick of things. (170)

He could be speaking for you, I think?

PA: Sometimes I have characters say the opposite of what I believe, but this passage corresponds to how I feel. It was the lesson I myself finally learned. When I was young, I wanted to make beautiful objects. That was the aspiration, but in the end I found it to be a self-defeating one. It must be the thing you're attempting to paint or the object you're trying to describe that takes precedence over anything else. It's the material you want to capture on canvas or on a page of writing. The form will find itself. If there's beauty in it, it's not because you're straining to create something beautiful. It's because you're straining to enter into the thing you're doing. That would imply that the process is more important than the result, and yet as an artist you have to be concerned with results. So, you're writing out of your guts, you're writing out of your unconscious, but at the same time it's not pure savagery. It's not all impulse. There's a lot of art and craft involved in trying to do it right. This is why writers spend so much time polishing their sentences and their paragraphs. Writing is essentially rewriting.

IBS: Is it a skill that can be acquired, do you think?

PA: I think you teach yourself. No one can teach it to you. You learn through experience, but it doesn't get easier. I've written all these books, and each time I think about a new one, I'm starting from scratch. I'm always at the beginning. I don't know anything. My past experience doesn't help.

IBS: Surely, you can draw on your knowledge of how to make sentences that work, building structures, forming characters, making leaps?

PA: I wonder. In any case, each time I start a new book, I've never written that book before. I'm going to have to teach myself how to do it as I go along. I have no formula to fall back on. The only change I've noticed over the years is that, when I was younger, if I came to a spot where I was blocked or confused or uncertain, I'd feel that the whole project was foundering. Now, I take it more calmly. If I'm stuck, it's for a reason. Usually, it means that I have to rethink something or find a new way to push on. That's a valuable lesson. Every book is different. Some books almost write themselves; for other books you have to grind out every sentence. The struggle doesn't show on the page. The reader will never be able to tell. That's the funny thing about it.

IBS: I see what you mean. Even if the reader is invited to participate, he or she is engaging with the result of your work, not the grinding process that preceded it.

PA: The effort all goes into making it look as though it didn't require any effort at all: making it seem inevitable and having everything fall into the right place. You don't want the reader to feel any hint of the labor you've put into the thing you've written. Even when I comment on this struggle inside my narratives, what you read is the result, not the work that went into achieving it. *Moon Palace* was a very long haul.

THE MUSIC OF CHANCE. (1990)
"The Mechanics of Reality"

IBS: Combining a Sisyphean task with Kafkian absurdity, moral awakening, and a touch of Buddhist philosophy, *The Music of Chance* recounts the strange story of a lonely fireman's quest for personal integrity. When Nashe inherits a large sum of money, he divests himself of all ties, sets off in his red Saab, and gives himself completely over to the freedom of the road until he meets the gambler Jack Pozzi. They lose everything to a pair of dangerously eccentric millionaires and end up detained at the end of a maze carting the stones from an ancient Irish castle across a meadow to build a wall that has no function whatsoever. Are there any elements in *The Music of Chance* taken from your own life?

PA: Essentially, no. I don't see any autobiographical component in *The Music of Chance*—except the scene when Nashe discovers Pozzi's beaten-up body. I wasn't aware of it while I was writing the book, but it probably has some connection to the boy who was struck and killed by lightning.* That scene had a tremendous emotional resonance for me, and I think it must go back to that terrible moment when I was holding the dead body of my friend in my arms. When you're writing a novel, you enter a state of hypersensitivity to everything around you. Things start bursting in on you, unexpected things that can wind up becoming a part of the book. Some of *The Music of Chance* was composed in Vermont. Siri, baby Sophie, and I were there for the summer, and my British editor, Robert McCrum, came to visit us. On a whim, we ate lobsters for dinner one night. The next day, when I sat down to write the scene about the prostitute visiting Nashe and Pozzi in the trailer, I used the lobsters. The other thing to say in this connection is that the day I finished the final draft of

---

* Described in *The Red Notebook*.

The Music of Chance was November 9, 1989. Can you imagine? I'm writing a book about the building of a wall, and then the wall that embodied the Cold War, the symbol of an entire era of history, was destroyed. Another one of those weird synchronicities . . .

IBS: Which have no meaning . . .

PA: No meaning whatsoever. Other than that, no, I can't think of anything taken from real life. The book was inspired by the end of the previous book, *Moon Palace*. Marco is driving out West in a red car, the car is stolen, and he makes the rest of the trip to the coast on foot. After I finished the novel, I said to myself, "I want to get back into that red car." So, the next book begins with a man driving around in a red car, in this case a red Saab.

IBS: There are often echoes from previous books in your novels, but, as far as I can tell, the red car is just about the only cross-reference in *The Music of Chance*.

PA: It's a self-contained work—part novel, part fable. Right from the start, I considered it a story about power. In some sense, even though not a word is mentioned about politics, I think it's one of the most political books I've written. There is, however, one element inspired by a play I wrote in my twenties, *Laurel and Hardy Go to Heaven:*[*] the idea of two men having to build a wall. I was always disappointed with the play, but this one image stayed with me, and I went back to it and started exploring it again.

IBS: Could we say that Nashe's journey in *The Music of Chance* goes from fairly radical divestment (of family ties) through unrestrained freedom (on the road) to bondage (in the meadow)?

PA: I would describe Nashe's journey as a slow process of moral

---

* In *Hand to Mouth*, "Appendix 1: Three Plays."

awakening. When he was free to do whatever he wanted, his life was empty. He had abdicated all his connections to other people: he reluctantly left his daughter behind and neglected his relationship with his girlfriend, Fiona. He was living what one might call a life of selfishness and self-indulgence. Essentially an absurd life. It's not until he's finally constrained and put in a position of bondage, as you put it, that he's forced to stop running away from himself and take responsibility for someone else: Pozzi. In this interaction with the Other, he grows into a different kind of human being, and the period in the meadow is fundamental for this development.

IBS: In fact, he jumps at the chance of applying himself to this preposterous task of building a wall, which has no purpose whatsoever.

PA: He sees it as an opportunity. Pozzi, of course, is horrified, as any normal person would be.

IBS: Prior to that, Nashe had abandoned his loved ones and spent thirteen months on the road in a kind of existential limbo.

> It was a dizzying prospect—to imagine all that freedom, to understand how little it mattered what choice he made. (6)

Choice, it seems, is of no consequence here. Does this mean that freedom renders him powerless to take charge of his own life?

PA: He thinks that cutting all ties will leave him completely free, but he's deluding himself. It's not freedom, it's an addiction. He becomes a prisoner of his own desire for freedom. The paradox is that he doesn't become free until he's prepared to be bound by friendship and moral obligation.

IBS: Quinn in *City of Glass* and Marco Fogg in *Moon Palace* also give their lives over to more or less aimless movement. They do so with little, if any, reflection on cause and aim, but for Nashe, as you say, there is an articulated purpose to his divestment:

> There was a certain pain involved in these transactions, but Nashe almost began to welcome that pain, to feel ennobled by it, as if the farther away he took himself from the person he had been, the better off he would be in the future. He felt like a man who had finally found the courage to put a bullet through his head—but in this case the bullet was not death, it was life, it was the explosion that triggers the birth of new worlds. (10)

PA: The idea of dispossession seems to recur fairly often in my early books. In each case, however, the circumstances are different. Fogg is a young person, alone in a way that few people are . . .

IBS: Nashe also lost his father at an early age.

PA: Yes, but Fogg is a much younger character. He's toying with the idea of living his life as a work of art. For him, divestment is a grand gesture, something characteristic of a late-adolescent romantic boy. With Nashe it's a mature and conscious act.

IBS: That's true, Nashe reflects on his actions. Something else triggers him.

PA: There's impulse as well as reflection. It was a big blow when his wife left him. Nashe feels he has failed, and he's hoping to find a new and better way to live. He misses that chance. After a year and a month on the road, the experiment is getting a little tired, but he's unable to stop. Pozzi becomes his excuse to rethink his life once again.

> The days passed, and even though there was rarely a moment when they were not together, he continued to say nothing

about what truly concerned him—nothing about the struggle to put his life together again, nothing about how he saw the wall as a chance to redeem himself in his own eyes, nothing about how he welcomed the hardships of the meadow as a way to atone for his recklessness and self-pity. (127)

IBS: Why is atonement so important for Nashe? As I see it, his sins are not that great.

PA: He atones "for his recklessness and self-pity"; he atones, essentially, for being stupid. Building the wall is an arbitrary, absurd task, but he decides that if he seriously applies himself to it and fulfills his obligations, it will become a redeeming act for him, no matter how meaningless the job might be. His desire to take it on gives it significance. He invests it with a purpose. Building that wall, isn't that like making a work of art? It's not useful, but you can look at it as a kind of sculpture in the meadow. Art has no utilitarian function either.

IBS: It's just that this wall is made of stones that used to be part of a castle that was once alive and vibrant and served a multitude of functions. Now they are just sitting there, ten thousand gray slabs in the middle of nowhere. They're being turned into something that has no purpose and, at least as I see it, no beauty.

PA: I think walls can be beautiful. You have these ancient Irish stones out there in a meadow in Pennsylvania. Maybe it will lead to something interesting.

IBS: All right, but it's just a perfectly straight line, no curves, nothing irregular or surprising—and nobody will ever see it!

PA: Walls are complicated; they can keep you in, but they can also keep you out. They have a double edge to them: imprisonment and protection.

IBS: It's certainly an image that stays with the reader.

PA: I just have to say, nothing is symbolic here. It is what it is. We're talking about the stuff of dreams. If you find a way to put those dreams into words, to form the precise image of those dreams, it can be haunting. I don't fully understand it myself. The only justification I have for writing it down and putting it in the book is that it feels right. It says something to me, even if I can't fully articulate what that thing is.

IBS: If we go back to the possible connection between Nashe in *The Music of Chance* and Quinn in *City of Glass*, in both cases we have a constitutive phase of aimless movement.

PA: Quinn walks, Nashe drives, yes, but the impulse is the same.

IBS: And they both reach a "nowhere": Quinn in the streets of Manhattan, Nashe here in the meadow. What are these voids?

PA: It's difficult for me to talk about these things. They rise up out of the unconscious and have little to do with rational thought. If you look at the two cases from a psychological perspective, Quinn is a person whose life has been interrupted and damaged. He's in mourning still. He's a suffering human being. His selfhood is a burden to him. The aimless walks help him to empty himself out. They give him the lightness-of-being he craves. Nashe is perhaps not quite as damaged as Quinn, but he's confused and unsettled. Then a bucket of money comes showering down on him, and he can afford to quit his job. They're different people, Nashe and Quinn, but they both find an escape from the burden of reflective self-consciousness in movement.

IBS: There's a feeling of inevitability about these wanderings, I think, and I'm intrigued by the ambiguous relationship between chance and purpose in your early writing. You are so focused on randomness, and yet, there's an undercurrent of something else: a sense of governance or direction that would seem to work entirely against the grain of contingency. It's suggested in *The Music of Chance*, for instance, when Nashe steals the miniature representation of Flower and Stone from the City of the World. This act unleashes a torrent of bad luck—or so it would seem.

> He was not sure why he had done it, but the last thing he was looking for just then was a reason. Even if he could not articulate it to himself, he knew that it had been absolutely necessary. He knew that in the same way he knew his own name. (97)

What is this knowledge that suddenly and inexplicably takes hold of him?

PA: The story is complicated by the fact that Nashe leaves the gambling room during their break. At that point, Pozzi is ahead, and Nashe thinks he's going to win. He's becoming a little bored, so he goes upstairs and ponders the City of the World. For reasons he himself can't understand, he steals the miniature of Flower and Stone. I have to say, that moment, when he pinches the figure, came as a surprise to me as well. When I sat down to work that day, I had no idea it was going to happen. Suddenly, he puts it in his pocket. It was almost as if Nashe did it himself and I was just writing it down. This often happens to me with my characters. You get inside them and pretty soon they're telling you what they're going to do. I'm not manipulating them. I had a fascinating conversation about this lack of "authority" with a Hollywood producer.* There had been several people interested in the film rights, among them an old veteran of Hollywood who had made some successful films in the past. He kept saying, in the exaggerated way of Hollywood producers, "Nobody in the world loves this book more than I do, and we have to make it into

---

* A film adaptation of *The Music of Chance*, directed by Philip Haas, was released in 1993.

a film." I said, "Well, that's nice to know." "But there's one thing," he continued, "those men who disappear, Flower and Stone, I think we should have them come back into the story because they're so interesting." I said, "No, they can't come back. It's extremely important that they don't come back." He said, "But you can change it. You wrote it, so you can do anything you want." I said, "No, actually, I can't do anything I want. I have to do what the characters tell me they have to do." We couldn't get past this idea, so I turned down his offer.

IBS: He didn't understand?

PA: He had no idea what I was talking about. He thought, "Well, if you're the author, you can tell any story you want, and therefore you can manipulate it in any way you want." That's not how it works. Not for me. There's some kind of inevitability in the truth of the things you've discovered and the way the story must develop. It never even occurred to me that Flower and Stone would reappear. They had to leave.

IBS: Of course, the reader also hopes they'll come back. We want to know what happened, but you leave everything in the dark.

PA: It's a book full of holes and ambiguities.

IBS: When Nashe removes the wooden figure, Pozzi believes some sort of divine balance has been upset:

> We had everything in harmony. We'd come to the point where everything was turning into music for us, and then you had to go upstairs and smash all the instruments. You tampered with the universe, my friend, and once a man does that, he's got to pay the price. I'm just sorry I have to pay it with you. (138)

It's strange how Pozzi, the very embodiment of chance and pot luck, needs to ascribe meaning to fluke events.

PA: Now we're talking about "mechanics of reality" again. I've never said, in any of my works, that chance is an all-dominant force that controls everything—it's one element in an infinitely complex totality of forces. We have the freedom to make decisions, to set goals for ourselves, but, as we know, accidents happen, random events often intervene. That's what I call chance. It can be a destructive force, it can be a positive force. It's neutral. Another word for it might be "the unexpected."

IBS: How does it tally with the title of this novel?

PA: I usually have the title of a book when I start, but the title for this one didn't come to me until I was about halfway through. There was a provisional title, but I was planning to drop it when something better occurred to me. It was named after a piece of music by Couperin, "Les Barricades Mystérieuses" (The Mysterious Barricades). It's a harpsichord piece in which, at any given moment, only one note is played. There are no chords. It's sublimely beautiful. I knew this title was too heavy, but I held onto it for a while, hoping I would eventually find another one. One Saturday, I was waiting in line at the supermarket here in Brooklyn, half-listening to the piped-in music wafting through the store. Suddenly, the phrase "the music of chance" popped into my head—out of nowhere. It was a strange moment. I thought, "That's the title of the book!" It's a contradiction, of course. Music is not chance, unless it's John Cage or something written intentionally against the spirit of music. Traditionally, music has always been about something close to mathematics: organized, orderly. The idea that chance creates its own kind of music means there's a pattern. If we substitute "pattern" for "music," you get a sense of what the title implies.

IBS: It would seem to suggest that there's a plan to randomness?

PA: Only in retrospect.

IBS: It's the impression I sometimes get from reading *The Music of Chance* and some of the earlier work, that you attribute a kind of meaning to coincidence. I realize that you don't. For you, it's all arbitrary, even so . . .

PA: I don't do it, but sometimes the characters do. They see things happening, and they think those random events are connecting in the same way Pozzi thinks that Nashe broke the rules by stealing the little figure. To me it's absurd, but that's his cockeyed view of the world. Nashe tries to argue with him.

> "It's a piece of wood, isn't it? A stupid little piece of wood. Isn't that right, Jack?"
> "If you say so."
> "And yet you believe this little scrap of wood is stronger than we are, don't you? You think it's so strong, in fact, that it made us lose all our money." (140)

IBS: This exchange reminds me of biblical Abraham in his father's workshop, remember? They were making wooden idols of gods and Abraham insulted the customers by insisting they were merely worshipping a carved piece of wood that couldn't possibly contain divine power.

PA: Yes, that's a good point.

IBS: If we look at *The Red Notebook*, it centers on these random but magical coincidences. Even so, it's an autobiographical text. The speaker is you.

PA: All I'm saying in those stories is that life is a lot stranger and more unpredictable than most of us want it to be. It's almost unbearable to think that so much of what happens is arbitrary. We just can't tolerate that.

IBS: There's solitude and loneliness in this book too. At the beginning, Nashe craves detachment:

> He wanted that solitude again, that nightlong rush through
> the emptiness, that rumbling of the road along his skin. (7)

Eventually, he ends up "crazy with loneliness" (201) and destroys himself in a mad act of revenge.

PA: I'm not sure he dies. It's not clear. There's definitely going to be a crash, but it may not be a fatal one. We don't know. The vehicle coming toward him has one headlight, so it could be a motorcycle. Or a car missing a headlight. I deliberately closed the story before the end. I wanted to show that Nashe had reached a new stage in his inner development, that he had come to a place where he was willing to accept anything that came his way. Whether it was life or death, whether it was freedom or not. What matters is that he's prepared to destroy himself. That was the point I wanted to make. He has transcended his own boundaries; he has become a greater person. He's been set free inside himself. It's a new awareness of who he is and who he can be. Of course, he's certain that they've murdered Pozzi, and Nashe loves Pozzi. When he picks up his broken body, it's devastating, and he's consumed with rage. Remember, he then goes through that long period when he wants to kill the child. He's so filled with a desire for revenge, as you say, that he even contemplates murdering a child. This, I think, is the most horrifying moment in the book.

IBS: We never learn what happened to Pozzi.

PA: We never know.

IBS: Nashe and Pozzi are an unlikely pair, and yet they form a strong bond of trust and loyalty. What's the magic between them?

PA: Initially, Nashe is simply amused by Pozzi. He's such a colorful character, such a confident character, one of those little guys who thinks he owns the world. Then he realizes that Pozzi is not stupid, he's got his own values, and Nashe respects him for that. In the end, Nashe looks on him almost as a kind of son. When they have to pay back their debt, he says to Pozzi,

> You're a free man, Jack. You can walk out now, and I won't hold it against you. That's a promise. No hard feelings.

Pozzi replies,

> Do you really think I'd leave you alone, old man? If you did that work yourself, you'd probably drop dead of a heart attack. (111)

IBS: Yes, Nashe places all his trust in Pozzi from the very beginning. He even invests the last of his money in Pozzi's poker game. Why does he have so much faith in this cocky little gambler?

PA: He wants to take the risk. He thinks it will embolden him— to know that he is strong enough to chuck everything away on a mere whim. Nashe and Pozzi met by chance, and their relationship is based on chance. They are in the gamble together, and for a while they form one of those special pairs of oddly matched men I wrote about in *Hand to Mouth*.

IBS: What about the other male pair in *The Music of Chance*, William Flower and William Stone?

PA: They were inspired by Laurel and Hardy, but I was also thinking about Bouvard and Pécuchet and most likely about Don Quixote and Sancho Panza as well. I've always been fascinated by these mismatched pairs. The skinny one and the fat one. So, I invented those two. They seem to be charming, silly, jovial fellows, but at bottom, no, they're crazy and brutal.

IBS: Yes they are. Flower and Stone also construct meaning where none apparently exists. They do it mostly in order to inflate their own sense of omnipotence. For instance, Flower insists that "each number has a personality of its own" (73) and is convinced that he and Stone have worked out "the magic combination, the key to the gates of heaven" (74) in something as quintessentially random as a lottery ticket.

PA: He was an accountant. He dealt with numbers all his life. I think the feeling that each number has a different personality comes from my childhood. It's something common in children.

IBS: But Flower is a middle-aged man.

PA: I know, but he hasn't given up this magical way of thinking. The arbitrary sign, whether a number or letter, can be invested with meaning if we choose to give it meaning. There's no real justification for it. It's a human impulse.

IBS: He is a bit of a megalomaniac, isn't he? For instance, he says, "It's as though God has singled us out from other men." (75)

PA: He's a bombastic, pompous blowhard. You have to understand that the two of them are stunted and infantile. Flower is the collector, and Stone is the artist. Flower collects historical artifacts with a kind of obsession, things owned by celebrated people. Stone is building an elaborate miniature model of a universal city with himself and Flower as centerpieces.

IBS: Flower describes Stone's City of the World as an artistic vision of mankind. He says,

> In one way, it's an autobiography, but in another way, it's what you might call a utopia—a place where the past and future come together, where good finally triumphs over evil. (79)

This is not the case at all, is it?

PA: No, it's a nightmare society of cruel punishments and savage laws.

IBS: Yes, they're playing god, an avenging god.

PA: That's right, and now they have two live prisoners. Stone is a skilled craftsman, and Nashe is astonished by the complexity and beauty of his work. At first glance, it seems to be a glorious project, but on closer inspection it becomes horrifying.

IBS: Flower's collection of objects is equally uncanny, I think.

> Flower's museum was a graveyard of shadows, a demented shrine to the spirit of nothingness. (84)

PA: Flower wants to possess things, and by obtaining these objects for himself, it's as if he's controlling the world. It's as if he owns the past. Here's the description of the items:

> The telephone that had once sat on Woodrow Wilson's desk. A pearl earring worn by Sir Walter Raleigh. A pencil that had fallen from Enrico Fermi's pocket in 1942. General McClellan's field glasses. A half-smoked cigar filched from an ashtray in Winston Churchill's office. A sweatshirt worn by Babe Ruth in 1927. William Seward's Bible. The cane used by Nathaniel Hawthorne after he broke his leg as a boy. A pair of spectacles worn by Voltaire. (83)

As it says here, "It was all so random, so misconstrued, so utterly beside the point" (83–84).

IBS: Exactly.

The fascination was simply for the objects as material things, and the way they had been wrenched out of any possible context, condemned by Flower to go on existing for no reason at all: defunct, devoid of purpose, alone in themselves now for the rest of time. It was the isolation that haunted Nashe, the image of irreducible separateness that burned down into his memory, and no matter how hard he struggled, he never managed to break free of it. (84)

I think this is a central passage in the book because it frames isolation through Flower's removal of objects from their natural context. Isn't this what they do also with the stones from the Irish castle? Removed from their origin and made homeless, suspended in a limbo of randomness—just like Nashe himself.

PA: That's right.

IBS: And there's no pattern?

PA: No pattern whatsoever.

IBS: It's this complete lack of purpose, or this context of nothingness, if you will, that upsets Nashe so deeply, right?

PA: He doesn't understand why anyone would want this. It confuses him.

IBS: It's as if it touches a raw nerve. Something that reminds him of his own life, perhaps?

PA: That's possible. It's just that Flower has severed these things from their context in such a way that they lose their meaning, and Nashe can't understand why this man, with all this money, would waste his time trying to assemble a collection of useless things. It's a splintering rather than a putting together. Nashe can't bear any more dissociation, he wants to reassemble things.

IBS: That makes sense. Even if there's no connection between the items in Flower's collection, each individual object is invested with meaning, isn't it?

PA: Sure, but it's entirely subjective. If you saw James Joyce's glasses and didn't know they had once belonged to Joyce, they would just look like a pair of glasses to you. This is what Nashe thinks. Who cares about Churchill's cigar or Fermi's pencil? Or the telephone on Woodrow Wilson's desk? It's just a telephone, it's just a pencil. They don't mean anything.

IBS: Can we compare these items to the abandoned objects in your other books?

PA: There are discarded objects in *In the Country of Last Things* and in *Sunset Park*, but here it's the opposite. Flower is acquiring things, collecting them.

IBS: Yes, but the context in which he places them is a "shrine to the spirit of nothingness." He's not giving them a home. And being abandoned is one of the things that defines the objects in the other books: They're lost, left, forgotten. They're masterless. They're just sitting there. There's no context. They don't belong.

PA: But there are many types of collectors and some very odd collections. Whatever patterns of meaning the collector attributes to what he owns is arbitrary and often highly idiosyncratic.

IBS: Okay, there are things that belong and things that don't. I'm just trying to make sense of this. I think I find it more difficult to get my head around *The Music of Chance* than any of your other books. I'm not quite sure why . . .

PA: It's difficult to talk about. Not just for you, but for me as well. Because it's irreducible. What else can we say but: *It is what it is*. It's filled with ambiguities, but at the same time, the truth of the story is in the tale that's told—a fable that is also a novel, firmly grounded in the real world and yet also projecting itself as a kind of nightmare or hallucination.

IBS: Yes, the ambiguity frustrates, and these perplexing images remain. But the lack of certainty doesn't make it any less interesting. On the contrary.

LEVIATHAN. (1992)
The Fall

No one can say where a book comes from, least of all the person who writes it.
Books are born out of ignorance, and if they go on living after they are written,
it's only to the degree that they cannot be understood. (36)

IBS: *Leviathan* is more explicitly political than your other books. It tells the story of Benjamin Sachs's astonishing route to anarchism. His fall off a fire escape on the Fourth of July triggers what becomes a quest for moral integrity where the personal history and the history of America interconnect. It seems to me that there's a new kind of realism here, a new take on ambiguity, which, I hope, we'll talk about. But first, are there are any autobiographical elements in *Leviathan*?

PA: Yes, there are. One element is the fall from the fire escape. I wrote about it in *The Red Notebook*, story number twelve. My father fell off the roof of a building when I was a boy. His fall was broken by a clothesline, and he was saved. The image of my father tumbling through the air—in all likelihood falling to his death—haunted my childhood and has continued to stay with me in the years since. That's one thing. Another thing is that a crucial aspect of the novel began as an idea for a film. Around 1989 or so, I was contacted by the British director Michael Radford, who said he would like to collaborate with me on a movie project. He told me about a friend of his, the French artist Sophie Calle—someone I had never heard of at that point—and a work she had made about a lost address book. I think you know the story: someone lost the book, she chanced upon it lying on a street in Paris and decided to talk to everyone listed in it in order to make a portrait of the owner—in absentia. Over the next month, she published daily interviews with the people she managed

163

to track down in the newspaper *Libération* (along with photographs of them). The owner of the lost address book was abroad during most of that month, and when he returned to Paris and discovered what was going on, he was so furious that he threatened to sue her unless she published her own picture in the newspaper—naked. She did it, and that was the end of the story. An intriguing bit of business, I thought, which possibly could lead to something, and so I agreed to explore it with Michael. We came up with an outline for a film—something quite sexy and steamy, I'm afraid, which didn't go down well with producers and was rejected everywhere—but by then the character I had invented for the film, Maria Turner, was so fully formed that I integrated her into the novel I had been dreaming about for the past year or so. I had met Sophie Calle by then, and when I asked her if I could appropriate some of her real works for my fictional character, she said yes. That explains the little note at the beginning of *Leviathan*: "The author extends special thanks to Sophie Calle for permission to mingle fact with fiction."*

IBS: What about the narrator, Peter Aaron? He has your initials.

PA: Yes, they're my initials, and Iris is Siri spelled backward. Iris was the protagonist of Siri's first novel, *The Blindfold*, which came out the same year as *Leviathan*. I imagined a kind of transfictional marriage between her character and mine. I wanted to use my initials because Siri had played with her own name for her character. They'd be married. It would sort of be us, and then, of course, it wouldn't. It was a little homage to my wife.

IBS: That's interesting: a transtextual marriage.

PA: There are other autobiographical elements: I did see the celebration for the centenary of the Statue of Liberty from the window of

---

* Sophie Calle then responded by thanking Auster for permission to mingle fiction with fact in her adaptation of Maria in her book, *Double Game* (Violette Limited, 1999; 2007).

someone's house in Brooklyn. It was a big party similar to the one I describe in the book. There's Columbia University, where Fanny and Aaron study, and Aaron was in France just the way I was. None of this is terribly significant. However, I did one thing with this novel I haven't done with any of the others: I used the place where much of it was written (Vermont) directly in the story.* It's probably of little interest to the reader, but I was fascinated by the idea of imagining my characters right there, in the same space where I was working. The house in Vermont in the story is the house where we were staying while I was writing the book. There I was, in that little shack,** writing at the green table, fictionalizing the real right in front of my eyes. Usually, I write from memory or imagination, but there the concrete world was turned into a phantom world. It had a strange, vibrating quality to it. Eerie.

IBS: Of course, in the book, you have the narrator, bearing your initials, move into this "real" house in Vermont, which, in the fiction, belongs to your central character. Peter Aaron here has an experience similar to the one you've just described:

> [I]t barely crossed my mind that I was sitting in the same chair that Sachs used to sit in, that I was writing at the same table he used to write at, that I was breathing the same air he had once breathed. If anything, it was a source of pleasure to me. I enjoyed having my friend close to me again, and I sensed that if he had known I was occupying his old space, he would have been glad. (218–219)

PA: That's true. There's a kind of projection here—or a double fiction.

IBS: As far as I can tell, there are a couple of echoes from the three novels that preceded *Leviathan*.

---

* Here, Auster uses the place where he lives; in *Sunset Park* he uses the time in which he lives. See opening of discussion of *Sunset Park*.
** Described in *Winter Journal*.

"Or, as my grandmother once put it to my mother: 'Your father would be a wonderful man, if only he were different.'"(82)

PA: It comes up again in *Winter Journal*, also in the script of *Blue in the Face*. I have Violet say to herself: "Auggie would be such a wonderful person, if only he were different" [*laughs*]. I think it's the funniest thing I've ever heard about marriage: perfectly understandable—but ridiculous: "You'd be great if you weren't yourself" [*laughs*]. I'd forgotten that I'd used it in *Leviathan*.

IBS: Is there an echo also of *The Locked Room*? I'm thinking of the way in which both narrators obsessively follow their best friend on what appears to be entirely aimless walks in the hope of detecting something—which, of course, they don't.

> Sachs wandered around the streets like a lost soul, roaming haphazardly between Times Square and Greenwich Village at the same slow and contemplative pace, never rushing, never seeming to care where he was. (125)

PA: Biography is something that interests me, and it comes up fairly often in my novels: one person writing the story of another. *Leviathan* is a good example of that. So is *Moon Palace*. So is *The Locked Room*. They're all books about friendship fraught with emotion, love, and worry. Male pairs: one of our recurring themes. In *Moon Palace*, Marco Fogg, the biographer as it were, is the protagonist of the book. Here in *Leviathan*, it's the opposite: the subject is a smaller character than the object. Aaron is less present and much less interesting than Sachs. Nick Carraway telling the story of Gatsby was a major source of inspiration here.

IBS: Like Nick Carraway, Aaron is also an unreliable narrator.

PA: Yes, Aaron is a flawed witness. There's so much he doesn't know or understand. Even though he's trying his best to tell the whole story, there are many blanks he can't fill in. He's earnest and has good intentions, but, finally, he's not up to the task.

IBS: *Leviathan* is firmly set in the political and cultural climate of America between 1950 and 1990, and this context is very important. Would it be fair to say that disillusionment with modern America is the principal determining factor in the shaping of the central character, Benjamin Sachs? You use Emerson's "Every actual State is corrupt" as the epigraph of the book, and Sachs suggests in the novel he wrote that

> America has lost its way. Thoreau was the one man who could read the compass for us, and now that he is gone, we have no hope of finding ourselves again. (38–39)

PA: It's really a novel about my generation and what we went through during those years; the war in Vietnam being the central, burning issue. Every young man had to make a decision about where he stood because everyone was going to be drafted into the army. If you were against the war, as so many of us were, it was an impossible choice: prison or exile. Sachs is a highly principled person. He's willing to put his ideas on the line, and so he goes to jail for a year and a half. That early experience determines who he becomes for the rest of his life. As things fall out, he begins writing his book in prison. It's a kind of historical novel, but then he loses interest in fiction and becomes an essayist, writing about many different subjects—always with strong political opinions.

IBS: So, his political views were formed against this background. Was it similar to yours?

PA: It's the background of our whole generation. Fortunately, I didn't have to go to prison for my views. By the time I wrote *Leviathan* in 1990 and 1991, we'd had eight years of Reagan and were already two years into Bush One. Ten years of right-wing leadership. It was terrible—the dismantling of everything we had fought for in the sixties.

IBS: *Leviathan* begins on the Fourth of July 1990 and curls back to its key event on the same date four years earlier on the eve of the hundredth anniversary of the Statue of Liberty. Sachs is very much a product of this time, as you say, and his story is intimately linked to the grand American icon of freedom. I was wondering whether we can see him as an embodiment of contemporary America? He refers to himself as "America's first Hiroshima baby" and his family background is truly a melting pot: his mother's family came to America "because of Sir Walter Raleigh" (the Irish potato famine), and his father because of "the death of God" (Russian pogroms). This is a strange, roundabout sort of logic, which is also very funny.

PA: Yes [*laughs*], Sachs is a witty fellow.

IBS: At the same time, there's that kind of American virtue about him: "he seemed to live in a state of perfect innocence" (50)—in a belated sort of Henry Jamesian way.

PA: Two things about Sachs: he's an enthusiast, and he's pure. He's not competitive in the way the rest of the society is. He's like a big child, he's kind, funny, hardworking. He loves his wife and his friend. There's nothing devious about him.

IBS: These qualities also characterize his writing, don't they? *Leviathan* is named after Sachs's unfinished novel. Aaron describes it in these terms:

> Sachs was on to something remarkable. This was the book I always imagined he could write, and if it had taken a disaster to get him started, then perhaps it hadn't been a disaster at all. (141)

I assume the title refers beyond Sachs's abandoned manuscript to Hobbes's notion of state absolutism and the tyranny and chaos associated with the biblical sea monster?

PA: It's a direct reference to Hobbes's notion of the state, and combined with the explicit references to Emerson in the text, it's clear from the beginning that this book will be commenting on the political climate of the day.

IBS: Would you say that *Leviathan* is among your most political novels?

PA: No doubt. The book talks directly about a series of real political events and ideas—anarchism for one, and environmental activism for another.

IBS: This is where the Statue of Liberty comes in, right?

PA: I should mention another autobiographical element. When I was six years old, my mother and I went to the Statue of Liberty, accompanied by one of her friends and that woman's two sons. As Sachs's mother does in the novel, my mother insisted that I dress up for the occasion—which made me feel foolish and uncomfortable—whereas the two other boys had been allowed to wear blue jeans and T-shirts. More significantly, my mother did indeed have a panic attack or a vertigo attack or some kind of crisis inside the statue, and she tried to cover it up by making a game of going down the stairs sitting instead of standing. She suffered from vertigo after that. The experience of seeing my mother nearly go crazy inside the Statue of Liberty had an important impact on my thinking about the statue. I couldn't separate the two things, couldn't think about one without thinking about the other, and I've never been back since that day. But, of course, the Statue of Liberty has a political significance here as well:

> It represents hope rather than reality, faith rather than facts,
> and one would be hard-pressed to find a single person willing

to denounce the things it stands for: democracy, freedom, equality under the law. It's the best of what America has to offer the world, and however pained one might be by America's failure to live up to those ideals, the ideals themselves are not in question. (216)

IBS: Early in the story, Sachs's mother says, "It's the symbol of our country, and we have to show it the proper respect" (33). Paradoxically, Sachs ends up systematically destroying replicas of this icon.

PA: In actual fact, there are not many replicas of the Statue of Liberty around the United States. I made that up. But yes, it's the political and moral statement that matters.

> Unlike the typical terrorist pronouncement, with its inflated rhetoric and belligerent demands, the Phantom's statements did not ask for the impossible. He simply wanted America to look after itself and mend its ways. (217)

He doesn't want to hurt anyone. He's not a terrorist in the sense that he wants to kill people. It's a symbolic act verging on performance art—political performance art. I remember that right after *Leviathan* came out, the Unabomber was caught, and several publications asked me to write articles about him. I didn't do it because my man was driven by completely different motives and had nothing in common with the Unabomber. Sachs and the Unabomber don't even live on the same planet.

IBS: Like Quinn and Nashe before him, Sachs divests himself of the life he has established with Fanny and sets out on the journey that will eventually destroy him.

> I want to end the life I've been living up to now. I want everything to change. If I don't manage to do that, I'm going to be in deep trouble. My whole life has been a waste, a stupid little joke, a dismal string of petty failures. (122)

Some of your other protagonists are tormented by a similar feeling of inadequacy. In connection with *Hand to Mouth* and *The Invention of Solitude*, we talked about failing in terms, in fact, of actually succeeding.

PA: Yes, but Sachs is talking about failure only. I don't think there's any double meaning to this. It's a depressed man who's talking here. He feels that he hasn't justified himself to himself, that he hasn't produced the work he wanted to do or become the man he wanted to be. We all feel that way sometimes, right?

IBS: Right. Solitude plays directly into this highly subjective perception of failure and success. Could we see it also as a precondition for development and achievement? In *Leviathan*, Sachs begins to write in prison and produces his best work up there alone in the studio in Vermont. Is his situation in any way similar to Effing's when he takes refuge in the hermit's cave in the canyon and produces his best paintings ever?

> [T]he two times I've sat down and written a novel, I've been cut off from the rest of the world. First in jail when I was a kid, and now up here in Vermont, living like a hermit in the woods. I wonder what the hell it means. (141)

PA: In some of my books people isolate themselves, hole themselves up somewhere in order to write or paint or reflect.

IBS: Is there something about seclusion that enhances the creative impulse? Sachs is imprisoned, Effing confines himself in the hermit's cave, and Fanshawe locks himself away in a room in order to write his book. In fact, they all produce brilliant work in these confined spaces; work that we never get to see or read.

PA: True, but each time it's a little different. I write about this in my new book:

> You wanted to isolate yourself as thoroughly as possible
> because you had started writing a novel, and it was your
> juvenile belief (or romantic belief, or misconstrued belief)
> that novels should be written in isolation. (*Report from the
> Interior*, 193)*

I had the mistaken idea as a young person that you had to lock yourself away from the world in order to do any kind of important work.

IBS: The notion of falling is a recurring theme in your work. We
discussed it in connection with *City of Glass* and will no doubt come
back to it again later. Here, in *Leviathan*, the fall is absolutely pivotal.

> His body mended, but he was never the same after that. In
> those few seconds before he hit the ground, it was as if Sachs
> lost everything. His entire life flew apart in midair, and from
> that moment until his death four years later, he never put it
> back together again. (107)

The fall unleashes Sachs's self-disgust, which matches his revulsion
against America's failure to live up to its own moral and political
ideals. The consequences are stupendous.

PA: Yes, but it's not just a symbolic fall. It's a physical fall as well.
It's an accident, inspired, as I said earlier, by what happened to my
father. It's several things at once.

IBS: Can we associate it also with your interest in the properties of
prelapsarian language? Sachs says, "It was as if uttering the word *fall*
had precipitated a real fall" (109). This suggestion of a causal connection between word and object is present especially in your later
books: saying the thing makes it happen.

---

* This conversation took place in March 2012, eight months before the publication of *Report
from the Interior*.

PA: Sometimes, yes, that's true. It's one of those weird synapses—even if it means nothing, it feels as if it does. I don't want to emphasize the symbolism of it too much. *You* can do it, but I won't. I know you read biblical fable into this story, and you're making an argument for that reading now, but I wasn't conscious of it while writing the story.

IBS: Could we look at my reading for a moment?

PA: Why not?

IBS: Leviathan, of course, is also the name of the ante-mundane figure of violence and chaos in Genesis. Here, in your *Leviathan*, we have a hero who is profoundly angry and distressed by the violence and lack of moral integrity of his country. "[T]here was something almost Biblical about his exhortations," you write, "and after a while he began to sound less like a political revolutionary than some anguished, soft-spoken prophet" (217). He suffers a dramatic fall at the very height of the celebrations of a national icon. It instantly and irrevocably changes Sachs's life: he shaves his head to exhibit his scars, then sets off on an unknown route into the backwaters of America. Aaron, his best friend, fails to keep up with him. Then, think of the biblical story of the golden calf and how Moses's brother, Aaron, brands the ram's head and sends it into the wilderness to atone for the sins of Israel.

> When Aaron has finished making expiation for the sanctuary . . . he shall bring forward the live goat. He shall lay both his hands on its head and confess over it all the iniquities of the Israelites and all their acts of *rebellion*, that is all their sins; he shall lay them on the *head* of the goat and send it *away into the wilderness.* (Lev. 16:20–23; my italics)

And here:

> But Sachs was driven to do penance, to take on his guilt as the guilt of the world and to bear its marks in his own flesh. (132)

As I read it, Sachs is Aaron's scapegoat, doing penance for America with the scars of guilt laid bare on his head. His fall is intimately associated with the grand icon of liberty, central to American self-understanding and celebrated almost to the point of worship. There is indeed an element of idolatry here, because it's merely an image, a symbol of freedom—not the real thing. And just like the biblical Aaron's brother, Moses, at first a "soft-spoken prophet," Sachs destroys the idol.

PA: I wasn't thinking about my story in those terms, but now that we've talked about these connections, I see them. This is the odd thing about writing novels: sometimes there's something going on underneath, and the writer is unaware of it. We keep coming back to this unconscious awareness in our discussions. As a writer, you're fixed on trying to tell the story, on trying to do it well, on trying to put the things you've been imagining on the page. Then this undercurrent of deeper meanings—it's there! You can feel it percolating underneath, but you don't always know exactly what it is. It's for the reader to explore. A number of years ago, Siri and I were invited to do an event in a theater in New York. She had agreed to interview me about *Oracle Night* and was asked not to discuss it with me in advance. Once we were on stage, she made a very strong case for her claim that the book is indebted to Kierkegaard's *Either/Or*. I was completely taken by surprise and said, "I don't know what you're talking about." I had never thought about it. Of course, I had read Kierkegaard's book many years earlier, and no doubt it had seeped into my unconscious and inspired elements in *Oracle Night*. It's the same with these biblical stories. I read them when I was a child and know them well, but I wasn't thinking about them consciously.

IBS: Not at all?

PA: Not at all, no.

IBS: I think it makes sense when you read the book: the worshipping of an icon and the marked scapegoat doing penance for a whole nation.

PA: It's a good way to read the book. Very clever.

IBS: Maria Turner is implicated in Sachs's fall in more ways than one:

> Maria was the embodiment of his catastrophe, the central figure in the drama that had precipitated his fall, and therefore no one could have been as important to him. (126)

PA: That's right.

IBS: It seems to me that she is doing with her camera what some of your characters do with words.

> It was an archeology of the present, so to speak, an attempt to reconstitute the essence of something from only the barest fragments: a ticket stub, a torn stocking, a blood stain on the collar of a shirt. (63)

Could we say that Maria "recreates" Sachs through the lens of her camera?

> Every time Sachs posed for a picture, he was forced to impersonate himself, to play the game of pretending to be who he was. After a while, it must have had an effect on him. By repeating the process so often, he must have come to the point where he started seeing himself through Maria's eyes, where the whole thing doubled back on him and he was able to encounter himself again. (130)

PA: Some primitive peoples think pictures rob a person of his soul. Here, it's the opposite.

IBS: Maria assists Sachs in this process of restoration, but he never fully recovers, does he? Something is irrevocably broken, inherently fractured.

PA: He's never quite well again. Then, of course, he has the protracted affair with Lillian, which is wrenching. She's a terribly complex character.

IBS: You have no fewer than three central female characters in *Leviathan*: Fanny, Lillian, and Maria. They all jump off the page. These wonderful women: strong, nuanced, unpredictable. Fanny really surprises, and she's so vivid in the reader's mind. Lillian, too, for different reasons—and Maria, obviously, with all her idiosyncrasies.

PA: Again, they're complete inventions, except for Maria's artworks. Other than that, there's little resemblance between my character and the real-life artist.

IBS: I was thinking of the way in which all three women are center stage in *Leviathan* and come across as nuanced and round. Since Anna Blume, I don't think you've given as much attention to any female character.

PA: This book represents a kind of shift for me. It's the first time I tried to write what you might call a realistic novel. Realistic in the sense that it's about people doing the ordinary things that people living in a society do together—something I had never addressed in any of my previous work. Until *Leviathan*, my books were almost exclusively about solitary figures.

IBS: We've often talked about recurrences in your work, but they are never repetitions: there's novelty to every one of them. Could we say that a new kind of "realism" plays into your take on ambiguity in *Leviathan*? Aaron, your narrator, repeatedly runs into a wall of indeterminacy and contradiction: "all my certainties about the world had collapsed" (84). His exchange with Sachs about the near-fatal fall illustrates this:

> "You told me you fell because you were too afraid to touch Maria's leg. Now you change your story and tell me that you fell on purpose. You can't have it both ways. It's got to be one or the other."
> "It's both. The one thing led to the other, and they can't be separated. I'm not saying I understand it, I'm just telling you how it was, what I know to be true." (121)

PA: That's right, but this is also about misinterpretation. Aaron is not a reliable witness, as we said earlier. A good example would be when he's at Fanny and Ben's apartment for dinner and doesn't know they've been trying to have a child for years and that, finally, they've been told she can't conceive. Sachs says, "Who wants children?" Aaron doesn't understand that he's doing this out of love for Fanny. We often mis-read other people because we aren't aware of their hidden motives. This kind of thing happens often in the book. Another example would be the uncertainty as to whether Fanny actually does have a love affair with Aaron in order to cure him.

IBS: The same goes for all those stories about Sachs's affairs.

PA: Yes, we don't really know.

IBS: Still, Aaron is not unaware of being in the dark.

> They had presented me with two versions of the truth, two separate and distinct realities, and no amount of pushing and shoving could ever bring them together. (98)

I think in *Leviathan* ambiguity becomes more concrete than in the earlier books. However perplexing it may be, it's quite clear now that there are many truths, and they can be equally accurate.

PA:

> In other words, there was no universal truth. Not for them, not for anyone else. There was no one to blame or to defend, and the only justifiable response was compassion. I had looked up to them both for too many years not to feel disappointed by what I had learned, but I wasn't disappointed only in them. I was disappointed in myself. I was disappointed in the world. Even the strongest were weak, I told myself; even the bravest lacked courage; even the wisest were ignorant. (98)

IBS: It really is a terrific passage. In a sense, it rounds up the process of "learning to live with ambiguity" that we talked about in connection with *The New York Trilogy*. It's as if here it falls into place for you. Could that be true?

PA: Of all my books, *Leviathan* was probably the biggest struggle for me. The work progressed very slowly, and I never felt happy writing it. I kept thinking I was doing it wrong. Artistically, it was an enormous challenge and extremely painful to do. I'm not sure why.

IBS: At some point Aaron says:

> No one can say where a book comes from, least of all the person who writes it. Books are born out of ignorance, and if they go on living after they are written, it's only to the degree that they cannot be understood. (36)

PA: My thoughts exactly. It could serve as the epigraph for our entire project.

MR. VERTIGO. (1994)
Levitating

IBS: The opening line of *Mr. Vertigo* is superb, and the first paragraph provides the perfect overture for this extraordinary story about an orphaned street urchin who becomes a famous levitator:

> I was twelve years old the first time I walked on water. The man in the black clothes taught me how to do it, and I'm not going to pretend I learned that trick overnight. Master Yehudi found me when I was nine, an orphan boy begging nickels on the streets of Saint Louis, and he worked with me steadily for three years before he let me show my stuff in public. That was in 1927, the year of Babe Ruth and Charles Lindbergh, the precise year when night began to fall on the world forever. (3)

PA: Yesterday, we discussed *Leviathan* as a story about falling. *Mr. Vertigo* grew out of a contrary impulse. I wanted to get my protagonist off the ground—to see him levitate. At first, I thought it would be a short story, somewhere between thirty and forty pages, but then the book started to grow. It took off. I wrote it in a kind of frenzy. *Leviathan* had been a slow, carefully worked out novel that took me over two years to finish. This one flew out of me in about eight months. I didn't have a definite plan to begin with, and unexpected things kept happening along the way. For example, when I started writing, there was no Mrs. Witherspoon. She came in later, and then she turned into one of the most important characters.

IBS: There's a dimension of magic realism to *Mr. Vertigo* that sets it apart from all your other early books.

PA: At the same time, everything about this book is down to earth. Literally, down to earth.

IBS: So is the flying, strangely enough. It comes across as if it's the most natural thing in the world: an art or a skill that anyone can learn.

PA: As an old man, Walt,* the narrator, believes that flying is connected to the desire for transcendence in all of us, the desire to do something extraordinary, to make something beautiful. At the end of the book he says:

> Deep down, I don't believe it takes any special talent for a person to lift himself off the ground and hover in the air. We all have it in us—every man, woman, and child—and with enough hard work and concentration, every human being is capable of duplicating the feats I accomplished as Walt the Wonder Boy. You must learn to stop being yourself. That's where it begins, and everything else follows from that. You must let yourself evaporate. Let your muscles go limp, breathe until you feel your soul pouring out of you, and then shut your eyes. That's how it's done. (278)

Needless to say, levitation is a metaphor. Even so, it's literal, it's concrete. An old friend of mine, the high-wire artist Philippe Petit,** read the book and said: "This is precisely what it feels like to be up in the air." Those words made me deeply happy. Because of this book, I've also become friends with the magicians Ricky Jay and David Blaine.***

---

* Walter Clairborne Rawley, homonymous with Raleigh. See Auster's essay "The Death of Sir Walter Raleigh," 1975, reprinted in *Collected Prose*.
** The French aerialist who gained fame for his high-wire walk between the Twin Towers of the World Trade Center in New York City, August 1974. Auster translated his book *On the High Wire* (New York: Random House, 1985) and wrote an essay on him in 1982, reprinted in *Collected Prose*.
*** Ricky Jay is an American stage magician, actor, and writer; David Blaine is an American illusionist and endurance artist.

They're big fans of *Mr. Vertigo*. That means a lot to me, because they understand better than other people what's involved here.

IBS: The book is set in Wichita, home of the American aircraft industry, and Walt's flight coincides with Lindbergh's.

PA: It's the 1920s, the so-called Roaring Twenties, a time that has always interested me. I tried to capture that time in the language: a semi-insane American vernacular, common speech shot through with biblical phrasing—a double language, in a sense. The slang is not authentic [*laughs*]. I invented it for Walt. Verbally, it's one of the wilder things I've attempted to do.

IBS: For me, one of the most brilliant aspects of this book is precisely the force of this peculiar language: the way in which the magic comes across as perfectly natural in a narration that shifts from the voice of a frightened street kid to a successful, mature man.

PA: I really wanted to let go. I found a way to do that by using a dumb, illiterate boy as the narrator.

IBS: Walt's language develops as he matures and becomes more tolerant and reflective, however. At the beginning, he's dreadfully biased.

PA: He's a racist.

IBS: And a misogynist.

PA: Among other things.

IBS: All that changes in the hands of Master Yehudi.

PA: The mysterious Master Yehudi . . . Earlier, I talked about *The Music of Chance* as a fable. *Mr. Vertigo* is pure myth. As in all myths, there are no psychological justifications for the way people act. The Master just *is*. You take him or leave him. Walt just *is*. Mother Sioux and Aesop, the most unlikely character, and Mrs. Witherspoon—they just *are*. Do you remember the comment by Peter Brook? "The distance of myth and the closeness of the everyday."* That's what I was trying to accomplish here.

IBS: Could we read *Mr. Vertigo* as an American myth about development from innocence to maturity? *Mr. Vertigo* is often regarded as a quintessentially American novel, a frontier novel. We might see it as a story about precisely that: America advancing into adulthood. Especially since it's set in the 1920s, a period so marked by crises—America's "growing pains," as it were—at the threshold of the American century. In connection with *Moon Palace* and *Leviathan*, we talked about possible parallels between the personal story and national history. Do we not have a similar correlation here between America and the protagonist, the unruly Wonder Boy's rise to fame and power?

PA: We're all products of our time and place, and time and place are critical here—America the beautiful, America the ugly, America way back when and America now.

IBS: We also have an archetypical American melting pot family in *Mr. Vertigo*—or substitute family, because, like so many of your other characters, Walt is an orphan. The father or master of the family is a Jewish immigrant from Hungary, the maternal figure is a Sioux Indian, and Walt's adoptive brother is a young black intellectual. It's in precisely this composite context that Walt turns from street urchin to Wonder Boy as he dances in the air above the crowd in a Huck Finn costume to the tune of "America the Beautiful." It's the American Dream fulfilled, isn't it? Then comes the stock market crash, which coincides with Walt's "fall."

---

* See conversation on *The Invention of Solitude*.

PA: Yes, all this is part of the fabric of the book. It's also connected with an American figure you may not be familiar with: Dizzy Dean. Dizzy Dean was a real baseball player, and everything about him in this book is based on fact. Dizzy Dean was one of the most celebrated bumpkins in American life. He wasn't terribly intelligent, but he was a great pitcher. Once, when he was hit on the head by a batted ball, he was rushed to the hospital and X-rayed. The joke headline read: "X-Rays of Dean's Head Reveal Nothing." So, I pick up Dizzy right at the end of his career in Chicago, but originally he came from Saint Louis, Walt's Saint Louis, and Walt says, "I'd latched onto Dizzy because he reminded me of myself" (252). Dean's story is also a story about Walt's failure.

IBS: Yes, it all goes up in smoke, basically, after Master Yehudi's death. It's downhill—for Walt and for America. The magic has gone out of it.

PA: Not quite. Walt does find a certain happiness with his wife, and he prospers.

> Those were the years when suburbs were spouting up around the cities, and I went where the money was, doing my bit to change the landscape and turn the world into what it looks like today. All those ranch houses and tidy lawns and spindly little trees wrapped in burlap—I was the guy who put them there. (264)

This is important: "doing my bit to change the landscape and turn the world into what it looks like today." We're talking about the postwar American world of suburban prosperity. As I look at the paperback edition now, I see that the *Boston Globe* review said that "nobody has produced a better parable about the condition of the national consciousness at century's end" and that *Mr. Vertigo* "achieves a kind of sublime craziness" [*laughs*]. That's wonderful.

IBS: That craziness is superbly reflected in the characters. Walt is the narrator-protagonist, and we have access to the other characters through him only. They develop and become more complex as Walt matures.

PA: His view of Mrs. Witherspoon, for example, changes completely over the course of those years.

IBS: Master Yehudi as well. In the beginning, we see him almost exclusively from a small boy's perspective as this strange figure in black clothes. Then, he gradually becomes rounder and more nuanced.

PA: Afterward, when I had finished the book, I discovered a certain resonance with *Pinocchio*: we could read Master Yehudi as Father Geppetto, Walt as Pinocchio, and Mrs. Witherspoon as the Blue Fairy.

IBS: Master Yehudi is such an enigmatic character: we know almost nothing about him. A Hungarian Jew. What is he doing out there in Kansas? Reading Spinoza. Why Spinoza?

PA: Spinoza is the only Jew in the pantheon of Western philosophers. He reflects on ways of thinking about the power of God in nature. That's the spiritual side of Master Yehudi. At the same time, however, he's just another con man. Later in life, Walt understands that his mentor wasn't the genius he had taken him for as a boy. The Master was winging it, improvising from start to finish.

IBS: Even so, Walt achieves something truly extraordinary under his guidance: he learns to fly! He also learns about ethics and morality from Master Yehudi. Is there a reason why you made Walt's instructor a Jew? Is there a connection here between Jewish law and American ethics?

PA: There's a religious dimension to it, for the fact is that Master Yehudi truly believes in these values.

> All men are brothers, and in this family everyone gets treated with respect. That's the law. If you don't like it, lump it. The law is the law, and whoever goes against it is turned into a slug and wallows in the earth for the rest of his days. (13)

It's a very Jewish thing: "The law is the law." This is the intersection between Judaism and American democracy. As I'm sure you know, certain ideas developed by the Jews became embodied in American law, especially the principle of "justice for all." That's the great lesson of the Book of Jonah, as we mentioned earlier. There can be no justice for anyone unless there is justice for everyone.

IBS: I suppose Master Yehudi is the closest you get to having a Jewish central character in any of your novels.

PA: The son of a rabbi, supposedly. There are many Jewish characters in my books, but questions of their ethnicity or religion are rarely emphasized.

IBS: I think the biblical stories and Jewish thought and experience are subtle but fundamental sources of inspiration in parts of your writing. Here, you have a pivotal figure straight out of an Ashkenazi background.

PA: The quintessential Other, floating through the hinterlands of the American Midwest.

IBS: They make a strange pair, the enigmatic Master and his acolyte united in this hazardous experiment. At some point, Walt hits rock bottom and must accept that death is part of life.

> A little seed of craziness has been planted in your head, and even though you've won the struggle to survive, nearly every-

thing else has been lost. Death lives inside you, eating away at your innocence and your hope, and in the end you're left with nothing but the dirt, the solidity of the dirt, the everlasting power and triumph of the dirt. (41–42)

PA: That's part of his training. He's just a little kid at this point, and he's learning about ultimate things here. He's going to be the boy of the air, and now, in order to achieve that goal, he must first be buried under the ground. Everything is working in opposites.

IBS: At some point, not too far into the book, Walt says, "I had taught *myself* how to fly, after all" (63; my italics). Is it his own achievement or Master Yehudi's?

PA: The Master has been grinding him through the thirty-three steps, but when Walt is finally able to rise up into the air, he does it himself—out of a feeling of loss and abandonment. He cries so hard, he feels as if his soul is dribbling out of him. In other words, his achievement is to turn misery and a feeling of emptiness into something spectacular.

IBS: Later in the story, he realizes that "Master Yehudi had launched a ship that was full of holes" (115). It's an interesting moment in the book because previously the Master had been in complete command of everything. Now the balance between them is upset for the first time.

PA: That comes after the unsuccessful first show.

IBS: Yes, where Walt was dressed as Jesus. It didn't work.

PA: It didn't work, no.

IBS: So, Walt takes over and suggests the Huck Finn costume.

PA: Walt might be uneducated, but he's not stupid.

> These rubes don't like no fancy stuff. They didn't take
> to your penguin suit, and they didn't take to my sissy
> robes. And all that high-flown talk you pitched them at
> the start—it went right over their heads . . . If you wear a
> plain old seersucker suit and a nice straw hat, no one will
> take offense. They'll think you're a friendly, good-hearted
> Joe out to make an honest buck. That's the key, the whole
> sack of onions. I stroll out before them like a little know-
> nothing, a wide-eyed farm boy dressed in denim overalls
> and a plaid shirt. No shoes, no socks, a barefoot nobody
> with the same geek mug as their own sons and nephews.
> They take one look at me and relax. It's like I'm a member
> of the family. And then, the moment I start rising into the
> air, their hearts fail them. It's that simple. Soften them up,
> then hit them with the whammy. It's bound to be good.
> Two minutes into the act, they'll be eating out of our
> hands like squirrels. (114–115)

IBS: In the end, Walt acknowledges his debt: "Without the Master I
was no one, I wasn't going anywhere" (229).

PA: If, technically, the Master does teach him how to fly, he also
teaches him how to become a human being. Tolerance and equality
are the bedrock on which everything else is built.

IBS: So, we have this male bond between teacher and pupil, master
and ephebe, father and son. Is there also an Oedipal element? I mean,
the "son" eventually takes control and finally replaces the "father" in
the marital bed. Mrs. Witherspoon talks about Walt having come
back to the beginning, taking over from Master Yehudi.

PA: Mrs. Witherspoon—how shall I put it?—is a compelling woman.

IBS: It's through her, rather than Mother Sioux, that Walt learns to respect women, isn't it?

PA: He loves them both. But Mother Sioux is killed at the end of part one, and Mrs. Witherspoon lives to a grand old age.

IBS: The book is also a close examination of how one turns oneself into an artist.

PA: Walt has some definite ideas on the subject:

> It was the unpredictability that excited me, the adventure of never knowing what was going to happen from one show to the next. If your only motive is to be loved, to ingratiate yourself with the crowd, you're bound to fall into bad habits, and eventually the public will grow tired of you. You have to keep testing yourself, pushing your talent as hard as you can. You do it for yourself, but in the end it's this struggle to do better that most endears you to your fans. That's the paradox. People begin to sense that you're out there taking risks for them. They're allowed to share in the mystery, to participate in whatever nameless thing is driving you to do it, and once that happens, you're no longer just a performer, you're on the way to becoming a star. (131)

IBS: You could be talking about writing, couldn't you?

PA: Absolutely. Any artist, any art.

IBS: Then, as in *Leviathan*, everything changes with a fall: Walt rises to stardom, then, literally and metaphorically, he plunges to the ground:

> I tumbled out of the air like a dead sparrow and landed forehead-first on the rim of a metal chair back. The impact was so sudden and so fierce, it knocked me out cold. (178)

Is rise inevitably followed by a fall?

PA: Things go wrong for him when he hits puberty. The gravitational forces in his body change, and once he becomes a man, it's over. Blinding headaches, horrible pain, agony beyond measure. Of course, Master Yehudi proposes the possibility of castration. Walt says no thanks.

IBS: [*Laughs*] Yes, it's a long process of success and failure that begins and ends with pain.

PA: The thirty-three steps, the crushing initiation that Walt is put through. He's nearly killed by those trials. He says that the physical ordeals were leading him "to places of such inwardness that he no longer remembered who he was" (49). The Master's idea is that, on the one the hand, he must break Walt's spirit so he won't resist and, on the other, he's disciplining him to withstand pain and fear. He's teaching him to become a real artist, to concentrate under adverse conditions. Soldiers are trained in that way. It's grueling. Often the training is worse than anything they experience in battle. Or boxers. It's very tough. Dancers: think of what those poor girls must go through—the rigors of performing the extraordinary. But Master Yehudi is also a bit crazy. He's imbued with mystical notions about "cracking open the universe." At the same time, he's making it up as he goes along. He wants Walt's devotion. And then there's what I would call the placebo effect. If he can convince Walt to believe in the program, then maybe something will happen. He even cuts off a part of Walt's finger, convincing the poor boy that the little joint has been weighing down his body. Then it works! Walt floats across the lake.

IBS: So, it's placebo, not magic?

PA: Maybe yes, maybe no.

IBS: It's not that you have to make a sacrifice in order to be able to do these extraordinary things?

PA: Maybe you do, but then again, maybe you don't.

IBS: No symbolism intended? No message about the state of America?

PA: If you want the message to be there, it's there. But what you see is not necessarily what someone else will see.

IBS: And what do you see?

PA: I can't say.

IBS: Can't or won't?

PA: Both.

TIMBUKTU. (1999)
"The Pure Pleasure of Language"

IBS: *Timbuktu* is the portrait of two lost souls, a homeless man, Willy, and his dog, Mr. Bones, facing the end of their lives. The story is told from the dog's point of view, and while his perspective on the world is determined by a domesticated animal's need for love, food, and shelter, there is much more going on than intelligent and witty canine observations: poetry, philosophy, theology, psychology, politics—and a lot of rambling on the edge between madness and vision.

PA: This was the first novel I published after the five-year gap following *Mr. Vertigo.** Those were the years when I was making movies. I didn't write fiction during that period, but I was thinking about a big novel, the book that eventually became *The Brooklyn Follies*. In the first version, the story was going to begin with Willy and Mr. Bones. Willy would die, as he does in *Timbuktu*, but Mr. Bones was going to be an important character throughout the book. Then, when I started writing it, I fell hopelessly in love with those two and decided to pull them out of the big narrative and make a short lyrical book about the trials and tribulations of my demented poet and his four-legged companion. That became *Timbuktu*. I wanted it to be a love story—but a love story without cynicism. There's a lot of me in Mr. Bones, I'm afraid. I love deeply and without much nuance—a dog at heart. The fact that Mr. Bones is a dog is almost incidental. He's a four-legged character in a novel, no more or less real than any two-legged character.

IBS: So that was the motivation: unconditional love?

---

* *Hand to Mouth* came out in this five-year period. However, it is an autobiographical text, not a novel.

PA: I think so. Willy is one of the broken souls of my generation. I borrowed a few things from people I knew when I was younger. For instance, I had a friend whose parents were Polish Jews who managed to escape from Eastern Europe during the war and made it to Brooklyn. It was a perilous journey, and the whole family suffered from the consequences. I adopted this for Willy's background. A very harsh father, whom he didn't like at all, and a loving but unhinged mother.

IBS: What's Mr. Bones's background? Is he inspired by your dog?

PA: I started writing this book before we got the dog, but, of course, once he was here, he helped me a lot.

IBS: There's an old school friend of Willy's called "Anster or Omster" (67). He's only mentioned in passing. Are you in the book?

PA: Yes, of course, that's me. Actually, now that you mention it, there's one autobiographical element in *Timbuktu*. The story of the typing dog, an amazing stunt, which I actually witnessed with my own eyes. When I was seventeen, I went to Europe for the first time. My mother's sister and her husband had been living in Italy for twelve years, and I went to stay with them for three weeks. My aunt had become good friends with a woman named Elizabeth Mann Borghese, Thomas Mann's daughter. She was a well-known scientist, and at the time she was involved in a field called animal psychology, which was a new discipline back then. She owned an English setter named Ollie, a lovely brown-and-white dog, and had devised a special typewriter with large round keys for him. The dog would hit the keys with his snout, and I actually saw him spell out, letter by letter: "Ollie is a good dog." Thomas Mann's daughter gave him food each time he got it right. I saw it: I saw a dog type! So, since I was on the subject of dogs and their ability to understand language, I had to tell this story in the book.

IBS: Obviously.

PA: Yes, so there you go. "Anster or Omster" briefly appears in the book reading Thomas Mann's *The Magic Mountain*. It probably comes across as the most far-fetched episode in the book, but it's the one thing that comes from real life.

IBS: You describe Mr. Bones as a "hodgepodge of genetic strains" with a "perpetual bloodshot sadness lurking in his eyes" (5). I was wondering whether the novel itself is a bit like that: a composition of different elements with a core of sorrow?

PA: Probably. The book is humorous, but there's a tremendous sadness in it, too. Mr. Bones's internal thoughts and Willy's verbal ramblings seem to combine both of those moods. It's certainly the most lyrical novel I've written. More than any other, *Timbuktu* turns on the pure pleasure of language.

IBS: In *Mr. Vertigo* you invented a rich vernacular for Walt, and here in *Timbuktu* you take language to another extreme—more poetic but also slightly mad.

PA: It was important to me to try to reproduce schizophrenic speech in Willy's monologues. I guess I've done that only twice in my novels: once in *City of Glass*: Stillman Jr.'s long, disjointed speech, and then Willy's soliloquies in this book. In both cases, I found that I had to go into a kind of hypnotic state to do it. You have to let the words bounce off one another and let it all flow out of you. Then you polish it later. This is essential, but initially you just need to get it all out in one big rush. Willy's language is crucial to the book.

> Know-how knows no borders, and when you think of the bounty that pours in from across the seas, it knocks you down a peg or two and puts you in your place. I don't mean obvious things like turkeys from Turkey or chili from Chile.

I also mean pants from France. I mean pain from Spain and pity from Italy and checks from Czechoslovakia and fleece from Greece. Patriotism has its role, but in the long run it's a sentiment best kept under wraps. Yes, we Yanks have given the world the zipper and the Zippo, not to speak of the zip-a-dee-doo-dah and Zeppo Marx, but we're also responsible for the H-bomb and the hula hoop. It all balances out in the end, doesn't it? Just when you think you're top gun, you wind up as bottom dog. And I don't mean you, Mr. Bones. Dog as metaphor, if you catch my drift, dog as emblem of the downtrodden, and you're no trope, my boy, you're as real as they come. (56–57)

IBS: Might we say that for Willy words fill an existential void?

PA: He's a word man. He's a poet, and he's ignited—a man on fire with words.

[Siri Hustvedt enters the room.]

SH: I taught writing for four years in a psychiatric hospital and learned that the linguistic creativity in psychosis is amazing. What they write is never clichéd. I think Willy's monologues match this kind of psychotic speech extremely well.

PA: Energized language. It's energy.

SH: It's a kind of manic brilliance . . .

IBS: And a different take on reality, I would have thought. A different take on meaning, the semantic side of language?

SH: Actually, it's just hugely creative, musical, and also, in a way, distanced. They're using language as an object.

PA: Yes, it's that kind of distancing that allows Willy to turn "Santa" into "Satan."

[*SH waves good-bye and leaves the room.*]

IBS: The overriding concern your canine character shares with his human colleagues is the question of how to communicate oneself to others. Of course, he's severely restricted when it comes to vocal communication, and the exchanges between man and dog are strangely asymmetrical. Mr. Bones apparently understands human language perfectly but can only express himself through body language, and Willy must learn to decipher this canine grammar of movement:

> There was so much to absorb, so much evidence to assimilate, decipher, and make sense of that Willy hardly knew where to begin. The wagging tail as opposed to the tail between the legs. The pricked ears as opposed to the flaccid ears. The rolling on to the back, the running in circles, the anus-sniffs and growls, the kangaroo-hops and midair turns, the stalking crouch, the bared teeth, the cocked head, and a hundred other minute particulars, each one an expression of a thought, a feeling, a plan, an urge. It was like learning how to speak a new language. (37)

This is wonderful. You capture dog communication so vividly. This is the body speaking, and it plays into what we've talked about several times already: the connections between verbal and physical modes of expression.

PA: A kinetic language, yes. It's a language of movement, dog movement, and Willy is trying to penetrate its precise meaning.

IBS: While linguistically and psychologically complex, structurally, *Timbuktu* is really rather simple. I was wondering, could we think of it as a kind of fable along the lines of what we talked about in connection with *The Music of Chance*? We have a dog with supernatural powers: he is transformed from dog to fly in order to be able to witness Willy's final words, and the magic number three determines the action. For instance, Mr. Bones has three dreams that predict the future:

> One by one, Willy touched on each and every topic that had come up in the dream, and when Mr. Bones realized that it was happening in precisely the same order as before, he felt a chill go down his spine. (80)

PA: Yes, the dreams, Santa Claus on television talking directly to Willy, Mr. Bones turning into a fly. Magic things happen. Free association and schizophrenia also play into the narrative. Willy's mind will turn one thing into its opposite by merely rearranging letters in peculiar word games. There are strange things going on inside their minds.

IBS: As always, you treat your characters, human and canine, with profound empathy and warmth. Take, for instance, Willy's last self-description:

> On the one hand, purity of heart, goodness, Santa's loyal helper. On the other hand, a loud-mouthed crank, a nihilist, a besotted clown. And the poet? He fell somewhere in between, I suppose, in the interval between the best and the worst of me. The man with voices in his head, the one who sometimes managed to listen in on the conversations of stones and trees, who every now and then could turn the music of the clouds into words. Pity I couldn't have been him more. (60–61)

This is very moving. Would it be fair to say that Willy becomes more human seen through the eyes of a dog?

PA: Mr. Bones doesn't judge. He doesn't care that Willy is crazy or that his body stinks. Their bond is absolute. By the end of the second chapter, however, Willy dies, and from then on he's essentially out of the book. He pops up a few times after that in dreams, but never again in the flesh. For instance—when the Joneses name the dog. Ah, the horror of being called Sparky! He's Mr. Bones, and they call him Sparky. Then, in the dream, Willy reassures him, "Just put it in its Latin form, and you'll feel much better. Sparkatus [*laughs*]. Behold yon Sparkatus, the noblest tail-wagger in all of Rome."

IBS: [*Laughs.*]

PA: We're not saying anything very serious here.

IBS: True. So, even if your central character is a dog, he has many of the same interests and concerns as your human protagonists. In fact, the book turns on his fear of loss and abandonment.

> Subtract Willy from the world, and the odds were that the world itself would cease to exist. (4)

Coping with loss is a recurring theme in your writing. Does *Timbuktu* resemble *The Book of Illusions* in that respect?

PA: Inevitably, I suppose. I'm always me, after all, and I'm interested in extreme emotional states. Losing people you love is the most terrible thing that can happen. It's worse than dying.

IBS: Here, loss has fatal consequences because an abandoned dog can't survive.

PA: Yes, that's it. What's going to happen to Mr. Bones?

IBS: In effect, he commits suicide, right? It's the only suicide in all of your work, isn't it?

PA: I hadn't thought of that. Stillman Sr. supposedly kills himself, of course. And then there are the Leapers and Assassination Club members in *In the Country of Last Things*. But we don't experience those deaths directly. We only hear about them.

IBS: Mr. Bones is not committing suicide to get away from his life as much as to get to . . .

PA: To Timbuktu, to be with Willy, yes. In a sense, it's a positive act. He doesn't have the greatest intelligence, Mr. Bones, and so he thinks this might be the means of transportation, so to speak. As I say here,

> It was called dodge-the-car, and it was a venerable, time-honored sport that allowed every old-timer to recapture the glories of his youth. It was fun, it was invigorating, it was a challenge to every dog's athletic skills. Just run across the road and see if you could avoid being hit. The more times you were able to do it, the greater the champion you were. Sooner or later, of course, the odds were bound to catch up with you, and few dogs had ever played dodge-the-car without losing on their last turn. But that was the beauty of this particular game. The moment you lost, you won. (185–186)

IBS: So, failure is success. After all, he is going to join Willy in Timbuktu, the serene "next world" where you become "one with the universe, a speck of anti-matter lodged in the brain of God" (49). Mr. Bones himself believes Timbuktu to be

> the land of words and transparent toasters, the country of bicycle wheels and burning deserts where dogs talked as equals with men. (185)

What is this place? A syncretism between Buddhist nirvana and Narnia?

PA: It just means the farthest, most remote place on earth. It's a common American expression: "You've got to go all the way to Timbuktu for that."

IBS: At the center of *Timbuktu* you have an Ashkenazi Jewish family. The entire family on both Willy's parents' sides perished in the camps, and Willy bears the burden of second-generation Holocaust victims. I think you capture the existence of first-generation survivors extremely well when you describe it as "a posthumous life, an interval between two deaths" (14). For many, this is exactly how it feels. You must have talked to Holocaust survivors to have this insight?

PA: Not expressly for this book, but I've known a number of survivors.

IBS: You did some work with Zosia Goldberg.

PA: I wrote the preface for the book she did with her nephew, my old college friend Hilton Obenzinger.* In fact, I did draw on a true Holocaust story in *Timbuktu*. There was a man in our family on my mother's side, Joseph Stavsky, whom I mention in *Report from the Interior* (69). He lost his wife and twin daughters in Auschwitz. He was the only person in his family who survived. My grandparents helped get him out of Europe and brought him to New York. He was one of the most elegant people I've ever known, the most sophisticated. He wore beautiful three-piece suits and smoked with a cigarette holder. He had been a lawyer in Warsaw. The once prosperous lawyer now made his living as a button salesman in New York's garment district. I give that job to Willy's father.

IBS: Holocaust survival also affects the second generation. Mr. Bones frequently reflects on that:

> Mrs. Gurevitch knew the world was out to get her, and she

---

* Zosia Goldberg, *Running Through Fire: How I Survived the Holocaust* (San Francisco: Mercury House, 2004).

lived her life accordingly, doing everything in her power to stay clear of harm's way. Willy also knew that the world was out to get him, but unlike his mother he had no qualms about fighting back. (16)

PA: Then her horror at the tattoo:

> Alas, when he returned to Brooklyn and proudly showed his mother this new ornament, Mrs. Gurevitch went wild, erupting in a tantrum of tears and angry disbelief. It wasn't just the idea of that tattoo that bent her out of shape (although that was part of it, given that tattooing was pro-scribed by Jewish law—and given what role the tattooing of Jewish skin had played in her lifetime), it was what *this particular tattoo* represented, and in that Mrs. Gurevitch saw the three-color Santa Claus on Willy's arm as a token of betrayal and incurable madness, her outburst at that moment was perhaps understandable. (22)

IBS: Willy grew up in a household severely marked by traumas, and he was a fairly lonely and unhappy child. Would you say that being a second-generation Holocaust victim is in part responsible for Willy's turning to drugs and his inability to settle down?

PA: No, not all survivors' children turn out that way. Willy has a genetic defect, and he's taken too many drugs. More than anything, he's one of the damaged souls from the sixties. So I wouldn't attribute his problems to trauma. He's a cantankerous fellow, he fights with his mother, he revels in his self-appointed role as outcast. Washed out. Washed up. A mess.

IBS: He finds his parents "alien," as you say,

> wholly embarrassing creatures, a pair of sore thumbs with their Polish accents and stilted foreign ways. (14)

Does any of this come from your own experience?

PA: No, no. I was out there in the New Jersey suburbs with Americanized, assimilated Jews. My parents didn't speak with foreign accents. My grandparents on my mother's side didn't speak with foreign accents.

IBS: So there's no echo from your own life here?

PA: No, I don't think so. Willy is a rebel rather than a victim. He has contempt for middle-class American life, and he gives his entire inheritance away. Mrs. Swanson, his old high school English teacher, has some significant things to say about Willy on his deathbed:

> "It was always touch and go with you, William," Mrs.
> Swanson continued, "so I can't really say I'm surprised. I'm
> sure you've done your best. But we're talking about highly
> combustible materials here, aren't we? You walk around with
> a load of nitro-glycerine in your brain, and sooner or later
> you're going to bump into something. When it comes right
> down to it, it's a wonder you didn't blow yourself up a long
> time ago." (76)

IBS: She never finds Mr. Bones, which is very sad. One keeps hoping that some miracle will happen. If only Willy had had the presence of mind to teach him how to read or write.

PA: Yes, that's Willy's principal regret.

IBS: There's this wonderful passage when he manages to convey the rudiments of his name to the Chinese boy, Henry:

> [H]e raised his head and emitted a series of three quick barks:
> wóof, wóof, wóof. It was a perfect anapest, with each syllable
> of his name accorded the proper stress, balance, and duration.

For a few brief seconds, it was as if the words Mis | ter Bones had been boiled down to their sonorous essence, to the purity of a musical phrase. (102)

And so, we come back to the importance of language again: how to express oneself through words and through the body.

PA: The book is about the language, and the characters, the moods and feelings of the characters as expressed in the language of the book. In the end, it's a very simple book—a book that explains itself.

THE BOOK OF ILLUSIONS. (2002)
From Page to Picture

IBS: *The Book of Illusions* can be read as a study of how human beings cope with tragedy. It's also the novel in which film is most extensively explored and woven into the fiber of your fiction. For me, this composition of arresting stories about David Zimmer's loss, Hector Mann's penance, Brigid O'Fallon's love, Frieda's fierce loyalty, and everyone's need for self-expression marks a new avenue in your writing, partly due to different combinations of compassion and complexity integrated at very deep levels. You capture your reader's attention from the very first line of the book: "Everyone thought he was dead" (1). So, there's death accompanied by the possibility of return, and an intimate relationship between narrator and reader is established from the very beginning, one that triggers expectation and suspense.

PA: The most important sentence in a book is the first sentence. Everything follows from it. The first words have to stop the reader in his tracks and tell him that he's in a different place now, that he's entered the world of the book.

IBS: How does the "world of the book" connect with the "world of the film"? Would it be wrong to say that *The Book of Illusions* marks a shift in your focus from the page to pictures?

PA: I've always been interested in movies. As far back as *Ghosts,** the second novel of *The New York Trilogy*, there's a long passage about the crime films from 1947 that Blue goes to see, along with an extensive description and analysis of *Out of the Past*. Since then, I've returned to films many times in my novels (*Man in the Dark*,

---

* Written in 1983, published in 1986.

for example), and in *Report from the Interior* I talk about the impact certain films had on me when I was a boy. Film has always been part of my writing.

IBS: But never to this extent.

PA: Never to this extent. But it turns out that years before I wrote *The Book of Illusions*, Hector Mann had already popped into my head. I'd been thinking about him for a long time. There he was—the mustache, the white suit, the light-footed dance steps—the "torques and pavanes" (33) and all his movements before the camera. I didn't quite know what to do with him. At one point, I thought I would write a series of short stories, each one a description of another make-believe film comedy. That was how *The Book of Illusions* began. Needless to say, it evolved into something much more complex.

IBS: How did you translate the images in your mind into words?

PA: Film moves quickly, words move slowly, and my job was to capture what it feels like to watch a film in words. If you put in too many details, the writing will bog things down and you'll lose the sense of watching a film. On the other hand, if you don't put in enough visual details, the reader won't see enough. The challenge is to find the proper balance between speed and detail. I hope I managed to do that. As a filmmaker friend said to me after reading the book, "You know, maybe these written films are better than real films [*laughs*] because they're perfect, because there are no mistakes."

IBS: I guess that's because here it's the reader who forms the images, not the camera.

PA: Yes. So in a sense, it's another way of exploring what writing does. You're putting words on a page in order to create images in the reader's mind. But, of course, *The Book of Illusions* is about more than just those films.

IBS: Absolutely. It's a fascinating story of loss and how we seek to overcome it, as you say early on in the book:

> What matters is not how well you can avoid trouble, but how you cope with trouble when it comes. (34)

PA: I suppose *The Book of Illusions* is essentially a novel about grief.

IBS: Why did you bring David Zimmer* back to life in this story?

PA: A good question. I'm not really sure. I always imagined him getting involved in film studies. In *Moon Palace*, he starts out as a poet and a student of literature, but toward the end of the book, when Fogg runs into him years later, Zimmer has changed course and is writing about film. Maybe that had something to do with it, I don't know. But the Zimmer in the second book is slightly different from the Zimmer in the first book. For one thing, he's become much taller.

IBS: You revive Zimmer from a previous novel, and you also resurrect historical figures as invented characters in different ways and at different narrative levels in *The Book of Illusions*: Alma brings David "back from the dead" (316), Chateaubriand** is translated from "beyond the grave," Hector lives on through his films and again, in Zimmer's book, Martin Frost destroys his work in order to restore Claire to life.*** Could we say that it's also a book about posthumous life?

PA: In many ways, this is what writing does: it "brings to life" and sometimes "keeps alive." When I started writing this book in 1999, I had been reading Chateaubriand and was growing more and more

---

* Zimmer, the protagonist of *The Book of Illusions*, is a minor character in *Moon Palace*, 1989, and reappears later in *Travels in the Scriptorium*, 2007.
** François-René de Chateaubriand (1768–1848). The others are Auster's characters; the latter, Martin Frost, a character invented by a character, Hector Mann.
*** For a discussion of the evolution of this film, see Auster's interview with Céline Curiol in "The Making of *The Inner Life of Martin Frost*" in *Collected Screenplays*, 409–425.

fascinated by him. I learned that there had been no new English translation of *Mémoires d'Outre-Tombe* in a hundred years. So I gave that job to Zimmer.

IBS: The translation is yours, isn't it?

PA: The excerpts? I did them, yes. The passages are quite beautiful.

IBS: Yes, they are, and they dovetail perfectly with the themes and plot of your story.

PA: That was why Chateaubriand's presence became inevitable. The epigraph also comes from the *Mémoires*:

> Man has not one and the same life. He has many lives, placed end to end, and that is the cause of his misery.

The idea that we have several lives, not just one . . .

IBS: This is a recurring theme for you, isn't it?

PA: People restored to life after suffering loss. I think that's what we're talking about here.

IBS: In *The Book of Illusions*, Hector's world is described both visually and verbally. In fact, you render one form of representation through the other: filming through words. This brings something new to your writing—indeed to writing in general, I think. Early on in this novel, you flaunt the intervention of the camera and refer to "the talking mustache" as "a creation of the lens" (29). As a matter of fact, it's not the lens's creation. It's yours. But herein lies part of the illusion, I imagine.

PA: I think the reader is automatically seeing it as film. We're talking about silent comedies, with a central character who doesn't quite resemble any other silent comedian. In retrospect, I understand that the physical model for Hector was Marcello Mastroianni in *Divorce Italian Style*. Have you ever seen that film? It's from the early sixties. Mastroianni in the white suit, Mastroianni with the mustache—I stole those things and used them for Hector.

IBS: You do make the reader feel that we are watching a film even if we are "reading" it. The illusion works.

PA: Well, film *is* illusion. Having worked in film, I've always been acutely aware of how unreal the whole thing is. The audience looks at a finished film and thinks, "Oh, it looks so real," but nothing could be less "real" than film. It's a series of images projected onto a two-dimensional rectangle. The feeling of depth we get when watching a movie is simply a product of photographic techniques. There *is* no depth. When you write a screenplay, you're writing for that rectangle, whereas when you write a novel you work in three dimensions. You're tasting and smelling things, too—and touching them. It's a much fuller experience.

IBS: What about the narrative perspective in *The Book of Illusions*? Does it make a difference that, in parts of the story, the narrator is reporting from an account already narrated: for instance, you have David writing Alma's description of Frieda's version of Hector's life?

PA: It's not just Frieda's account, it's Hector's biography. It shifts into a third-person narration when they get on the plane and fly to New Mexico. Until then, the information Zimmer has dug up about Hector has been filled with contradictions. The story starts to become a little clearer to him.

IBS: You translate body language into verbal language throughout *The Book of Illusions*:

> A twitching filament of anxieties, a metaphysical jump rope,
> a dancing thread of discombobulation, the mustache is a

seismograph of Hector's inner states, and not only does it make you laugh, it tells you what Hector is thinking . . . the mustache is the instrument of communication, and even though it speaks a language without words, its wriggles and flutters are as clear and comprehensible as a message tapped out in Morse code. (29)

And this is interesting: Hector and the other comedians "had invented a syntax of the eye, a grammar of pure kinesis" (15). It's a striking idea and I was wondering, would you say that there's also a "grammar of movement"?

PA: What I'm describing here, I think, is something very close to dance.

IBS: As in the dance rehearsal that inspired *White Spaces*?

PA: Yes, and dance is a difficult thing to put into words, a difficult thing to talk about, even if it does create its own language. There are always limits to a dance piece—it's not just free movement. There are patterns, rhythms, thoughts that go into it. That's the grammar, and each piece will have its own syntax. It sets up its own limits, its own possibilities, and therefore its own expectations.

IBS: Language and the body completely merge in Hector's eloquent "soliloquy of the mustache" (30).

PA:

Hector can charm you with any one of a thousand different gestures. Light-footed and nimble, nonchalant to the point of indifference, he threads himself through the obstacle course of life without the slightest trace of clumsiness or fear, dazzling you with his backpedals and dodges, his sudden torques and lunging pavanes, his double takes and hop-steps and rhumba swivels. (33)

I wanted the reader to *see* him moving through all this.

> Observe the thrums and fidgets of his fingers, his deftly timed exhales, the slight cock of the head when something unexpected catches his eye. (33)

IBS: All this is possible, of course, because it is *silent* film.

PA: People move in talking films as well. And there are many scenes in talking films when the characters don't talk. But yes, in this book I'm exploring the lost world of *silent films.*

IBS: And so, silence is a kind of vehicle here, right?

PA: I think that's why silent movies continue to exert a strange power over us, why they feel more universal than talkies.

IBS: Silence is a cornerstone in much of your writing, and when we were talking about *Moon Palace*, you said that silence produces meaning. That's also the case here in *The Book of Illusions*, isn't it, through your focus on the mechanisms and effects of Hector's films. "They were like poems," you say, "like the renderings of dreams, like some intricate choreography of the spirit," and "their muteness," you continue,

> relieved the images of the burden of representation . . . we no longer had to pretend that we were looking at the real world. The flat screen was the world, and it existed in two dimensions. The third dimension was in our head. (15)

"The burden of representation," what's that?

PA: I'm referring to the type of film that seeks to represent the reality of a particular world, in contrast to silent comedies, in which these concerns are basically unimportant.

IBS: The same goes for books, right?

PA: It can. Certain books by certain writers. Kafka, for example—but not Proust.

IBS: In *The Book of Illusions*, as elsewhere in your work, silence goes hand in hand with death. Chateaubriand speaks from beyond the grave—indeed, for the second time, through your translations. Just as Zimmer is trying to keep his dead sons alive by playing with their Lego and sorting out their baseball cards. So, here we have another instance of "restoring to life" by making present the absent in order, ultimately, to ward off complete loss.

PA: Yes, but these are simply the gestures of grief. This is what people do. As time goes on, the need to behave like that gradually diminishes—for most of us, in any case—but I think it's a necessary part of the process many people go through in the early days of mourning. And then there's the scene when David runs into his friends at the supermarket and is pressed into accepting an invitation to a party he has no desire to go to. He misbehaves badly and insults the sweet German professor, who has been nothing but kind to him. He's just so angry, so devastated. Not at all ready to become part of the world again.

IBS: Yes, these are strong scenes that stay with you. I was wondering, is there a connection between silence, that which you cannot hear, and invisibility, that which you cannot see, in your work in general? In *The Invention of Solitude*, A. is terrified of being reduced to silence:

> In the interim, in the void between the moment he opens the door and the moment he begins to reconquer the emptiness, his mind flails in a *wordless panic*. It is as if he were being forced to watch his *own disappearance*, as if, by crossing the threshold of his room, he were entering another dimension, taking up residence inside a black hole. (*The Invention of Solitude*, 77; my italics)

Similarly, in *Moon Palace*, Effing reaches the point where he

> was no longer afraid of the *emptiness* around him. The act of
> trying to put it on canvas had somehow internalized it for
> him, and now he was able to feel its indifference as some-
> thing that belonged to him, as much as he belonged to the
> *silent power of those gigantic spaces* himself. (*Moon Palace*,
> 170; my italics)

"Wordless panic," "emptiness," and here, in The Book of Illusions,
the emphasis on silent gesture combined with loss.

PA: I never thought of it that way. I think silence has a different cause
and a different effect in each of these cases, but you may be right that
ultimately they're different manifestations of the same thing. Here,
Hector's silent films had a healing effect on the suffering protagonist.
They drew him out of himself. They made him laugh.

IBS: So, there's inspiration from silent movie comedy in *The Book
of Illusions*. There are also two prominent literary sources: Chateaubriand, whom we mentioned earlier, and then, of course, Hawthorne.

PA: Yes, "The Birthmark," which is an astonishing story.

IBS: When you bring in stories from outside your own work, as with
the Hawthorne story or the Chateaubriand, you do so, obviously,
because they . . .

PA: . . . Are connected to the story I'm writing or can serve as metaphorical representations of certain aspects of the book as a whole . . .

IBS: In other words, they inform your story.

PA: I'm interested in the idea of collage—a picture with multiple
pictures in it, a story composed of several stories that bounce off

one another. I feel that when you put diverse elements together in the same frame—or the same field—new energies are created in the spaces between them. If you have three or four or five elements interacting with one another in various ways, for example, they generate a force field of narrative energy—something stronger and more compelling than any of the single parts could generate on its own.

IBS: It's the space in between, isn't it? This is where meaning, a plurality of meanings, is fostered.

PA: If you do it right, it can have a tremendous cumulative power.

IBS: Perhaps it's this combination of heterogeneous materials that one of the reviewers is referring to when he says that you are "brilliant at making the intellectual life sexy."*

PA: I don't know what that means.

IBS: Well, you have an unusually intricate structure here: Paul Auster invents the story of Zimmer, who is narrating the story of Hector Mann, who is narrating the story of Martin Frost, who is narrating the story of Claire—and this, of course, is later turned into a full-length cinema production. It's bewitching! You have ontological layers overlapping, books within books within books, voices within voices, genres in flux—and everything is accompanied by reflection.

PA: That's what I mean by the collage effect.

IBS: I think it's more than that. You write a book in which there are multiple perspectives, one within the other, where narratives move across different levels inside the novel and outside in a kind of intertextual dialogue with writings by Hawthorne, Chateaubriand, and

---

* D. T. Max, "'The Book of Illusions': Paul Auster's Professor of Despair," *New York Times*, September 1, 2002, http://www.nytimes.com/2002/09/01/books/review/01MAXLT.html.

others. There are several imaginary films playing inside the verbal universe of the book—one of which then becomes a real film! This is really something. Beyond collage and Chinese boxes.

PA: And yet some of these things just happen on their own. Making the film of *Martin Frost*, for example. It came before the book—and then after the book. Life taking over . . . Is there anything else to say?

IBS: There's so much to talk about here. It's a complex and hugely interesting book.

PA: Well, one thing is certain: *The Book of Illusions* is one of my longest, most complex novels. Some of my books have been consciously written as chamber pieces. This one is large—a work composed for full orchestra.

ORACLE NIGHT. (2003)
"The World Is in My Head"

IBS: *Oracle Night* is not just the story about the marriage of an ailing writer, Sidney Orr, who is struggling to get back on his feet both physically and mentally. It's also a book about the processes, the labor and the mystery of writing. Orr struggles to complete his haunting narrative of Nick Bowen, who, one day, for reasons that are not entirely clear, decides to divest himself of his former life and ends up trapped in an underground bomb shelter that serves, strangely, as a Holocaust archive. We're not always sure whether we're inside or outside Orr's mind.

PA: *Oracle Night* developed very slowly. As far back as 1982, I started writing something about an enchanted notebook—a book you could enter and actually walk around in—a strange little poetic text that never amounted to anything and that I stopped working on after ten or fifteen pages. But the idea stayed with me and eventually transformed itself into the Portuguese notebooks in *Oracle Night*. I remember that I started the novel not long after finishing *Timbuktu*—in 1998—but after writing the first twenty pages or so, I stopped. I still didn't understand what I was doing, so I put it aside and worked on other things—the screenplay of *Martin Frost*, then *The Book of Illusions*—and didn't get back to it for another three years, when I started writing it in earnest. It took that long to figure it out—and even then, I still ran into problems.

IBS: A difficult book to write.

PA: Yes, very difficult, especially toward the end. I had an ending in mind, but then I realized that I didn't like it. I was stuck—in the same way Sidney gets stuck with his story. I didn't know what to do. I must have written seven different endings until, finally, I found what I was looking for. What a strange business. Sometimes, a book is there for you: you know what you want to do, and you do it. Other times, you believe you know, but in fact you don't, and you have to keep searching for the right solution. That's why every book is a different experience.

IBS: Are you in the book? Trause is an anagram of your name, isn't it?

PA: Yes, but he has nothing to do with me. He's from a different generation, and he's a different kind of writer with an altogether different biography from mine. And yet—how shall I put it?—I think of the writers in the book as representations of my younger and older novelist selves. But not in an autobiographical sense—in a spiritual sense. The protagonist, Sidney Orr, may be the same age as I was in 1982, the year I began thinking about this book—but he shares none of my history: I was never a schoolteacher, I never had a near-fatal illness, my books don't resemble his. As for Trause, he fought in World War II, for God's sake. I hadn't been born then.

IBS: Then why give him a version of your name? It's almost as if you are writing "Auster" into a book again.

PA: I know. I saw the anagram and I liked the name, but other than the fact that Trause is in his mid-fifties—as I was when I wrote the book—I don't think we should make too much of this.

IBS: *Oracle Night* is very much a book about writing, especially about being stuck, as you just said. Sidney begins but never manages to complete the Nick Bowen story.

> That morning, however, as I sat at my desk for the first time in almost nine months, staring at my newly acquired notebook and struggling to come up with an opening sentence that wouldn't embarrass me or rob me of my courage, I decided to give the old Flitcraft episode a shot. (14)

PA: Another piece of old resurrected material. The Flitcraft episode goes back to 1990, when I was first contacted by the filmmaker Wim Wenders, who remains a close friend. Wim had been reading my books, and he proposed that we work on a film together. We talked about a number of possible ideas, then he suggested that we do something with the Flitcraft story in *The Maltese Falcon*. Not a straight adaptation of Hammett, just the premise: the story of a man who walks away from his life. "That's interesting," I said. "I like it." So I mapped out the tale of Nick Bowen (which is nearly identical to the one in *Oracle Night*) and boiled it down to a fifteen- or twenty-page treatment—an outline of the film. Unfortunately, the financing never came through, and the project fell apart. For ten years, those pages sat in a drawer of my desk. I never knew what to do with them, but the idea continued to fascinate me—a man who abandons everything and winds up getting stuck in a room. *Oracle Night* gave me a chance to go back to the idea, and the pages came out of the drawer. In the original outline for the film, I was planning to get Bowen out of the room, but for the novel, no. It would have been absurd to release him. Sidney is not in good shape: he's confused, he's weak, and his writing is going nowhere. He's not up to figuring out a way to get Bowen out of the room. Still, this attempt to begin writing again is itself a sign that Sidney is recovering. It's a first step. Even if it fails, it's nevertheless a step toward taking hold of his life again.

IBS: And so, the secondary narrative reflects the primary narrative, and this is why Sidney Orr's story about Nick Bowen should not be finished?

PA: It shouldn't be finished. I'm sure a lot of readers were frustrated by that.

IBS: Absolutely! You abandon the poor man trapped in an old bomb shelter with no means of escape. It's such a cliff-hanging moment: we desperately want to know whether Rosa Leightmann rescues him.

PA: It happens to writers all the time. You start on a project and run out of gas. Sidney runs out of gas. How else to show that except by stopping the story before it ends?

IBS: That makes sense. So, we have aborted writings and an aborted baby. Is there a connection between the two? I mean, one of the big questions in *Oracle Night* concerns the capacity of words to create and to kill, right?

PA: Okay, I want to tell you three things: first, the story about the French writer who stopped writing is a true story. Louis-René des Forêts. Do you know about it?

IBS: I just know it was a real event.

PA: The newspaper article is real. I rewrote it very slightly and changed the name of the author, but it was a real news story. I was horrified, I have to say. Third, the Warsaw phone book. It's also real. I have it. My Polish publisher gave it to me because there was an Auster listed in it—perhaps a relative—and I wanted to include these fragments in the book as documentary evidence alongside my inventions. Have I told you the story about the journalist? Not long after *Oracle Night* was published, a Polish journalist came here to interview me. He was in a sweat, hyper-excited, about to jump out of his skin. He said, "You'll never believe this, but the people in the phone book, the Orlovskys—they were my grandparents." Now, that is strange! I'd picked them out at random.

IBS: That's unbelievable! All this connects with the notion of the oracular, doesn't it, when you place a writer between the present and the future, propelled by words whose impact he hasn't quite understood.

> The future was already inside me, and I was preparing myself for the disasters that were about to come. (223)

Is this what the title refers to: the writer as a medium for oracular words?

PA: Yes, that's exactly right. Another interesting thing about the title is that I stole it from another book—and wasn't even aware of it. A book of poems written in the late seventies or early eighties by someone named Michael Brownstein—an acquaintance of mine but not a close friend. A book with the title *Oracle Night*. Michael called me and said, "Do you remember my book?" I felt like an imbecile. No, I hadn't remembered, and now that I did remember, I was mortified. "Don't worry about it," Michael said, "it doesn't matter in the least"—a generous and gentlemanly response, but I still felt like an imbecile. It's the only time I've ever done anything like that. But what a beautiful title—ideal for my purposes—and my unconscious mind reached out and stole it.

IBS: It seems fitting, then—almost "oracular" in fact—that you throw into doubt the origins of the title in the book:

> I thought maybe I'd read a book by Sylvia Monroe as a boy and had since forgotten about it, only to dredge up an unconscious memory of her in the person of Sylvia Maxwell, the pretend author of the pretend *Oracle Night*. But it seemed I'd plucked Maxwell out of thin air and *Oracle Night* was an original story, with no connection to any novel other than itself. I probably should have felt relieved, but I didn't. (184)

PA: So, there must have been something stirring inside that unconscious of mine.

IBS: I think *Oracle Night* is also a book about the impossibility of getting to the truth of things.

PA: Sidney keeps analyzing Grace's behavior, again and again he tries to figure out what's going on. He thinks he's probably right that she had an affair with Trause, but she has never confessed. Which means that he can't be one hundred percent certain.

IBS: Why is she so enigmatic? Why doesn't she tell him what's going on? She asks him to trust her . . .

PA: She can't, she can't. I've known many people like this, people who can't talk, who can't reveal things about themselves. She's warm and loving, but she has secrets, and she can't share them. That's her personality, that's who she is. One has a sense, I do anyway, that as life goes on she'll evolve into something a bit different.

IBS: Yes.

PA: By the end of the story, Sidney reaches a conclusion that makes sense to him—but then again, he may not be right. In an almost Kierkegaardian way, he makes a leap of faith and decides that it doesn't matter whether he's arrived at the truth or not. He can live with the uncertainty because he cares enough about Grace to feel that, whatever betrayals might have occurred, they are finally unimportant. He wants her too much. Those are the spiritual under-pinnings of the book.

IBS: There's also something inexplicable about Sidney's pres-ence-slash-absence in their apartment. There are several instances when Grace insists that Sidney was not in his study when, in fact, he was sitting right there at his desk completely absorbed in his writing: "[Y]ou weren't there" (27), she insists. Sidney explains (as much to himself as to Grace and Trause) that

> It's not so unusual for a person to be so preoccupied as to appear absent—but the point was that I wasn't absent. I was there, fully engaged in what was happening, and at the same time I wasn't there—for there wasn't an authentic there any-more. It was an illusory place that existed in my head, and

that's where I was as well. In both places at the same time. In the apartment and in the story. (29–30)

It's as if Sidney has fallen "into his own story," as one of your best critics suggests,* and I was wondering whether you are using the mysterious Portuguese notebook to illustrate the fact that the writer is lost to the world but fully present to himself *only* when absorbed in writing?

PA: It's ambiguous. We can't know. What matters is that Sidney himself believes it.

IBS: When I read *Oracle Night*, I have the feeling that there's an obscure, almost arcane dimension to it: to the words, to the relationships between characters, to the notebook. You don't often do that. There's a magic element in *Mr. Vertigo* and *Timbuktu*, but this is different. I think it has to do with the notion that words hold the power to create reality here and now, directly.

PA: It *is* different. This is a very strange book, on the borderline of real madness. I thought of it as a dream book. I think it has to be read like that. There's something so immediate about the way it's written that it comes across as a realistic novel. It isn't, of course, even though we could probably break it down and explain everything in terms of conventional realism if we were interested in doing that. I'm not. In *Oracle Night*, I write about states of mind and emotional reactions—and about the power of writing, the power of words, the power of stories.

IBS: And about being literally absorbed in writing, right? Sidney disappears . . .

PA: You do disappear when you're writing. I feel that all the time.

---

* Mark Brown, *Paul Auster* (Manchester: Manchester University Press, 2007), 95.

It's uncanny how I can go into my little office at eight o'clock in the morning, get to work, then glance at my watch and realize that it's one o'clock in the afternoon. It feels as if only ten minutes have gone by. I've been utterly immersed during those five hours: I'm not hungry, I don't even know I'm there. I think this book is a reflection of that kind of "vanishing."

IBS: Is Sidney on the border of madness?

> The world would bounce and swim before my eyes, undulating like reflections in a wavy mirror, and whenever I tried to look at just one thing, to isolate a single object from the onrush of whirling colors—a blue scarf wrapped around a woman's head, say, or the red taillight of a passing delivery truck—it would immediately begin to break apart and dissolve, disappearing like a drop of dye in a glass of water. Everything shimmied and wobbled, kept darting off in different directions, and for the first several weeks I had trouble telling where my body stopped and the rest of the world began. (2)

PA: Sidney has been damaged, but he's slowly regaining his coherence and his strength, slowly but surely. Those sentences are from the beginning of the book, and they introduce what we would call a classically unreliable narrator. He's being as honest as he can, but his perceptions are off.

IBS: So we shouldn't trust anything he says?

PA: The only thing we can trust is that he's *trying* to be trustworthy.

IBS: That brings me to the footnotes. Sidney is trying to be as precise as he can, and footnotes, generally speaking, are intended to add precision to the text, right? This is the first time you use footnotes. But they're not just ordinary footnotes: they're part of the fiction and add quite considerably to the story, even if they're physically subordinate to it.

PA: This is what I was thinking: the book takes place over a nine-day period, what I would call "the narrative present." The footnotes are concerned with things from "the narrative past." I didn't want to interrupt the story with explanatory digressions and decided that footnotes would be the right place for them.

IBS: They start out as explanations, reasonably brief explanations of action, especially in connection with Grace, but then they become longer and longer and at some point threaten to take over. One of them goes on for four pages.

PA: The first long one is number three, which describes Sidney's first meeting with Grace, his first encounter with the beloved.

> Bodies count, of course—they count more than we're willing to admit—but we don't fall in love with bodies, we fall in love with each other, and if much of what we are is confined to flesh and bone, there is much that is not as well. We all know that, but the minute we go beyond the catalogue of surface qualities and appearances, words begin to fail us, to crumble apart in mystical confusions and cloudy, insubstantial metaphors. Some call it *the flame of being*. Others call it *the internal spark* or *the inner light of selfhood*. (19)

IBS: Why put that wonderful description in a footnote? It's hugely relevant to the story.

PA: I know, but I wanted to have different levels of discourse in the book, the past and the present to begin with, but also different kinds of texts and typefaces: the news article, the footnotes, the illustrations—they're all sitting next to one another on the page, each one distinct from the others and yet coexisting simultaneously.

IBS: One of the pivots in the book is the intimate and somewhat enigmatic bond between Orr and Trause.

PA: They have a warm relationship, but at the same time there's a certain edginess to it. There's also something competitive between them, which could suggest that Trause did in fact have an affair with Grace. And yet, Trause genuinely likes Sidney. He thinks he's a good writer and a dependable person (why else would he ask Sidney to visit his son?). But he's not above making an occasional nasty dig—as with poor Sidney's "menstruating schnoz." So many tangles. Another example of what you call "the male bond."

IBS: Yes, and partly because of the asymmetry between the younger and the older man with regard to the nature of their writing and to the woman they both love.

PA: Their love for Grace is a connection here, of course, but as two artists from different generations, they do have something of a "master-apprentice" relationship. Sidney admires Trause's work. He feels both awe and gratitude that Trause has accepted him as a friend, and the friendship is exceedingly important to him. Then, of course, he loses Trause's manuscript—which, by the way, is the manuscript about the imaginary country that pops up later in *Travels in the Scriptorium*. Just so we don't forget . . .

IBS: There's also an important connection between Sidney and Trause's son, principally because of the violence it triggers, which results in Grace's miscarriage.

PA: That's the tragic part of the book.

IBS: The third male relationship is with Mr. Chang. It also ends in violence.

PA: Yes, violence again. Chang is an incomprehensible person, a figure from a hallucination.

IBS: The beating he gives Sidney is truly vicious. That moment seemed to me to be the exotic element in the novel: the violent clash with the "Other" culture, the culture we don't understand.

PA: Yes, but it's also relevant, as Sidney speculates, that Chang might have been a member of the Red Guard as a teenager, someone who learned violence from an early age. The incident from the Cultural Revolution discussed in the novel was drawn from real events, by the way. Bits of twentieth-century history keep slipping into the book in peculiar, unexpected ways. Not just the Cultural Revolution in China but World War I (Flagg and his ability to predict the future), World War II (Ed Victory and Dachau), the Kennedy assassination (Sidney's film version of *The Time Machine*), and Duvalier in Haiti (the "African Princess"). Real events, as it were, embedded in a fictional world.

IBS: That's also true of your commemoration of Holocaust victims through Ed Victory's collection of telephone books. As you mentioned earlier, you have the real one from Warsaw and picked random names for your characters from it. Storing away an arbitrary selection of phone books underground is indeed a strange way of commemorating the horrors of the death camps.

PA: Ed has his reasons. After Dachau, he felt the world had come to an end.

IBS: But why phone books?

PA: Because they contain the names of people, the living and the dead, the roster of the human race. He wants to collect all of humanity in his underground archive. It's mad, I know, but Ed's passion for this makes sense to me. It comes directly out of his war experiences.

IBS: Ed is quite a character. Of course, he's invented by Sidney Orr, and Orr has very intimate relationships with his protagonists:

As for Bowen, however, I expressly made him someone I was not, an inversion of myself . . . I didn't model him on anyone I knew (not consciously, at any rate), but once I had finished putting him together in my mind, he became astonishingly vivid to me—almost as if I could see him, almost as if he had entered the room and were standing next to me, looking down at the desk with his hand on my shoulder and reading the words I was writing . . . watching me bring him to life with my pen. (17–18)

Do characters sometimes feel as real to you as Bowen does to Orr here?

PA: They generally do. I don't know if this is a sign of mental immaturity, some kind of magical thinking, or just an effect of the time and emotion you invest in people who are not real. I wrote about this in *Travels in the Scriptorium*. They live inside you so vividly that they become people, even though they're not. When we read, they *are* real people: characters who feed our imaginations and help us understand the world.

IBS: Even if, in fact, they belong between the covers of the book or inside someone's skull. Just like your many characters trapped in confined spaces, locked away in bare rooms, immobilized in graves. It's a very strong image.

PA: I think this is something that's been driving me ever since I started writing. If you look at some of my early poems—that's what they're about. The title of my first little collection (which was never published) was *Captives*. Then there's *Wall Writing,** a title that refers to the fact that you can be on either side of a wall: included or excluded, as we said in connection with *The Music of Chance*. I was mostly thinking about walls surrounding a person as a metaphor for

---

* *Wall Writing* (1971–1975) in *Collected Poems*, 63.

consciousness, the way thoughts trap us inside ourselves. I'm interested in trying to represent that—physically, in images. Or, to say it again: "The world is in my head. My body is in the world."

THE BROOKLYN FOLLIES. (2005)
"An Escape from American Reality"

IBS: *The Brooklyn Follies* is at once complex, hugely allusive, and superbly easygoing. It's set in your own neighborhood just before the disaster of 9/11 changed the world, with a cast of intriguing characters: the ailing narrator, his group of friends who are all ordinary people living through everyday trials and tribulations, the slightly obtuse but perfect and beautiful mother, the nephew with his literary obsessions and dreams of an escape from modern American reality. The book is especially critical of the political climate around the 2000 election and takes a very dim view of fanatical Christian sects. At the same time, it's one of your funniest books.

PA: *The Brooklyn Follies* is the only book I deliberately set out to write as a comedy. By comic I don't mean farce. The characters suffer, and, of course, the book has a dark, dark conclusion: it ends forty-six minutes before the first plane crashed into the World Trade Center on September 11, 2001. I wanted to talk about life in New York before 9/11. How lucky we were to have our small problems, our little pains and aches and sufferings—the things that make us human. Then, when the cataclysm comes, it wipes out all our trivial concerns. I kept thinking about something Billy Wilder once said: "If you're feeling good about yourself and the world, that's the moment to write a tragedy. But when you're down in the dumps, write a comedy." I was down in the dumps about, well, just about everything when I wrote *Brooklyn Follies*, not just 9/11 but also the Bush administration, the 2000 elections, and the buildup to the war in Iraq—the whole bloody American mess. I needed to look at life in a different way.

IBS: Yes, there's a lightness here that the critics have perceived either as a new avenue in your writing or as a return to pure storytelling.

One thing I've learned through our discussions is that what is easy to read was often very challenging, very difficult to write, and so, I was wondering whether this was the case with *The Brooklyn Follies?*

PA: It was a problem book. There was something I couldn't figure out, and when I finally sat down to write it in around 1997–1998, the structure was . . .

IBS: So you started it *before* 9/11?

PA: Yes. It began as a different book altogether. But we've already talked about that in our discussion of *Timbuktu*. Once I removed Willy and Mr. Bones, the structure of the book collapsed, and I didn't know what to do with it anymore. I had Tom and Aurora, Harry and Rufus, the B.P.M., but I no longer knew what to do with them. So, the whole thing went into a drawer for a number of years. It wasn't until I came up with the idea of using Nathan as the narrator that I was able to reassemble the characters and make a story out of it.

IBS: Everything revolves around him.

PA: Yes, but the book doesn't dwell that much on Nathan. It's about everyone else around him. Nathan's story is a kind of resurrection story: he goes through divorce, cancer, a phase of bitter disgust, and a general feeling that his life is over. Little by little, he finds a new way to live, new friends, new loves—a way of rejoining the human circus.

IBS: Just like Sidney in *Oracle Night*. I mean, in later years you've often focused on weakened characters.

PA: It's true. There was a whole sequence of them. In one way or another, all those characters were in decline.

IBS: Aging and ailing.

PA: Aging and/or ailing, I guess. But putting that aside for now, let's talk about the rascals and straight shooters. Most of the protagonists in my books have been straight shooters—what I would call earnest seekers. They are not people who commit crimes. They have moral integrity. Then there are the rascals like Pozzi in *The Music of Chance*, Willy in *Timbuktu*, and Walt in *Mr. Vertigo*. In *The Brooklyn Follies*, Nathan is a bit of a rascal, but he's also a grown-up, a man with a past carrying around his accumulated burdens. Think of the chapter entitled "On Rascals." I think it's fundamental to understanding the book, even if, at first glance, it doesn't seem terribly important. As you'll remember, Nathan and Tom are discussing Jacob and Esau.

> "The bad guy wins, and God doesn't punish him. It didn't seem right. It still doesn't seem right."
> "Of course it does. Jacob had the spark of life in him, and Esau was a dumbbell. Good-hearted, yes, but a dumbbell. If you're going to choose one of them to lead your people, you'll want the fighter, the one with cunning and wit, the one with the energy to beat the odds and come out on top. You choose the strong and clever over the weak and kind."
> "That's pretty brutal stuff, Nathan. Take your argument one step further, and the next thing you'll be telling me is that Stalin should be revered as a great man."
> "Stalin was a thug, a psychotic murderer. I'm talking about the instinct for survival, Tom, the will to live. Give me a wily rascal over a pious sap any day of the week. He might not always play by the rules, but he's got spirit. And when you find a man with spirit, there's still some hope for the world." (53–54)

This is the comic force driving the story.

IBS: Well, "the bad guy wins," but in your work they do so only after they've suffered and developed a measure of integrity.

PA: Bad guys with integrity. I like that. *The Brooklyn Follies* is a bit of a departure for me, but only a bit, since in some ways it resembles the screenplay of *Smoke*. A group of ordinary people in a Brooklyn neighborhood, the struggles of being alive, the forming of new friendships, new alliances, new loves, an ensemble work dealing with several characters at once. My two comedies. One a book, the other a film.

IBS: Are there any autobiographical references? Nathan's heart attack, which turned out to be an inflamed esophagus?

PA: Yes, that was something that happened to me. What else? The B.P.M.* is based on a real person. When my daughter Sophie was little, I used to walk her to school on Carroll Street every morning, and—just as I describe it in the book—every morning there was a lovely young woman sitting on the front steps of her house with her two little children—waiting for the school bus. I never talked to her, but I saw her every single day, five days a week for several years. She seemed so comfortable with her children, so deeply in harmony with them that I started calling her the "Beautiful Perfect Mother," the B.P.M. I based that character on her. As I said, I don't know the real person at all, but a strange thing happened while I was writing the book. By then, Sophie attended a different school, so I hadn't seen the B.P.M. in a number of years. Then, on the very day I introduced her into the book, I went out for lunch and saw her walking down the street.

IBS: Amazing.

PA: There she was, going to the subway decked out in high heels and a lovely dress, looking like a million dollars. A part of me wanted to run up to her and say, "I've just started writing about a character inspired by you." No doubt she would have thought I was insane. I've never seen her again.

---

* The Beautiful Perfect Mother.

IBS: That's very strange.

PA: What else could be considered autobiographical in this book . . .

IBS: Well, the entire setting, I suppose. I mean, it's very much *here*, in this part of Brooklyn, isn't it? I'm thinking of the description of houses and streets. To me, they seem to come straight out of your own neighborhood.

PA: That's true. There's also the story I stole from Siri:

> One Sunday morning, I went into a crowded deli with the absurd name of La Bagel Delight. I was intending to ask for a cinnamon-raisin bagel, but the word caught in my mouth and came out as *cinnamon-reagan*. Without missing a beat, the young guy behind the counter answered, "Sorry, we don't have any of those. How about a pumpernixon instead?" (5)

That really happened to her. Some of the restaurants are real places and others are invented. La Bagel Delight (believe it or not) is real.

IBS: What about the Hotel Existence? Harry's Hotel Existence is a place for inventing new places, an elegant world of erotic fantasies, but it begins as "a refuge for lost children" (102). Is there an echo from Woburn House in *In the Country of Last Things*? After all, Dr. Woburn turned his house into a shelter for the sick and homeless, a place of refuge:

> If he could not save thousands, he said, then perhaps he could save hundreds, and if he could not save hundreds, then perhaps he could save twenty or thirty. (*In the Country of Last Things*, 131)

PA: But Woburn House is a real place—real in the fiction, that is. The Hotel Existence in *The Brooklyn Follies* is a fantasy, a utopia—in the fiction. It's your ideal world, your dream world. Everyone has one. Tom's college paper on Thoreau's *Walden* and the three pieces by Poe is important in this connection. The ideal landscape, the ideal house, the ideal room—which for both writers meant a place to think and work, an escape from American reality.

IBS: In *The Brooklyn Follies* it's a place where children are rescued, among other things. It's a place to be safe.

PA: It was the middle of World War II, and Harry was only ten years old. The hotel was inspired by stories he'd read about refugee children in Europe. But you're right, the Hotel Existence always brings a sense of safety and protection. Or, in his adolescent fantasies, erotic excitement.

IBS: That's true. Harry says, "It was a retreat, a world I could visit in my mind. That's what we're talking about, no? Escape" (102). "Every man has one," he continues.

PA: Yes, "each man's Hotel Existence is different from all the others" (105).

IBS: So, the question of course is whether you have your own "Hotel Existence"? Perhaps your books provide that kind of refuge?

PA: I've always found it interesting to think about perfect worlds, to look at flawed reality and imagine ways of improving it. I mean, what would you want the world to look like if you had the power to remake it? If nothing else, it's an excellent question to ask if you want to know where someone stands politically. Please, sir, describe your perfect world to me.

IBS: There's also a rural version of the Hotel Existence: the Chowder Inn.

PA: Oh, I should also mention that Stanley Chowder is based on a real person.

IBS: In Vermont?

PA: Yes. The man who lived down the road from us was always mowing his lawn. He and his wife had been planning to turn their house into a bed and breakfast, but then she died, quite suddenly, and the poor man mowed his lawn as a way of coping with his grief. He wasn't old, maybe sixty, still vigorous, but he was lonely. We talked to him just a few times. He said he liked to go to Atlantic City to gamble. That was the big adventure of his life now—gambling. Then he would come back—and continue to mow his lawn. Thus was born the figure of Stanley Chowder.

IBS: You've returned to the Vermont countryside a few times in your work.* Nature, or the natural world, plays into the names you've chosen for the characters in *The Brooklyn Follies*: Wood, Flora, Aurora, Bright, Dunkel, Glass, Marina.

PA: Brightman-Dunkel is obvious. A reinvented self. An ex-jailbird's stab at a new life.

IBS: Flora, Marina?

PA: I don't know. It was probably something in the air—or in the drinking water.

IBS: So no reason?

PA: Probably not. Although Nathan does make the joke, "We could start an architectural firm named Glass, Wood & Steel."

IBS: As opposed to most of your other work, *The Brooklyn Follies* doesn't challenge literary conventions.

---

* In *Leviathan*, *The Book of Illusions*, and *Man in the Dark*.

PA: I deliberately wanted to write a more traditional narrative, and for the purposes of a comic novel, I think it's better to be reasonably straightforward. There was a certain simplicity of tone that I wanted to establish with this book. Depending on the material, impulses find different ways of expressing themselves. In this story, the approach had to be blunt and straightforward, largely because the narrator, Nathan, is that kind of person. He's not deeply reflective. He's direct and at times fairly crude. The style of the book is a reflection of his character.

IBS: Your chapter headings are also a natural part of this particular narrative fabric, aren't they? Some of them are really funny.

PA: I've always loved the chapter headings in eighteenth- and nineteenth-century novels, and, yes, I hope they're funny: "The Sperm Bank Surprise," "Hawthorn Street or Hawthorne Street?," "Riding North" (a reference, by the way, to John Donne's poem "Riding Westward"). What else? I'm trying to remember. "Farewell to the Court." That's the title of a poem by Sir Walter Raleigh. "Our Girl, or *Coke Is It*." "Coke Is It" was a line from a TV commercial back in the seventies or eighties. "A Knock on the Door," "Monkey Business" . . .

IBS: So, you had fun writing this book?

PA: Yes, it was fun.

IBS: Did it cheer you up?

PA: It did while I was writing it, but then, of course, I came home and read the newspaper [*laughs*].

IBS: And it's not all comedy, as you said earlier. You weave in a substructure of references and allusions. Kafka's story about the doll is prominent here, in fact, a key to the book, isn't it?

By that point, of course, the girl no longer misses the doll. Kafka has given her something else instead, and by the time those three weeks are up, the letters have cured her of her unhappiness. She has the story, and when a person is lucky enough to live inside a story, to live inside an imaginary world, the pains of this world disappear. For as long as the story goes on, reality no longer exists. (155)

PA: The Kafka anecdote seems to be a true story, by the way. They tried to track down the little girl. Never found her. Which doesn't diminish the power of the story, of course. It's terribly moving.

IBS: So it found its way into your book.

PA: Because Tom's head is crammed full with such things—an inexhaustible supply of useful and useless bits of junk and flotsam—because he's a literary man through and through.

IBS: There's a kind of discord between language and the body in *The Brooklyn Follies*. I mean, it's as if kinetic movement is more eloquent than speech. For instance, when Lucy arrives and refuses to talk, Nathan realizes that he

> should have known better than to count on language as a
> more efficient form of communication than nods and shakes
> of the head. (183–184)

PA: Yes, often a shake of the head is more than sufficient.

IBS: The other day, we talked about *The Book of Illusions*, in which silence is an important generator of meaning. Here, silence becomes a form of sacrifice.

PA: I was thinking of the blind religious fanaticism that has become so prevalent in America these days. Rather than investigate an existing sect, I decided to make up my own. I thought it would be more interesting. Reverend Bob is forcing a brutal process of dispossession on his congregation—and the first thing to go is words.

IBS: And Aurora's husband, David Minor, falls for it.

PA: David means well, but his faith is unquestioning, and it leads him to commit acts of tremendous cruelty. But give him credit. In the end he backs off and lets Aurora divorce him.

IBS: Fortunately.

PA: David is a lost soul, and he finds comfort in his devotion to Reverend Bob—who, of course, turns out to be a charlatan, an unholy holy man whose mind is set on fucking the beautiful Aurora.

IBS: Aurora is beautiful, indeed, and like the other central female characters in the novel, Lucy, Rachel, and Honey, she is also a complex character. Nancy, the B.P.M., less so, I think. She's almost too good to be true, isn't she?

PA: Not really. Beautiful, yes, but once Nathan meets her, he discovers that she's rather stupid, a dim bulb of the New Age claptrap variety. Sweet and kind, but in other ways a disappointment.

IBS: Yes, she's not very bright. Of course, we see her through Nathan's perspective only.

PA: He's the one who's telling the story.

IBS: Perhaps he's not the most reliable of narrators. Take, for instance, his description of his own daughter, Rachel:

> [M]uch like her mother before her, it's a rare day when she speaks in anything but platitudes—all those exhausted

phrases and hand-me-down ideas that cram the dump sites
of contemporary wisdom. (2)

PA: He's unreasonably critical of her. Probably because he sees his
ex-wife every time he looks at her, and he hates his ex-wife so much
that he can't even write her name anymore. For much of the book, he
refers to her as "Name Deleted." Fortunately, Nathan changes, and
his reconciliation with Rachel is crucial to the outcome of the story.

IBS: Yes, it lifts the dark mood set in the opening line—"I was
looking for a quiet place to die" (1)—and with the new connections
he forms with the other female characters, his life improves considerably: Lucy, Aurora . . .

PA: And Joyce, let's not forget Joyce. All those women. Tom gets his
Honey, but Nathan is surrounded by women, and I think living in
that female world is good for him.

IBS: We've touched upon the Christian religious dimension of
The Brooklyn Follies, but there's an interesting perspective also on
Judaism—for instance, when Nathan explains his sense of Jewishness
to Aurora's extremist Christian husband:

> All Jews are atheists, except for those who aren't, of course.
> But I don't have much to do with them. (251)

There's a lot of humor here. "All Jews are atheists"? Where does that
come from?

PA: I don't know. Most Jews *are* atheists, aren't they? Judaism, as far
as I can tell, is the only Western religion you can belong to without
having to believe in God.

IBS: This is precisely what some of the most interesting Jewish
thinkers say: atheism can be part of being Jewish.

PA: Then you agree with me.

IBS: I do, and you are right, of course, that one of the major differences between Christianity and Judaism has to do with notions of the divine being. For the Jews the godhead is much more opaque. Here it's infinity, it's scripture . . .

PA: And it's laws. Judaism is about human life, how to organize human life.

IBS: As far as I know, even the most devout Jews cannot have any direct connection with the divine.

PA: That's right, you can't talk to God in the way born-again Christians can supposedly talk to Jesus.

IBS: For the Jew, the way to approach God, of course, is through scripture. Everything is in the Book. The Book is the door. Worship is exegesis: you must interpret, discuss, read between the lines. In fact, everything depends on how *well* we read. Isn't that fascinating?

PA: Well, that's the Jewish tradition, isn't it? Lots of discussion, lots of disagreement, but very little certainty.

TRAVELS IN THE SCRIPTORIUM. (2006)
One Dark Day of Amnesia: "The Writer Rewritten"

IBS: As you said the other day when we were talking about *Oracle Night*, *Travels in the Scriptorium* is essentially a book about the relationship between the author and his characters. It's also a story about an old man who wakes up to find himself in a kind of laboratory undergoing an experiment or a treatment he doesn't understand. He's seriously troubled both physically and mentally: he can barely walk, he's uncertain about the correct connection between words and the objects they name. Infrequent flashes of memory haunt him, and he fears the revenge of characters who have suffered at his hands. But Anna Blume is there to look after him. Fanshawe, Quinn, Marco Fogg, Benjamin Sachs, and other protagonists from previous novels also reappear. It all takes place in the course of a single day.

PA: For some reason, I started seeing a picture in my head of an old man sitting on the edge of a bed—dressed in striped pajamas, with slippers on his feet and his hands on his knees. I had no idea what it was about. The image kept coming back to me, and the more I thought about it, the more I came to suspect that it was a vision of myself as an old man, a very old man. That's how this novel started—out of that image. Yesterday, you said to me, "All your books took years of thinking before you wrote them." Not this one. It poured out of me.

IBS: Is there any inspiration from real life in this strange setting?

PA: As you noticed, the book is dedicated to Siri's father, and he inspired some of the things that are in it. Years before he died, a tumor was discovered in one of his legs, and after the tumor was cut out, walking became close to impossible for him. He was still mentally active, but more or less immobilized. He had emphysema, too, which is awful, and that restricted his movements even further. Through it all, he forged on with a number of writing projects—a personal memoir and a family history—sitting in his desk chair in his room in Minnesota, a chair with wheels, just like the chair in my book. Another thing that comes from him is the joke about the man who goes into the bar and orders three drinks. Siri's father told me that joke, and I used it as a secret homage to him. And also because it's spectacularly funny.

IBS: Did he know you were going to dedicate it to him? Did he see the manuscript?

PA: No, he was already dead before I started writing it. There's also a minor autobiographical reference in the book: the little memory Mr. Blank has about trying to kiss the girl while they're out on a pond ice-skating. That comes from when I was quite young, probably ten or eleven years old. When I tried to kiss her she had no idea what I was doing. "Why would you want to kiss me?" she said. She simply wasn't old enough to understand. Such a painful memory. Those are about the only private things I can think of.

IBS: Could we argue that, in a sense, there's an autobiographical dimension to the cast of characters in *Travels in the Scriptorium*? I mean, they're all figures you have invented for other novels now revived from your previous work, indeed recalled from your memory—where they still live—restored to life in this new book.

PA: They're my characters, of course. Which in some way turns me into Mr. Blank. Then again, I'm not Mr. Blank. He doesn't realize he's written novels, he thinks he's sent real people out on dangerous missions, and so fact and fiction overlap—even if it's all within the world of the book. Still, we mustn't forget that there's also a humorous side to all this. And a certain eeriness to it as well.

IBS: Yes, it's an unusually multilayered narrative. This is very much reflected also in the way the novel was received.

PA: You said there's a website that has gathered together conflicting reviews and interpretations. This is interesting to me.

IBS: Ah yes, *Open Letter Monthly* issued an essay reviewing the reviews.*

PA: I think it's good that a book can inspire many different readings.

IBS: I've rarely seen such diversity as in the reviews of *Travels in the Scriptorium*. Some claim that it's "a fable about Guantanamo and the CIA's secret prison networks"; others that it's an "homage to Beckett" with "nods to Kafka"; still others that it's an elegantly construed comment on the modern human condition in general.

PA: There's probably some truth to all of them. Not the Beckett-Kafka business, but the other readings are plausible. As for me, I was primarily thinking about old age and how many people there are like Mr. Blank: elderly people alone in rooms, unsure of who and where they are, living in a kind of haze. I was trying to capture that, but then, of course, there's a lot more going on, and, yes, there are explicit political references in this book. The horror called "extraordinary rendition" was very much on my mind as I was writing it—one of the nastiest, most brutal things the American government has ever done. And then, buried in the center of the novel, there's the story about the "Confederation" written by a supposedly young John Trause, which was inspired by my response to the war in Iraq. Empires need an enemy in order to unite their people. If you don't have a real enemy, you invent one.

---

* Sam Sacks, "Peer Review: Paul Auster Perplexes," *Open Letter Monthly*, http://www.openlettersmonthly.com/peer-review-paul-auster-perplexes/.

IBS: Your readers are also intrigued by the crossing-over of characters from your other novels.*

PA: I kept asking myself, "Will *Travels in the Scriptorium* be comprehensible to someone who has never read anything else I've written?"

IBS: That's also what the reviewers ask, and some of them argue that it's actually an advantage not to have read your other novels. But that's just one opinion among others.

PA: In the end, I don't think it matters. That was the conclusion I came to, in any case. The book is a work unto itself. Even if it refers to things outside itself, you don't have to know what those references are. If you do know, well, it only becomes richer.

IBS: Where did the idea come from of bringing characters from previous books back to life? Were their stories somehow not finished?

PA: I don't know. Or can't remember. When I realized that Mr. Blank could be an imaginary version of myself at an advanced age, I started looking back at what I've done with my life. We were talking about this the other day. Mostly, I've made up stories with imaginary people in them. And those characters are going to outlive me. What a strange thought that is. As the narrator explains, without the author

> we are nothing, but the paradox is that we, the figments of another mind, will outlive the mind that made us, for once we are thrown into the world, we continue to exist forever, and our stories go on being told, even after we are dead. (129)

---

* Anna Blume and Samuel Farr from *In the Country of Last Things*; Daniel Quinn, Peter Stillman, Sophie, Fanshawe (and J. P. Flood) from *The New York Trilogy*; Marco Fogg from *Moon Palace*; Ben Sachs from *Leviathan*; John Trause from *Oracle Night*.

IBS: I see what you mean. The *Guardian* reviewer* asserts that the purpose of *Travels in the Scriptorium* "seems to be to prove that the inside of Auster's skull can become extremely crowded at times." Would that be accurate?

PA: Well, it *is* crowded, yes.

IBS: We've talked quite a bit about the special bond between male characters in your books, but here, of course, by far the strongest connection is between Mr. Blank and Anna Blume.

PA: She was his first "charge," and he has a deep affection for her. Just as I do. And now we learn that Anna was the second wife of David Zimmer, who died of a heart attack in *The Book of Illusions*, the same David Zimmer who was waiting to hear from her in *Moon Palace*. Mr. Blank sent Anna on a dangerous mission—to the country of last things—and she suffered terribly because of it. But she's forgiven him now, and because of that forgiveness, she's the one who takes care of him, who treats him with the greatest tenderness. There's also Sophie, whom he likes as well, but it's a different relationship. He doesn't feel the same intense attachment to her—even if he does want to touch her breasts [*laughs*]. Without humor this book would be deadly. It would be impossible to read it.

IBS: That's true.

PA: Then there's Quinn. Good old Quinn reappears. Again and again, Quinn comes back into my books, which we noted earlier. But, of course, it's always a different Quinn. This one says, "I was your first operative." There's also the British police detective, Flood, who comes in from *The Locked Room*. Originally, he was mentioned only in a passing remark—he had no life.

---

* Alfred Hickling, "Where's the Exit?," *The Guardian*, October 14, 2006, http://www.theguardian.com/books/2006/oct/14/fiction.paulauster.

IBS: Exactly. He appears in Fanshawe's book, *Neverland*, which is one of the brilliant books we never get to read. And so, he's the invention of an invention: doubly fictitious.

PA: In fact, he's not even there as a person—only by virtue of a dream. Oh, here it is: "(Montag's house in chapter seven; Flood's dream in chapter thirty)" (*The New York Trilogy*, 324).

In parentheses only. Then, here in *Travels in the Scriptorium*, Flood says, "Without that dream, I'm nothing, literally nothing." (53)

IBS: That's a very small part indeed.

PA: Yes, the smallest allusion possible.

IBS: But you hadn't forgotten him, obviously.

PA: No. I thought it would be interesting to bring back the most minor character from all the books I've written. I turned him into a cockney policeman [*laughs*].

IBS: [*Laughs*] There was no life. There was nothing more than a dream invented by a writer who is himself a figment of someone's mind—mentioned in parentheses only! That's really funny.

PA: Given this background, he's very resentful, of course, and he has evil designs on the old man.

> You play with people's lives and take no responsibility for what you've done. I'm not going to sit here and bore you with my troubles, but I blame you for what's happened to me. I most sincerely blame you and despise you for it. (53)

IBS: Flood and the other transtextual characters are referred to as "charges" and "operatives." Can you possibly see your work as a kind of "operation"? The setting here is almost like a laboratory: there's a camera for round-the-clock observation, and the narration is written in a very clinical, scientific tone.

PA: Mr. Blank is clearly undergoing some kind of treatment, an experiment of some sort that he himself seems to have initiated. Again, you can read this in different ways: it could be standard treatment for the elderly, it could be a method for recovering or even reliving his past, it could be something else entirely. There are some mysterious things going on. Think of all the difficulties he has with the simplest functions of his body—and his mind.

IBS: As the inventor of all this hardship for your protagonists, do you think you are possibly a little troubled by their predicaments? Do you feel responsible for sending them out on difficult and perilous missions?

PA: Well, that's what I did. These poor people have suffered, some of them have died, they've had injuries . . .

IBS: Suffered losses. Sometimes terrible losses.

PA: Yes, all these different people . . . I've put them through their paces, as they say.

> The damned specters, Mr. Blank says. They're back again.
>   Specters?
>   My victims. All the people I've made suffer over the years.
> They're coming after me now to take their revenge. (81)

If you took it seriously, in other words, if these were real people, what a monstrous person I would be. Still, it seems that it was necessary somehow. It's Sophie who says, "You did what you had to do." I can't remember where. Do you know what I'm talking about?

IBS: Yes, it's when she's talking about her marriage to Fanshawe and we learn that she had two boys—named after you, I assume: Ben* and Paul.

PA: [*Laughs.*]

IBS: Earlier, you said that Mr. Blank is and is not you. I was wondering, given the fact that your work is reviewed, even judged, all the time, do you sometimes feel as if you're being watched like Mr. Blank? He's under constant observation. You may not be, but certainly your work is being assessed and weighed all over the world all the time.

PA: Under microscopes and magnifying glasses. It's true. I never really thought about it in that way.

IBS: Just look at what I'm doing [*laughs*].

PA: I know. Well, that's an interesting interpretation. Maybe there's some truth to it. It may be how the idea came to me.

IBS: If we look at the opening lines:

> The old man sits on the edge of the narrow bed, palms spread out on his knees, head down, staring at the floor. He has no idea that a camera is planted in the ceiling directly above him. The shutter clicks silently once every second, producing eighty-six thousand four hundred still photos with each revolution of the earth. Even if he knew he was being watched, it wouldn't make any difference. His mind is elsewhere, stranded among the figments in his head as he searches for an answer to the question that haunts him. (1)

---

* Auster's middle name is Benjamin.

PA: Yes, the camera clicks every second.

IBS: It's in the ceiling, so the camera is inside the room. And so, of course, we think, "Aha, there's somebody operating that camera, somebody outside looking in." Mr. Blank is being observed—like Black in *Ghosts*.

PA: I wanted to see if I could write something confined to a small space—something with no geography, so to speak—an entire book set in one room.

IBS: Yes, there's a kind of claustrophobic feeling to it.

PA: It was intentional. I definitely wanted that.

IBS: What is it about the door? The "eternal enigma of the door" (101). Why doesn't he just try the door?

PA: Because he keeps forgetting, and then he's afraid because he doesn't want to accept the fact that he's locked in—even if he's agreed to his confinement. I think the inconsistencies in Mr. Blank's thinking have to do with the effect of the drugs he's taking. His judgments are wobbly, uncertain. He has trouble following a train of thought. And then—the discovery about the nailed-shut window horrifies him. After that, he's too scared to deal with the door.

IBS: Scared of what he might find?

PA: Exactly.

IBS: What he finds inside the room also upsets him. Photos of characters from your previous novels and manuscripts he recognizes but cannot place.

From the look of disgust that comes over his face as he scans these sentences, we can be fairly confident that Mr. Blank has not lost the ability to read. But who the author of these sentences might be is still open to question. (5)

PA: This story, the story within the novel, is something I started working on back in the 1980s. It turned out to be one of those projects I could never quite figure out how to do. But nothing is ever completely lost, is it? It remains in your head, and fragments of earlier, unfinished work can sometimes find their way into later work. We talked about this in connection with the Nick Bowen story in *Oracle Night*.

> Ancient material, written when I was still in my teens and twenties. None of it was ever published. Thankfully, I should add, but in reading over the stories, I found one that wasn't half terrible. I still wouldn't want to publish it, but if I give it to you, you might be able to rethink it as a film. Maybe my name will help. (*Oracle Night*, 167)

This story, originally one of my own abandoned projects, which Trause gives to Sidney in *Oracle Night*, is then developed in this later novel [*laughs*]. Without it, *Travels in the Scriptorium* would be impoverished, I think. You need that material about another imprisonment outside the room in order to give the book a little air. It's an imaginary exit from the confinement.

IBS: I see, yes, it's the only thing that points beyond the room.

PA: The political subtext of the novel is reinforced by Trause's story of that figment country. Every now and then, Mr. Blank thinks he's being held by government authorities for something he's done—but which he can't remember, of course.

IBS: Yes, there is that Kafkian sense of paranoia.

PA: Again, this book isn't one of those puzzles in which every piece fits neatly together. It's a collection of different pieces with spaces in between them for you, the reader, to fill in for yourself.

IBS: [*Laughs*] All right. Speaking of the reader, your narrator addresses his audience directly a few times, for instance, here:

> [A]s the reader has already learned, his thoughts have largely been elsewhere, lost in a fogland of ghost-like beings and broken memories as he searches for an answer to the question that haunts him. (16)

Who delivers the impassive, at times almost scientific account of Mr. Blank's day in this confined space? It's somebody who is studying him like a rat in a cage. Who is the coldly objective—and radically omniscient—narrator?

PA: Toward the end of the book, we find out that the author of *Travels in the Scriptorium* is Fanshawe—don't ask me what N. R. stands for. Fanshawe never had a first name. Here, he's one of the people who've been observing Mr. Blank.

IBS: This is where the narrative curls back upon itself and repeats the first two or three pages in verbatim repetition: "The old man sits on the edge of the narrow bed."

PA: Yes, it continues for a couple of pages to the point where:

> By now, Mr. Blank has read all he can stomach, and he is not the least bit amused. In an outburst of pent-up anger and frustration, he tosses the manuscript over his shoulder with a violent flick of the wrist, not even bothering to turn around to see where it lands. As it flutters through the air and then thuds to the floor behind him, he pounds his fist on the desk and says in a loud voice: When is this nonsense going to end? (126–129)

Then the voice changes, and this is no doubt Fanshawe: "It will never end. For Mr. Blank is one of us now" (143), meaning he's now a character in a book, "and struggle though he might to understand his predicament, he will always be lost."

> Mr. Blank is old and enfeebled, but as long as he remains in the room with the shuttered window and the locked door, he can never die, never disappear, never be anything but the words I am writing on this* page. (129–130)

IBS: Has the author now been subsumed or circumscribed or imprisoned by his linguistic creations?

PA: One of those things, surely. It's interesting that he can now predict what will happen because he is writing the story:

> In a short while, a woman will enter the room and feed him his dinner. I haven't yet decided who that woman will be, but if all goes well between now and then, I will send in Anna. That will make Mr. Blank happy, and when all is said and done, he has probably suffered enough for one day. Anna will feed Mr. Blank his dinner, then wash him and put him to bed. Mr. Blank will lie awake in the dark for some time, listening to the cries of birds in the far distance, but then his eyes will at last grow heavy, and his lids will close. He will fall asleep, and when he wakes up in the morning, the treatment will begin again. But for now it is still the day it has always been since the first word of this report, and now is the moment when Anna kisses Mr. Blank on the cheek and tucks him in, and now is the moment when she stands up from the bed and begins walking toward the door. Sleep well, Mr. Blank.
>
> Lights out. (144–145; closing paragraph)

---

* The Faber and Henry Holt editions mistakenly say "his."

IBS: So the narrative focus keeps shifting between subject and object?

PA: It's like receding mirrors. Everything is contained in everything else. At once inside and outside. Remember Thomas Carlyle's *Sartor Resartus*, "the tailor stitched"—or "the tailor re-tailored"? Well, here I suppose you could say we have "the *writer rewritten*."

IBS: Yes, the passages we have just read are radically self-reflexive. They open to questions your readers and interpreters naturally ask: Does the author, does Mr. Blank, now exist in the book only? Is he being drawn further and further into fictions within layers of fiction?

PA: Yes, because what you finally have is the book: This is the world. And this is the only place where he can be now.

IBS: Even if a page is only two-dimensional, made of ink and paper? The rest is in the reader's interpretation, isn't it? Characters come alive, images are conjured up as we read . . .

PA: Ink and paper form a three-dimensional world in our minds. But in the end, books are just paper.

IBS: Yes, I can see why you are intrigued by the idea that imagined beings made of ink and paper outlive real people. Words are stronger than the body in *Travels in the Scriptorium*. And speaking of words, you play with the relationship between language and the concrete world: at the beginning of the day, they match, but later—just as in *In the Country of Last Things*—the word is divorced from the object it's meant to name.

> The wall now reads CHAIR. The lamp now reads BATH-ROOM. The chair now reads DESK. (103)

PA: Someone has switched the labels on him.

IBS: This "switching operation" astonishes and upsets Mr. Blank, and he's desperately trying to understand what's happened:

> He has suffered a stroke or brain injury of some kind; he has lost his ability to read; someone has played a nasty trick on him. (103)

PA: Again, it's the people involved in the experiment. It's another test.

IBS: What is being tested?

PA: Whether he believes in and is still capable of understanding the coherence of a world in which things have one name and one name only—that "table" can only be a table. It's not a bed. If suddenly it becomes a bed, then all order would break down. Language would disintegrate into chaos, and Mr. Blank rebels against it. He's horrified.

IBS: Yes, not unlike Stillman Sr. in *City of Glass*, Mr. Blank struggles to put signifiers and signifieds back in order. It's hard work, he breaks three fingernails in the process and suffers an attack of nausea as a consequence. Is there an intimate relationship, in this book, between linguistic and digestive mechanisms: between word movements and bowel movements?

PA: "Word movements and bowel movements." [*Laughs*] That's funny.

IBS: [*Laughs*] What about his amnesia?

PA: He has some brief flickers of memory. For instance, he remembers holding a little child in his arms—maybe his child? He's not sure, but he thinks so. Then he can't remember who the child might have been. It's the blur of dementia that I was so interested in trying to capture—not in medical terms, but in some kind of interior way. I know it's a strange book. It can stand on its own, but maybe it makes more sense if you read it as the first part of a diptych. The other is the next book, *Man in the Dark.*[*]

---

[*] In the United States, *Travels in the Scriptorium* and *Man in the Dark* are now available in a single volume: *Day/Night: Two Novels* (New York: Picador, 2013).

MAN IN THE DARK. (2008)
One White Night of Insomnia: Confronting One's Past

IBS: *Man in the Dark* embraces the entire adult life of your insomniac protagonist in a single night. It's a complex composition of interlacing stories at different levels of narrative reality. In the primary story, August Brill is passing yet another sleepless night by analyzing film scenes and telling himself a story of civil war in a parallel America partly to ward off the horror—which is at the center of the book—of the real war in Iraq that haunts his family. The book revolves around the point of divergence between the two stories within the book: one set in a "real" America, the other in an alternative America, "which hasn't lived through September 11 or the war in Iraq" (50). Brill, here, is in a very dark place, and he leaves his protagonist in an even darker one.

PA: As I said yesterday, this book is a companion to *Travels in the Scriptorium*. Even though the two novels are very different, the circumstances are identical. In both cases, the protagonist is an elderly man who is damaged or injured and therefore immobilized. Neither one of them leaves his room. *Travels in the Scriptorium* takes place in the course of one day; *Man in the Dark* takes place in the course of one night.

IBS: In contrast to *Travels in the Scriptorium*, there's action and interaction between "real" characters leading "real" lives, as it were.

PA: It's also set in an identifiable space: a house in Vermont. We know that the house is owned by the narrator's daughter, we know that his granddaughter is living there now and that he, August Brill, suffers from insomnia. We spend one night with him as he lies in the dark making up stories to pass the time. All kinds of stories:

humorous stories, adventure stories, continuations of novels he's read. We understand that this is how he often spends his time while the rest of the household is asleep. On this particular night, he tells himself a story about someone named Owen Brick. He also fiddles with other stories. Then Katya, his granddaughter, knocks on the door, she comes in, and from that moment on, the narrative takes an abrupt turn. The rest of the book is different. I understood that this was a radical and even risky way to construct a story, but the shift functions as a kind of hinge, and the narrative within the narrative, big as it is, throws the primary story into relief.

IBS: The story Brill invents that particular night turns on political issues. It's about civil war in an alternative America.

PA: There's some talk in *The Brooklyn Follies* about the 2000 presidential election. The civil war story in this novel is inspired by that election. I have to say that I was horrified and disgusted by what happened then. I think it's one of the darkest moments in American history. An election was actually stolen in plain sight. Everyone could see it happening. The United States Supreme Court made a decision that was completely at odds with all legal precedents when it overturned the ruling of the Florida Supreme Court. By all rights, they should have thrown the election back to Florida, which would have led to a recount of the whole state. What the Supreme Court did was to carry out a "legalized" illegal coup for Bush. Gore won the election, and the Republicans stole it. What surprised me, as a citizen of this country, was that there wasn't more outrage from the public. After all, it was almost a declaration of war by one half of the country against the other. Al Gore was in a tough situation, I'll admit that, but he shouldn't have rolled over. He should have fought. He should have fought if only for the principle of the thing.

IBS: Yes, it was almost incomprehensible, certainly from an outside perspective.

PA: It meant that we had Bush for eight years. Bush—who did so much damage to this country. I was in a seething rage all during the eight years he was president. I couldn't believe that we'd allowed this man to take office and do all the terrible things he did. America was on the brink of collapse when Obama was elected. We were losing eight hundred thousand jobs a month. Every month! The country was in free fall. These were the catastrophic consequences of Bush's policies. Not to speak of the war in Iraq, which was the single greatest tactical blunder in American history. Eight–nine years of war—for nothing! Because Iraq had weapons of mass destruction? No, they didn't. Because somehow Saddam Hussein was in league with Osama bin Laden? No, he wasn't. All the justifications they came up with were false. For people simply to swallow those lies and not react—it's beyond comprehension. The Brick story embedded in the main narrative of *Man in the Dark* was born out of my anger, my frustration. In Brill's imaginary world, people do get angry, and they start a civil war:

> This is America, and America is fighting America.
> What are you talking about?
> Civil war, Brick. Don't you know anything? This is the fourth year. But now that you've turned up, it's going to end soon. (8)

IBS: And so, Brill is inventing a kind of counter-history?

PA: The story becomes more and more complicated the more deeply he involves himself in it. He can't detach himself from what he's telling, and therefore he begins to question his role as inventor of this imaginary world: if he's the creator of the story in which the war takes place, logically speaking, the only way the war can end is for him to be eliminated. At one level of the fiction, the people wanting to end the war will enlist the imaginary character, Brick, to cross the line and go into the "real" world and kill Brill. But, of course, this leads to a standoff: you can't cross back and forth between different levels of (narrative) reality. And so, Brill just gives up and kills his protagonist, and that's the end of it. Again, he has complicated things to such an extent that there's no possible resolution. He becomes tired of this mind game and wants to think about something else. The speculative "counter-history" adventure story has served its purpose for a few hours, and now he'll move on to the next story. Then he's interrupted by Katya, and the narrative turns at an abrupt angle. Now it's the two of them lying in the bed together, talking about his life and his marriage. She wants to know *everything*. And so, he's forced to abandon his fictions and start confronting his own past.

IBS: So, we have stories within the story with a perfectly clear distinction between first-, second-, and third-order narratives, and, as in *Travels in the Scriptorium*, it has become possible to cross over from one ontological level to the other: from one world of fiction to another. What sets these two novels apart from, say, *Oracle Night*, is that the characters here are fully aware that they exist only in the imagination of their creator:

> And he invented you, Brick. Don't you understand that? This is your story, not ours. The old man invented you in order to kill him . . . and every night Brill lies awake in the dark, trying not to think about his past, making up stories about other worlds. (70–71)

PA: This is spoken when Frisk and Brick are discussing Giordano Bruno's theory about the infinite plurality of worlds.

> There's no single reality, Corporal. There are many realities. There's no single world. There are many worlds, and they all run parallel to one another, worlds and anti-worlds, worlds and shadow-worlds, and each world is dreamed or imagined or written by someone in another world. Each world is the creation of a mind. (69)

Brill is trying to find a way out of the deadlock of his story. Again, he's confronted with a problem of inconsistency, so he's seeking a way around that by considering the notion of multiple worlds.

IBS: So, in a sense, your protagonist, Brill, is speculating here about the narrative structures *you* employ. Here, as in *Oracle Night*, you have fictional worlds clearly delineated and side by side.

PA: Yes, but the difference is that in *Oracle Night* no one is crossing the boundary. Sidney Orr is writing a story, and that story remains a second-order narrative in its own world. That world is strange because it also includes the book, *Oracle Night*, which Nick Bowen is reading, and before long we realize that the book is relevant to what's happening to him. Still, it's confined to its own realm, whereas this one isn't. Bit by bit, Brill is implicating himself in the story he's created, and so, the boundary between levels of fiction is eroded. It has a different effect altogether.

IBS: Of course, the radical example of characters crossing over is *Travels in the Scriptorium*, where they come in, not just from other levels of fiction, but from other novels entirely.

PA: I'm fascinated by the porousness between the invented and the real; the intersection of different imaginary spheres.

IBS: Brill gives quite a bit of thought to the implications of allowing this to happen:

> By putting myself into the story, the story becomes real.
> Or else I become unreal, yet one more figment of my own
> imagination. Either way, the effect is more satisfying, more
> in harmony with my mood—which is dark, my little ones,
> as dark as the obsidian night that surrounds me. (102)

PA: Yes, the embedded story is a reflection of Brill's state of mind.

He's in a very dark mood. He's thinking about Titus—and he doesn't want to think about Titus—the beheaded boy. He's also trying to keep Sonia at bay, "the ever-present absent one" (102). He can't let go. And so, the book emanates outward from that core— the double core of Titus and Sonia. I wanted to encompass my protagonist's whole life in that one night. The story of the civil war is a reflection of his inner state, which is filled with the torment of his wife's death, of Titus's death, his daughter's divorce, Katya's depression, as well as his own wounded leg, which was injured in a car accident.

IBS: Yes, that's how we find him as the book opens with the description of his distress enhanced by contrasts:

> Bright light, then darkness. Sun pouring down from all corners of the sky, followed by the black of night. (1)

We have the "white night in the great American wilderness" and later "the black void of oblivion, a nothingness as deep and dark as death" (72). It seems to me that it's the hinge itself, or the moment *in between* light and dark, day and night, when his imagination is most actively at work.

PA: Yes, you're in that hole, so to speak, where the only thing to keep you alive is your thoughts.

IBS: I was wondering whether insomnia is as terrifying as the claustrophobic blank spaces in some of your earlier writing? Silence, wordlessness, solitude—now insomnia. Are they similar?

PA: That's a good question . . . No, not really. Insomnia is not so much a void, because your mind is racing. That's why you can't fall asleep. You're almost too full. You must empty yourself out to be able to fall asleep. So it's almost the opposite. But you're right, there is something fertile about insomnia, even though it's maddening.

We've all had insomnia. Those horrible nights when you simply can't close your eyes.

IBS: There's a central blankness inside the protagonist himself, isn't there?

> I walked around with a feeling that my life had never truly belonged to me, that I had never truly inhabited myself, that I had never been real. (153)

PA: Brill is talking about a character flaw in himself. This is a sort of self-psychoanalysis. I think many of us have the feeling that we're living to the side of our own life, that we're not truly experiencing anything, that we're a little dead to ourselves and to other people. As a young man, Brill felt detached from his core, and Sonia was the one who brought him into a better relation with himself, but it took a long time. What he's talking about here is the affair he had with Oona. He allows himself to fall for her because he didn't feel his actions had any consequences.

IBS: I think, perhaps, there's a similar kind of "black hole"—or a white space—at the core of many of your male characters. A flaw, as you say, or an incompleteness they seek to remedy. It's not just an absence or the loss of a loved one, but something deeper, more existential.

PA: A disintegration of self. I've seldom met anyone I would call fully integrated. We're all scattered, we're all fragmentary.

IBS: Could it be more than fracture, perhaps? It's as if there's something that remains blank. In the narratives, it functions as a fertile space; in the characters, it's something that drives them. I mean, they go on, they reinvent themselves, and they establish new lives that are satisfactory. But you don't get a sense that the void is ever filled.

PA: Many of my protagonists cope with loss, as we've already mentioned, and eventually move on to new lives, different lives. That was one of the reasons why I wanted the biography of Rose Hawthorne in this book. The special relevance of Rose Hawthorne is that she floundered through half her life: "a confessed 'stranger to herself'" (45). She then reinvented herself completely and became a nun. Rose was one of the first to go against the theory, which was prevalent at the turn of the last century, that cancer was a communicative disease. Cancer patients were isolated. She managed to get hold of a building on the Lower East Side, the poorest part of New York City, and housed and cared for terminal cancer patients. The Rose Houses* still exist as hospices. She was a remarkable woman and a fine writer. I quote that page from her book about her father. It's so beautiful.

> It seemed to me a terrible thing that one so peculiarly strong, sentient, luminous as my father should grow feebler and fainter, and finally ghostly still and white. (48)

Hawthorne knew he didn't have much time left. He didn't want to die at home in front of his wife and daughter, so he went on a little trip to New Hampshire with Pierce** and ended his days in a hotel room. The last time the family saw him was when he was walking away from the house. I find this heartbreaking:

> Like a snow image of an unbending but old, old man, he stood for a moment gazing at me. My mother sobbed as she walked beside him to the carriage. We have missed him in the sunshine, in the storm, in the twilight, ever since. (48–49)

IBS: Another thing that Brill thinks about in the night is films. They play a significant role here as well.

---

* Rosary Hill Home, New York.
** Franklin Pierce, president of the United States (1853–1857), had been Hawthorne's roommate at Bowdoin College.

PA: Of course, Katya is a film student. She and Brill have been watching movies together, two or three movies every day. The films are an integral part of the book. They're especially important because the scenes Brill and Katya discuss are all about women.

> How women are the ones who carry the world. They take care of the real business while their hapless men stumble around making a hash of things. Or else just lie around doing nothing. (21–22)

IBS: Is this the opinion of a widowed grandfather, or is it your view too?

PA: No, no, I really do believe this. And Brill believes it, too. It's not always the case, not one hundred percent of the time, but for the most part women keep the world going.

IBS: Is this the reason you chose these particular films?

PA: Well, they're masterpieces, all of them, on a level with the greatest works of fiction.

IBS: Katya's theory about objects conveying human emotions is very interesting.

PA: I agree. I think she's really on to something—and I think she knows it, too.

IBS: Brill sees Katya's obsession with films as a form of self-medication:

> Escaping into a film is not like escaping into a book. Books force you to give something back to them, to exercise your intelligence and imagination, whereas you can watch a film— and even enjoy it—in a state of mindless passivity. (15)

PA: Most people don't watch films as closely as Katya and Brill do. They're glued to the screen, watching in a state of absolute attentiveness. And they're watching good films,* the best films. Brill finally admits that some films are just as good as the best books.

IBS: Brill comments extensively on what he calls the "homeopathic drug" of each of the inhabitants of the house: for Katya it's the films, for Miriam it's her work on Rose Hawthorne, and for Brill it's the mechanisms of narration, for example, when he says:

> I'm treading water because I can see the story turning in any one of several directions, and I still haven't decided which path to take. Hope or no hope? Both options are available, and yet neither one is fully satisfying to me. Is there a middle way after such a beginning, after throwing Brick to the wolves and bending the poor sap's mind out of shape? Probably not. Think dark, then, and go down into it, see it through to the end. (88)

PA: Brill is making up the story as he goes along. So, he's considering where to go with it next.

IBS: Brill's considerations are similar to Sidney's in *Oracle Night*— and both their embedded narratives are abandoned in mid-story.

PA: That's true. They don't go anywhere. One stops before the end, and the other comes to an abrupt end. I think those are the only two cases in which I've written about someone in the act of writing something or making up a story. Right? I don't think I've done it anywhere else.

IBS: What about Benjamin Sachs in *Leviathan* leaving his big book unfinished up there in the house in Vermont?

---

* *The Bicycle Thief,* dir. Vittorio de Sica, *The World of Apu,* dir. Satyajit Ray, *Grand Illusion,* dir. Jean Renoir, *Tokyo Story,* dir. Yasujiro Ozu.

PA: We know he's writing it but from a narrated perspective only. We're not inside him. In *Moon Palace* we hear about Barber's early novel, but that's a recapitulation of something that has already been written. I'm talking about the process.

IBS: Well, we certainly get inside the head of Ellen Bryce in *Sunset Park*, who draws these strange pictures, which, I think, is a process similar to that of writing, and we follow Alice Bergstrom in the process of writing her dissertation.

PA: That's true. But still, nothing quite as involved as those two cases.

IBS: Brick is a common soldier, a pawn, a simple building block in the elaborate structure erected by Brill. The name "Brill" strikes me as similar to "Braille": the alphabet for blind people, who are "in the dark." And so, I have to ask you again whether the semantic content of the names bears any relation to the nature or function of the characters?

PA: My son had a Mrs. Brick as his teacher when he was in elementary school. I was always fascinated by that name. In my poems and in *City of Glass* I talk about bricks in a wall. How they're all identical and yet each one different from the others.

IBS: Also in *Moon Palace*.

PA: *Moon Palace*?

IBS: Yes, when Marco is describing the bricks in a wall to Effing. It's one of my favorite passages in that book.

PA: Of course, how stupid of me. New York is filled with brick walls. I particularly like the red brick buildings in the oldest parts of the city. Some of the most sublime visual moments of my life have occurred while walking downtown in Manhattan or in Brooklyn as the sun is setting. In spring and early summer, the glow of the sun on the bricks is one of the most beautiful things in the world. Edward Hopper captured this in some of his paintings. Bricks are part of my visual world. Brick is also the individual in the group. You have ten thousand bricks—as if a wall were a city of bricks. Part of the whole, the individual connected to others. Owen Brick is part of the world, he's not isolated from other people.

IBS: That's how he's presented—at least in the beginning. He's like biblical Adam, a fully grown man without memory or past, created by an identified maker. Then he's given an impossible mission. What about Brill?

PA: I was thinking of light, you know, *briller* in French. Interestingly enough, there's a famous building in Manhattan called the Brill Building. It's on Broadway and Forty-ninth Street. In the old days, it was the place where all the popular music in America was written— Tin Pan Alley. In every room, there was someone with a piano making music. All that died away, and now the building houses one of the largest post-production film centers in New York. I spent about a year and a half in the Brill Building editing *Smoke* and *Blue in the Face*. The lobby is a stunning art deco creation with the most beautiful elevators in the city. You should go in there sometime just to see the elevator doors, which are made of brass and are polished every day. Not that the Brill Building has anything to do with *Man in the Dark*. I just liked the name, that's all, and I wanted the names of the three protagonists in the two books to begin with *B*: Blank, Brill, and Brick.

IBS: Because it comes straight after *A*, which must be primary, and *B*, secondary?

PA: [*Laughs.*]

INVISIBLE. (2009)
Three Seasons and an Epilogue

> *"[A]nd isn't it intriguing that thought cannot exist without language,*
> *and since language is a function of the brain, we would have to say that*
> *language—the ability to experience the world through symbols—is in some*
> *sense a physical property of human beings, which proves that the old*
> *mind-body duality is so much nonsense, doesn't it? Adieu, Descartes.*
> *The mind and the body are one." (197)*

IBS: In *Invisible* we follow the life of Adam Walker by way of the relationships that form him: the intense bond with his magnificent sister Gwyn and the ties with their dead brother, the disturbing alliance with Rudolf Born, and his sexual obsession with Margot. The stories are told through a prism of shifting perspectives set in very different types of writing. The *New York Times* names it the finest novel you have ever written. It really is an unusually absorbing story of violence, loss, sex, and difficult love firmly set in the political climate of 1968. You were a student in those days. Did you take part in events similar to those you describe in the book?

PA: The facts are that Adam Walker is my age and he's a student at Columbia University. He has the same job in the library that I once had. The Paris hotel is based on a hotel where I stayed: a dump that cost seven francs a night, which was the equivalent of a dollar and forty cents back then. I was there in 1965, he goes there in 1967. It was a difficult time in my life, amply illustrated by the letters I'll be publishing in my next book.* The West End Bar, where certain things happen in the novel, was a real place. It still exists in a different form. It was famously one of Dylan Thomas's watering holes, and it was the bar to go to in those days. I spent most of my undergraduate years hanging out in there.

---

* *Report from the Interior* was not yet completed when this conversation took place.

IBS: So, in many ways, this book is a walk down memory lane?

PA: I wrote *Invisible* in 2007 and 2008. The previous year, we started celebrating fortieth anniversaries of many of the crucial events from the late 1960s: the Six-Day War, the Newark and Detroit riots, the nationwide student strike against the Vietnam War. And then, of course, even more of these fortieth anniversaries occurred the following year—after all, 1968 was the year of years. You were probably just a little baby then.

IBS: I was born in 1961.

PA: Well, it was an important time. It was the year of the Tet Offensive, which greatly intensified the fighting in Vietnam; it was the year Johnson announced his decision not to run for reelection. The country had split down the middle. It was a crazy time, an impossible time. It was the year of the assassinations of Martin Luther King and Robert Kennedy. It was the year of the violence at the Democratic convention in Chicago. I don't know if these long-ago events ring any bells for you.

IBS: Absolutely, but more from a European perspective.

PA: So you know it was the year of immense student upheavals in Europe as well. Politically, there were radical things going on in Germany and France. There was the Russian invasion of Prague. All the media attention in connection with the anniversaries made me want to go back to those days. That was one of the inspirations for this book. We had our big demonstrations at Columbia, where the university was shut down during eight days of sit-ins. There was a police riot on campus, and seven hundred of us were arrested one violent night at the end of April. In April 2008, there were fortieth anniversary events at Columbia—a weekend of panel discussions, readings, and films. I went to a couple of those gatherings and met people I hadn't seen in decades. It was very moving, I have to say.

One always hears about how the student radicals of the sixties sold out to become bankers, stockbrokers, and corporate lawyers, but with my Columbia classmates that wasn't true. Most of the people I saw that weekend had maintained the ideals of their youth. They were community organizers, legal aid lawyers, people still fighting the good fight. I mention all these things because it's important to know the historical context in order to understand my protagonist, Adam Walker. He's one of those people: he becomes a lawyer and a community activist, mostly in poor black neighborhoods. Walker is a product of that time. So is the Frenchman Rudolf Born, but in a radically different way, since he's older and has lived through France's misadventure in Algeria as a soldier, an interrogator, and, finally, a torturer. When I lived in Paris in the early seventies, I had many conversations with people of Born's age and older about the Algerian War. How bloody it was. The Paris police were continually rounding up people, arresting people, and there were many murders in the city, political murders of Algerians, whose bodies were dumped in the Seine. It was a dangerous time, the assassination attempt on de Gaulle, dark mayhem everywhere. Born is someone who emerges from that darkness.

IBS: Yes, he certainly is ominous.

PA: Anyway, that's the background of the novel. The book itself, of course, doesn't dwell much on those things. But they're all there, hovering around everything that happens.

IBS: Are there any autobiographical elements in your narrator, James Freeman? He's a mature celebrated writer.

PA: Freeman is a shadowy character. Not much information is given about him, but I imagine him to be someone rather like myself.

IBS: Also: Adam Walker is trying to write something about George Oppen. Oppen is one of your favorite poets, isn't he?

PA: Yes, and he later became a friend. The reason Oppen is in the book is because he was one of the few American poets of that time who managed to take the personal and integrate it into the political. He's both a private and a public poet. His work is impregnated with a kind of wisdom that is rare in American poetry. My character, Walker, is very attracted to this.

IBS: He's also attracted to the medieval poet, Bertran de Born,* whose work celebrated war and violence.

PA: One of the finest poets who ever lived, the man who appears in Dante's *Inferno* holding his own severed head. I've never read poetry like his. It's the most savage call to battle I've ever come across. I translated his poem for the book myself because I wasn't satisfied with the existing versions in English. It was very hard work. I don't know Provençal, but I managed to get hold of some French translations, and those helped me.

IBS: In the novel, you attribute the translation to Walker. You also have the young girl, Cécile, struggling with her translation of Lycophron.**

PA: Lycophron you probably remember from *The Invention of Solitude*. In "The Book of Memory," I discuss the translations of Lycophron's long poem about Cassandra. Q., here, is Pascal Quignard, now a well-known novelist and essayist in France. When he was about twenty years old, he did an extraordinary translation of Lycophron into French, a masterpiece of translation. Pascal told me there had been only one English translation of this poem. It was by a certain Lord Royston, the Earl of Gloucester. I tracked it down in the Columbia University Library. This was in 1974. I found the Lord Royston translation amazing: a brilliant, wild English poem based on Lycophron's poem—another masterpiece of translation by another

---

* The Provençal troubadour Bertran de Born (1140s–1215).
** Classical Greek poet, Alexandria, third century.

young man. Lord Royston, it turned out, drowned in a shipwreck off the Swedish coast in 1808 at the age of twenty-three or twenty-four. He would have been a great English writer, but this translation is pretty much the only major thing he did. It's a poem that has stayed with me all my life, and I wanted to reexamine it in the novel. So, both of the translated texts in *Invisible* are dense and difficult poems by largely forgotten writers. It's impossible to produce a literal rendering of them. As Walker says about Lycophron, "It's like trying to translate *Finnegans Wake* into Mandarin" (215). So, yes, there's quite a bit about translation in *Invisible*.

IBS: I think you said to me the other day that you took up Bertran de Born on impulse?

PA: Because of the name, first. Born. What a good name that is. And then I remembered that he was a poet. And then I remembered that he appears in Dante. And then . . . all those things became a part of the book. But Born began as Rudolf Born for me, not Bertran de Born, the poet.

IBS: So you weren't trying to resurrect Bertran de Born from Dante's *Inferno* and "put him back together again"? There are so many "broken" people in *Invisible*.

PA: No, I was interested in Born's violence. The man in my novel is such an ambiguous character. He's a villain, brutal and unpredictable, but not evil. He's also very intelligent and slightly crazy. More disturbed than wicked, I would say. The imbalance is in his character, but exacerbated by experience: I think the Algerian War unhinged him. Margot more than implies this. That's why he can take out a knife and stab a boy to death. He reacts like the soldier he once was: he's under attack, so he kills.

IBS: Why does he seek out Adam in the first place?

PA: Gwyn's theory is that it was a homoerotic attraction. It's possible.

IBS: You don't really get a sense of that, though, do you?

PA: Not really, no, but then, why is Born offering to set up the magazine for Walker? He's certainly not doing it because Margot has asked him to.

IBS: No, he's the older man playing God to his Adam. He wants to see what happens. It's just an experiment.

PA: Walker, in retrospect—how naive he was, how stupid, how in the world could he have allowed himself to get sucked up into all this? But these are the kinds of things that happen to us when we're young and inexperienced.

IBS: It's in *Invisible* that you first introduce the second-person narrative and begin to play with shifting points of view across the four heterogeneous parts that constitute the novel:

> 1. "Spring," Adam's narrative presented in the first person, past tense
>
> 2. "Summer," second-person perspective, present tense
>
> 3. "Fall," adapted from Adam's shorthand, third person, present tense
>
> 4. Cécile Juin's diary

The perspective changes more radically than ever before in your writing, and you have both Adam and Jim comment on the implications:

> By writing about myself in the first person, I had smothered myself and made myself invisible, had made it impossible for

me to find the thing I was looking for. I needed to separate myself from myself, to step back and carve out some space between myself and my subject (which was myself), and therefore I returned to the beginning of Part Two and began writing in the third person. *I* became *He*, and the distance created by that small shift allowed me to finish the book. (89)

This is also an allusion to *The Invention of Solitude.* Is it a key to understanding the composition of *Invisible*?

PA: As I told you a long time ago, I started "The Book of Memory" in the first person as a natural outcome of the first part, "Portrait of an Invisible Man." Then it suddenly came to me that I had to write about myself in the third person. Once I did that, I was able to complete the project.

IBS: Later on, in *Sunset Park*, *Winter Journal*, and *Report from the Interior*, you add a striking new dimension to your writing through second-person narration, but it's here, in *Invisible*, that you first begin to fully explore the mechanisms and effects of altering perspectives, isn't it?

PA: All the novels I'd written up until *Invisible* had one narrator only. The overall perspective never changes, even if, inside the novels, there are many first- and third-person shifts, say, in *Moon Palace* or *Leviathan* or *The Book of Illusions*. There's an "I" who's telling the story about himself and his relation to the other characters, then, suddenly, he's telling the story about someone else in the third person. For instance, you get Effing's story in the third person in *Moon Palace.* The same goes for Benjamin Sachs's story in *Leviathan*, and in *The Book of Illusions*, Hector's story is also narrated in the third person. So, there are shifts in the earlier novels, but it's not as extreme as in the last two books.*

---

* *Invisible* and *Sunset Park*.

IBS: Multiple perspectives make the narrative more complex, don't they?

PA: Yes, probably.

IBS: Not just with regard to the narrative perspective, it also affects the structure. Maybe the two go hand in hand?

PA: It's possible. This was the first time I felt the need to use multiple voices. It was also my first foray into writing in the second person, something I found so intriguing that I've used it now in *Winter Journal* and *Report from the Interior*.

IBS: The effect of the shift in Adam's narrative from first to second person is dramatic. It's like watching a cubist painting, where all angles are represented within one frame:

> Yes, you are impossible. You and your life are impossible, and you wonder how on earth you managed to find your way into this cul-de-sac of despair and self-loathing. Is Born alone responsible for what has happened to you? (132)

PA: Without this kaleidoscopic perspective, I didn't think it would work. The passage you just quoted would be no good in either the first or the third person. It needs another point of view. Then, of course, you don't know if Walker is telling the truth or not.

IBS: That's right, we don't know that. He refuses to tell us.

PA: Freeman, the narrator, says, "Everything has been invented, and the reader can be assured that Adam Walker is not Adam Walker." I can't remember the page, oh, here it is:

> Not even Born is Born. His real name was close to that of another Provençal poet, and I took the liberty to substitute the translation of that other poet by not-Walker with a

translation of my own, which means that the remarks about Dante's *Inferno* on the first page of this book were not in not-Walker's original manuscript. Last of all, I don't suppose it is necessary for me to add that my name is not Jim.

Westfield, New Jersey, is not Westfield, New Jersey. Echo Lake is not Echo Lake . . . (260–261)

IBS: Ah, so even "real" places in the fiction like Westfield, New Jersey, and Echo Lake, where Andy drowns, or your "real" interest in Bertran de Born are twisted here?

PA: Yes, very twisted.

IBS: The narrative structure of *Invisible* is also twisted as the final of the four sections sets itself apart from the other three: it's in diary form, and it's not named after a season. Was there a reason for leaving out "winter"?

PA: Walker's narrative is in three parts, and the fourth part, Cécile's diary, is a kind of epilogue to the book.

IBS: Still, it's quite strange because it so radically breaks the rhythm and the mood.

PA: I've done this once before—in the screenplay for *Smoke*.* Nearly every American film is devised in three acts. It's considered to be the one foolproof method for writing successful scripts, and there's not a man or woman in Hollywood who doesn't accept this structure as the bedrock premise of all filmmaking. I don't believe in any rules, so when I wrote *Smoke* I operated with a completely different structure of interlinking parts. The ending of the movie has nothing to do with what comes before, but without it the movie wouldn't make any sense. I remember how worried Wayne was about this. He said, "They're going to kill us. No one will understand what's going on, the

---

* *Smoke*, 1995, dir. Wayne Wang.

structure is so unusual it's going to be attacked." I said, "Don't worry. It hangs together, it's going to work." And it did. No one ever made a fuss about it. As I see it, the fourth and final part of *Invisible* is similar to that last part of *Smoke*. It appears to have little to do with what comes before, but if it weren't there, the book would lose its sense of fullness. So, Cécile is essential here. This is the first book in which I have three narrators. The first book to shift so radically between past and present tense, first-, second-, and third-person narration. It's a narrative collage. The material seemed to demand it: the way the story was evolving, the way the characters were developing—I simply needed these different perspectives to be able to tell the story.

IBS: It's strange how the book emerges from the material and takes form as you go along, when, from the reader's perspective, a novel like *Invisible* comes across as very carefully structured: part one, first person, past tense; part two, second person, present tense; part three, third person, back to present tense.

PA: I have to tell you, I kept running into problems with this book. The original idea was to structure the novel around three encounters between Walker and Born, each one twenty years apart: 1967, 1987, and 2007. I finished the first part (which stands in the book as is), but then I started writing the second part and didn't like it. I didn't like it at all. I wasn't sure if I could continue with the project. I put everything away and spent several months rethinking the book. Finally, I managed to find a new structure, but it was a rough go there for a while. So much doubt, so much confusion. Some books resist you. Others take you by the hand and tell you everything you need to know. This one was a struggle, but once I found my way, I sprinted to the end.

IBS: In *Invisible*, the word is not just representative and creative, it's also resurrective. Hence, I assume, your interest in Dreyer's *Ordet*[*]:

---

[*] *The Word*, dir. Carl Th. Dreyer, 1955, winner of the Golden Lion at the Venice Film Festival, 1955. The film is based on the play by Kai Munk, *Ordet*, 1932.

[I]f not for the end, *Ordet* would not have affected you more than any other good film you have seen over the years. It is the end that counts, for the end does something to you that is wholly unexpected, and it crashes into you with all the force of an axe felling an oak. (133–134)

I realize that it's Dreyer's film version and not Kai Munk's play that had such an effect on your central character, but the extent of the impact still surprises me. What is it that's so powerful here?

PA: I looked up Dreyer a few months ago in my film encyclopedia and found that we have the same birthday. I was very pleased [*laughs*]. Have you seen the film?

IBS: I think all Danes my age and older have seen it. It's based on Munk's work, and everybody knows about Kai Munk, certainly. He was the wild visionary vicar from Western Jutland, killed by the Nazis during the war.

PA: What I describe in the book is Adam's experience of watching Dreyer's film adaptation in the New Yorker Theater on Broadway— which happens to be where I saw the film for the first time myself.

IBS: But the film is ancient.

PA: It's not ancient. It's from the fifties. That's not old.

IBS: [*Laughs.*]

PA: I think I saw it in 1966. Just as I describe in *Invisible*, most of the audience burst out laughing when Inger sits up in her coffin. I didn't laugh. I thought it was extraordinary.

IBS: They laughed?! I thought it was generally perceived as uncanny and haunting.

PA: I agree. Nevertheless, half the audience responded with derision and hoots of laughter.

IBS: It's very simple, the film, don't you think? The play, too, it's unbelievably naive.

PA: There's that wonderful line when the other pastor comes to the house and says to the husband, Johannes's brother, "What's wrong with him?" and the husband replies, "Too much Kierkegaard" [*laughs*]. Anyway, going back to *Invisible*, Adam sees the film at a time of great emotional distress, and the resurrection scene gives new life to something inside him, or lifts something inside him, and he walks out of the theater in better shape than before.

IBS: Of course, there's also an element of resurrection in the annual celebrations of the deceased brother's birthday. In a sense, Andy is brought back to life every time Adam and Gwyn exchange memories of him; even more so when they begin to invent the life he would have lived had he not drowned at the age of seven. They're rather obsessive about these rituals, aren't they?

PA: Yes, the protocols have been firmly established. First dinner, and then a series of three conversations: one about Andy's past, one about the present, and one about the future.

IBS: Exactly. This is a way of keeping him alive, isn't it?

PA: Definitely. But then the moment comes when Gwyn can't take it anymore. It's over.

IBS: She feels that words can no longer bring Andy back, and she loses contact with him. "He's gone now, and we'll never find him again" (140), she says.

PA: Yes, too much time has passed. He's been dead longer than he was alive. The space is too great to cross. She can't go back anymore.

IBS: From this moment, the bond between brother and sister is no longer predicated on grief, it seems, but on sex. We cannot be certain that they actually have an incestuous relationship, but it's more than likely, and the focus of the book shifts quite radically from "the word" as the principal medium of communication to "the body": "Sex is the lord and the redeemer, the only salvation on earth" (181).

PA: Andy's death has destroyed their mother, and in some sense Gwyn and Adam have been orphaned. They spend their lives in the attic of the house and are more or less on their own.

IBS: Can you say something about the connection you make between verbal and sexual communication?

> He wonders if words aren't an essential element of sex, if talking isn't finally a more subtle form of touching, and if the images dancing in our heads aren't just as important as the bodies we hold in our arms. (181)

PA: This is in connection with Margot. My dear, damaged Margot . . .

IBS: She's mysterious . . .

PA: Very mysterious. In any case, Adam is feeling awful, and he doesn't want to have loveless sex. But then they go ahead and do it anyway:

> Margot tells him that sex is the one thing in life that counts for her, that if she couldn't have sex she would probably kill herself to escape the boredom and monotony of being trapped inside her own skin. Walker doesn't say anything, but as he comes into her for the second time, he realizes that he shares her opinion. He is mad for sex. Even in the grip of the most crushing despair, he is mad for sex. Sex is the lord and the redeemer, the only salvation on earth. (181)

IBS: Sex plays such an essential part here, probably for the first time since *The Book of Illusions*.

PA: There's a lot of sex in *The Book of Illusions*, of course, but in *Invisible* it's much more explicit.[*]

IBS: Why is that?

PA: It's so difficult to write about sex. Sex in novels is almost always inaccurate and uninteresting. In films it's usually terrible. I'm rarely swept up in it. Maybe you feel differently? It took me all these years to find the courage to write about it in such an open way.

IBS: You were so preoccupied with the properties of language in your earlier work, you still are, but now, it seems to me, a shift has occurred where the senses are much more directly in focus.

PA: Well, let's see. In thinking about my past books . . . there's actually some fairly vivid sex in *The Music of Chance* between Nashe and Fiona. In *Leviathan*, also, eroticism plays an important role in the story. It's not described at length, but there's the scene of Maria posing as a prostitute, Sachs's affair with Lillian, and Aaron's affair with Fanny. Now that I think about it, I would say it starts with *Mr. Vertigo*. That book signals a shift toward the body.

IBS: Lady Marion?

PA: Yes, but also Walt's incessant masturbation during puberty. As a grown-up, he becomes quite a randy fellow, Walt. When he encounters Mrs. Witherspoon in Chicago, he actually walks out on a business opportunity because he doesn't want to be late for his hotel tryst. Sex dominates him. *Timbuktu* is a very physical book as well.

---

[*] Later, in *Sunset Park*, Bing is actively exploring his own sexuality and Ellen is haunted by hers in a somewhat extreme manner.

We're inside the dog, we're inside Willy. The senses are prominent here: think of the olfactory experiment, the symphony of smells. What comes after *Timbuktu*? It's *The Book of Illusions* and, of course, at one point Hector becomes part of a sex-show porn act. What I'm saying is that, over the years, the physical has become more and more important in my stories. In a book like *City of Glass* there's one kiss, that's it. No sex. Even in *Ghosts*, Blue picks up a prostitute, Violet, but it's not discussed. My characters make love, but it's not central to the story in any way.

IBS: When I ask about a gravitation toward the body, I'm also thinking about a new interest in the aging and ailing body in your last six books.

PA: Well, I'm not getting any younger, am I? [*Laughs.*]

IBS: I suppose one pays more attention to the body as one gets older?

PA: I don't know, I don't know. Part of it is my desire to keep pushing into new realms, to explore new things.

IBS: Ah, but the word and the body have always interacted in your writing, all the way back to *White Spaces*. It's there from the very beginning: the strange bond between verbal and physical communication. It has been explored in many, many different ways and it takes many different forms in your writing—but it's always there.

PA: I think you're right.

IBS: This new, sharpened focus on the impaired or aging body often has to do with movement, I think, the distressing decline from agility to restricted activity.

PA: Yes, pains and pleasures.

IBS: Exactly. It seems to me that while previously your characters experienced the world principally through language, now it's as if reality is mediated more acutely through the senses. I don't know . . . this is probably a gross simplification that doesn't quite make sense.

PA: No, it makes a lot of sense. Maybe when you're young, you don't think about your body at all. Your body is working. Your appetite is good, your sexual potency is at its peak, you can stay up all night for days on end. You're young! You don't inhabit your body in the same way you do when you're older. I guess the older I've gotten, the more I've come to realize that we *are* our bodies.

IBS: Earlier you would have said, "We are our words." Think of Stillman Jr., he *is* his own speech. He's nothing more than the vocables he utters.

PA: Yes, but this is because his body has been mistreated, abused. So, it's a physical thing for him as well.

IBS: At any rate, words, your words, bring to life and keep alive. In *Invisible*, Adam has a posthumous life through Jim Freeman's completion of his shorthand drafts:

> Walker was dead, and now he was talking to me again, a dead man was talking to me, and I felt that as long as I held the letter in my hand, as long as the words of that letter were still before my eyes, it would be as if he had been resurrected, as if he had been momentarily brought back to life in the words he had written to me. (165)

In more senses than one, he's made "visible" as Jim is filling in the blanks of Adam Walker's life. Just as he and Gwyn were filling in the blanks of Andy's life.

PA: But then, isn't that what human beings are doing all the time? Isn't that what you're doing, what we're both doing, in these conversations? Filling in some—but only some—of the blanks.

SUNSET PARK. (2010)
Broken Things

IBS: In *Sunset Park* the kaleidoscopic perspective is taken a step further as the story about five major characters and their inner lives breaks into several narrative points of view. The portraits are sketched with more empathy than ever before as Morris Heller nearly goes mad with worry when his son, Miles, runs away from home and his marriage begins to fall apart. Miles spends more than a year photographing abandoned things in vacant houses, then, forced to leave Florida because of his relationship with a minor, Pilar, he returns to Brooklyn to become a squatter in a derelict house with his friend, Bing Nathan, who runs the Hospital for Broken Things, and two women equally absorbed in their work: Ellen in her pornographic drawings and Alice in her doctoral research.

PA: Yes, Alice has been studying the 1946 movie *The Best Years of Our Lives* for her dissertation on postwar America, and this is significant for the book as a whole, which is a kind of multi-generational portrait of America in the present moment. I consciously thought of it that way.

IBS: Most of the book revolves around a derelict house that was actually situated in Sunset Park here in Brooklyn, wasn't it?

PA: It was a real place, yes. I roamed around the neighborhood a few times, and one morning I came to a street that runs along the edge of Green-Wood Cemetery, with vacant lots and a partially built house that had clearly been abandoned in mid-construction. The wooden house was on that street. It was boarded up. No one lived there. I couldn't get inside, of course, but I took about a dozen pictures of the house, and I kept them on my desk while I was writing the book.

My descriptions of the house are taken directly from the real thing. After the book was published—in November 2010—National Public Radio wanted to do an interview with me, and the journalist suggested that we do it while walking around Sunset Park. I said, "Okay, let's go to the house first." When we arrived, it wasn't there anymore! It had been demolished. My photos were the only evidence that the house had ever existed—just as the only traces left of Miles's "abandoned things" are the photos he's taken of them. I felt I had been thrust into the world of my own fiction. Very strange.

IBS: So, the boundary between the real and the imagined is blurred once again?

PA: I know. Even so, the book has a kind of documentary quality to it. There are many real events woven into the fictional events in the novel. Green-Wood Cemetery is a real place, of course, and so are the people I mention who are buried there. All the baseball players are real; their deaths took place when and how I've described them. PEN and the Freedom to Write Program, all that is true. Steve Cochran was a real actor who died that strange death on the boat with those women— and yes, my mother apparently dated him for a while when she was young. This was the first time I ever set out to write a book located in the *Now*, with a capital *N*. Some of the real events I wrote about in the book had taken place just two or three months earlier, so, in effect, I found myself writing a chronicle of the moment—and what a rough moment it was: the closest thing to the Great Depression we've experienced in my lifetime. It was an odd feeling, I have to say, because I had never written a novel (as opposed to autobiographical works) in the space of the present. All my novels (nearly everyone's novels, for that matter) are set in the past. This one was set in the present.

IBS: *Sunset Park* revolves around a specific identifiable place: the house. It's described in different ways depending on who is speaking. It's almost as if there's a correlation between house and character. From Bing's perspective, it's a dopey little two-story wooden house with a roofed-over front porch, looking for all the world like something that had been stolen from a farm on the Minnesota prairie and plunked down by accident in the middle of New York. (80–81)

Miles feels that

[t]he house is like no house he has ever seen in New York . . . but this house in Sunset Park is neither suburban nor historic, it is merely a shack, a forlorn piece of architectural stupidity that would not fit in anywhere, neither in New York nor out of it. (124–125)

PA: "A forlorn piece of architectural stupidity" [*laughs*].

IBS: Yes, Miles is a little more reflective. Ellen sees the house almost exclusively from "inside." I mean, she rarely goes out, and when she finally does, it's because she has been "transformed by love." Perhaps I'm reading too much into this, but it seems to me that Ellen, much more so than any of the other core characters, lives so much "on the inside"—inside herself and inside the house.

PA: That's true. Even if she does have a job and goes to the office every day. It's just that we don't see her engaged in those activities. She also visits her sister and the baby. It's one of the good moments for her in the book.

IBS: Even so, there's very little action in *Sunset Park*. The book centers almost exclusively on portraits formed on the basis of reports from the inside perspective of each character.

PA: Each section catches a character in the middle of something and then the narrative spreads out from that moment, sometimes going backward into the past. The characters remember their lives and sometimes reflect on their memories. It's almost like a series of tableaux. An example of that approach would be when Ellen gets up early one foggy but warm December Sunday. Everyone in the house is asleep, and she's just standing on the porch thinking about who she is, who she's been, who she wants to be. There are other scenes like that: New Year's Eve, when Morris is alone in his apartment, or when Alice sits down to watch *The Best Years of Our Lives* for the twenty-eighth time—then remembers her grandparents. Yes, that's the way the book works. It's true, there's very little action. Miles falls in love with Pilar, he gets into a squabble with her sister, and he leaves Florida for New York. Morris has an affair, marital problems ensue, and his business is in trouble. Bing, Ellen, and Alice become squatters. Those are the important events. Alice breaks up with her boyfriend. Mary-Lee plays Winnie in *Happy Days*. Bing poses for Ellen. Little action, as you say, because most of the book takes place inside the heads of the characters.

IBS: This comes across also in the style of writing, I think.

PA: Mostly because I've been growing into a new way of writing sentences. I think it started in *Invisible*, but in *Sunset Park* I broke through into something else: there are sentences that go on for two or three pages. I've rarely done that before, but it seemed to me that these long, propulsive run-ons were better at capturing the meanderings of thought and reflection than short sentences. Not quite stream-of-consciousness, but something similar. It gives momentum and urgency to the characters' thoughts partly because it doesn't pretend or seek to be logical—it's associative. So you follow the twists and turns. I must say it's galvanizing to write like that. One gets swept along, and another kind of force field is generated in the process.

IBS: I felt there was almost a Proustian quality to some of those sentences that go on and on. Then, by association, of course, I thought about the name Swann.

PA: I loved the name "Mary-Lee Swann." What better name for an actress? And I'll tell you, one of the things I enjoyed doing most in the book was the Mary-Lee chapter. When she's waiting for Miles to come to her apartment for dinner, she's in an absolute frazzle. She changes her clothes four times, she orders two different dinners, her mind is spinning like a gyroscope.

IBS: Yes, she really comes off the page. Morris Heller is perhaps your most decent—most human—character ever. He has integrity, he suffers, he copes with suffering: his own and that of others. One immediately warms to him.

PA: He's the moral center of the book.

IBS: All the characters are described with tremendous compassion. For instance, here, through the narrator's take on Bing's unrequited love for Miles:

> [I]n the same way you have already vanished from his heart, have never been in his heart, have never been in anyone's heart, not even your own. (224)

"Not even your own"!

PA: I know. It's wrenching.

IBS: One of my favorite passages in *Sunset Park* is when Morris reflects on the compulsion of his best friend and his former wife to express themselves artistically:

> He has never been able to put his finger on the line that separates life from art. Renzo is the same as Mary-Lee, they are both prisoners of what they do, for years both have been plunging forward from one project to the next, both have produced lasting works of art, and yet their lives have

been a bollix, both divorced twice, both with a tremendous talent for self-pity, both ultimately inaccessible to others—not failed human beings, exactly, but not successful either. Damaged souls. The walking wounded, opening their veins and bleeding in public. (192)

It goes hand in hand, doesn't it, with Bing's perception that

[d]rumming has always been a way for him to scream, and Ellen's new drawings have turned into screams as well. (249)

Is suffering the principal source of creativity?

PA: Yes, I'm afraid to say: suffering is the principle source of creativity. There's no question about it. Perfectly happy people, if there are any, don't need to write novels or play the drums.

IBS: I think perhaps some of your best writing ever is in these portraits. They are so vivid and moving.

PA: Writing this book utterly drained me. I wrote it in an astonishing burst—and then, complete mental and physical exhaustion. It's taken me all this time* even to begin to think about writing more fiction.

IBS: You must have put a lot of work into the tailoring of style to match the inner states of the individual characters. For instance, you suddenly use stage directions in passages describing Mary-Lee Swann and diary form toward the end when communication between Morris and his wife, Willa, has come to a halt. These fairly abrupt shifts into another mode immediately link form and content, I think, and they strengthen the individual portraits. In previous novels you have changed style and tone in mid-chapter—but not genre, right?

---

* Until the autumn of 2012, when this conversation took place.

Let's look at that first difficult reunion of Mary-Lee and Miles when, suddenly, you weave in stage directions that hugely enhance the awkwardness of the moment:

> If you still cared, why run away in the first place?
> That's the big question, isn't it? (*Pause. Another sip of wine.*) Because I thought you'd be better off without me— all of you. (262)

The narrative switches over into Mary-Lee Swann's mode as the most natural thing in the world. It's as if a screenplay is being written for her, which is appropriate, given that she's an actress. We're in her world.

PA: Most of those things just came to me—without much conscious thought. But they felt right.

IBS: The intricate structure adds to the urgency, I think. The four parts are sharply focused and very dense. Two are named after father and son, Miles and Morris Heller, each divided into four numbered chapters. One is dedicated to Bing Nathan and Company and comprises four chapters, each named after a member of the group. The last part, simply entitled "All," consists of eight chapters bearing the names of six central characters. So, you use names in some headings and numbers in others. Why is that?

PA: Miles and Morris are the two most significant characters, and they stand out individually, while Bing is part of the group: "Bing Nathan and Company." That's why the different chapters in that section are named after the four members. The structure reflects this hierarchy of importance.

IBS: It makes a fine symmetry, doesn't it, where chapter division and character hierarchy go hand in hand: 4 + 4 + 4 + 8.

PA: The fact is, I'm always thinking about numbers when I compose my books. For a long time, I only wanted to write books—this is a weird confession—with an odd number of chapters, so there would be one chapter that fell dead center. There are just three of my books that don't have chapters but sections. *Mr. Vertigo*, *Invisible*, and *Sunset Park*. Those are the only books with even numbers [*laughs*]. I always thought of *Invisible* as three parts and an epilogue, and in *Mr. Vertigo* it's essentially the same, three parts and an epilogue. Then there are the books of continuous writing, with no chapters at all—*Travels in the Scriptorium*, *Man in the Dark*, *In the Country of Last Things*. In *Ghosts* there aren't even any breaks. But four somehow seemed right for *Sunset Park*, a perfect square.

IBS: It seems to me that there are several new and very exciting avenues in *Sunset Park*: the present-tense mode, for instance, the run-on sentences, the tailoring of genre to match particular thoughts and moods in a given character. You also play with narrative perspective in a different way. Except in the last section on Morris Heller where you switch to the second-person point of view, everything is reported by a third-person narrator who is entirely omniscient—even, in one instance, to the point of moving freely between Morris Heller's journal and narrative reality.* There is little direct speech, little dialogue, very few direct exchanges between characters. Even so, there's a high level of understanding and compassion between them. That's most unusual, isn't it?

PA: Most of the characters are alone throughout most of the book. They're remembering conversations, which are summarized in the narrative. That passage where Mary-Lee and Miles are reunited is one of the few times we actually have two people together. There's also the dinner at the restaurant with Morris, Mary-Lee, and her husband, Korngold. Bing and Miles talk at times, so do Alice and Ellen. Actually, maybe there's more direct communication than you think.

---

* See *Sunset Park*, 292.

IBS: Very often, we see the characters only through several layers of narration, for instance, when Miles is introduced to the squat, it's only through Alice's-report-of-Bing's-description-of-Miles.

> A man named Miles Heller will be joining them tomorrow or the day after. Bing says he is hands down the smartest, most interesting person he has ever known. (92)

Or, more radically, at one of the peak moments in the story, when the effects on Miles of the first call to his mother in over seven years are reported—not by Miles, but by Bing:

> How did she sound? Very well, Miles says. She called him a no-good shithead, an imbecile, and a rotten coward, but then she cried, then they both cried, and afterward her voice became warm and affectionate, she talked to him with far more kindness than he deserved, and hearing her again after all these years was almost too much for him. He regrets everything, he says. (250)

Why the distance here? After all, it's one of the most important moments in the story. Why will you not let us have a more direct glimpse of Miles?

PA: The indirection makes it more powerful. I describe how Bing is assimilating information. That's how we learn things in the book, almost always through another point of view.

IBS: It certainly has an interesting effect on the reader. We're doubly removed from the scene, and, at the same time, privileged by a very private and intimate take on the different characters and what goes on between them. I haven't seen this before, certainly not in your writing, this stepping back at peak moments only to provide more clarity.

PA: I wasn't even thinking about this. It just came naturally.

IBS: I think it works extremely well. Look at the way Pilar speaks. It's always through Miles, and his tone changes when he reports her speech. We never hear Pilar herself.

PA: Or the narrator reports through Miles.

IBS: Exactly! It's speech doubly reported: twice removed from the object and yet strangely intimate. And it's not a mode of narration consciously constructed?

PA: No, the spirit of the book was so alive for me, I didn't have to ask any questions. I knew what I wanted it to sound like. I knew the tone. I always do. Every book is born out of some inner music, some sense of music, and the music of each book is different from the music of every other book. I can hear it—and therefore I know what it's supposed to sound like. I think I'm repeating myself, but all I can say is that this is how it feels to me while I'm working. I'm lost in the book—the whole book, the totality of the book, even as I'm working on the individual parts of the book. I have a sense of how everything is supposed to connect. So much of it has to do with tone, and tone is all about sentences: writing the words correctly.

IBS: So, the tone shifts according to character, mood, emotion, thought—even age, for instance, when Alice remembers herself as a child thinking about Ayatollah Khomeini's fatwa on Salman Rushdie:

> [A]nd then came the news about a man living in England who had published a book that angered so many people in distant parts of the world that the bearded leader of one country actually stood up and declared that the man in England should be killed for what he had written. (227)

The voice changes completely.

PA: She's back inside her ten-year-old self.

IBS: Yes.

PA: I'm glad you're so sensitive to this. Many people don't get these shifts of tone.

IBS: I guess it's my job to notice these things [*laughs*]. Tone is crucial also in connection with Pilar. She's the most important of the female characters, right? Even so, she doesn't have a voice of her own, and, unlike Alice, Ellen, and Mary-Lee, she doesn't have her own chapter. Why is that?

PA: It wasn't necessary. You learn everything about her through other points of view. Pilar is essential, but I wanted to leave a blank. Even so, there are many intimate passages about her. Remember when Miles has a vision of her future:

> He wasn't telling her what to do, he was merely asking her to consider the matter carefully, to weigh the consequences of accepting or turning down what in all likelihood would be offered to her, and for once Pilar was silent, not willing to share her thoughts with him, and he didn't press her to say anything, for it was clear from the look in her eyes that she was already pondering this very question, trying to project herself into the future, trying to imagine what going to college in New York would mean to her or not mean to her, and as they walked among the deserted grounds and studied the facades of the buildings, he felt as if she were changing in front of him, growing older in front of him, and he suddenly understood what she would be like ten years from now, twenty years from now, Pilar in the full vigor of her evolving womanhood, Pilar all grown into herself and

> yet still walking with the shadow of the pensive girl walking beside him now, the young woman walking beside him now. (206–207)

It didn't seem necessary to give her a chapter of her own. She's so present.

IBS: Through him.

PA: Yes.

IBS: In terms of action, the pivotal moment in *Sunset Park* is when Miles overhears Morris and Willa discussing him in the kitchen:

> They were chopping him into pieces, dismembering him with the calm and efficient strokes of a pathologist conducting a post-mortem, talking about him as if they thought he was already dead. (29)

This is when he decides to disappear, and so, like several of your male protagonists, he abandons everything on the spur of the moment.

PA: Yes, it's a sudden decision. There are people in my novels who throw everything to the four winds and leave, and, of course, divestment has been one of our themes in these discussions. Think of Nashe in *The Music of Chance*. He has his reasons for disappearing: his wife has left him, he's inherited a lot of money, so he feels free to do what he wants.

IBS: Marco does it.

PA: Marco does it. He's evicted from his apartment, but of course, in his case it's willful and self-sabotaging. There are ninety ways he could have stayed there, but the boy's brain is addled, and he believes in the spiritual value of passivity [*laughs*]. Who else is there? Benjamin Sachs takes off. That's because he's killed someone. Hector Mann takes off as well. Another murder, but not one he committed himself.

IBS: They all have a reason to make their divestment abrupt and radical.

PA: With Miles, it's a little different: radical but not so abrupt. Bobby's death has been eating away at him for a long time. Then he overhears the fatal conversation between his father and stepmother. It's so devastating to him that he runs away.

IBS: And abandons everything. Of course, your interest in abandoned things is taken to another level in *Sunset Park*: here it has become a regular job to clear them out of the empty houses. Miles not only removes these traces of absent people's lives—he also takes it upon himself to record them. It's announced already in the opening line: "For almost a year now, he has been taking photographs of abandoned things." Later, Miles is stirred by his realization that

> [t]here were the abandoned things down in Florida, and now he has stumbled upon the abandoned people of Brooklyn. He suspects it is a terrain well worth exploring. (133)

PA: I read an article in the *New York Times* about these trash-out workers. It made a big impression on me, and I gave that job to Miles because it seemed to fit his personality.

IBS: I can see why it would make an impression on you. You've been writing about this for more than thirty years [*laughs*].

PA: [*Laughs*] Perhaps. But I never knew there was such a job— trash-out worker, subcontracted by the banks that have foreclosed on unpaid mortgages.

IBS: It's trash removal only, right? They're not hired to make a record of what was left behind in these houses.

PA: No, their job is to clean them up so the banks can sell them.

IBS: Right, so taking photos is Miles's own idea.

PA: It's his own idea. The other guys are stealing things, but Miles just takes his photos. He doesn't want things. He wants *the pictures* of things, the images rather than the objects.

IBS: Since *In the Country of Last Things* you've had people collecting trash, treasuring objects left behind, renaming broken items, writing about them. As I see it, these acts serve to situate or to preserve the abandoned things—if only for a little while.

PA: That's right. Here, as in *Smoke*, things are captured and recorded—not in words but in pictures.

IBS: Ellen is also seeking to represent an absence in her somewhat disturbing drawings:

> She wanted to make pictures that would evoke the mute wonder of pure thingness, the holy ether breathing in the spaces between things, a translation of human existence into a minute rendering of all that is *out there* beyond us, around us, in the same way she knows the invisible graveyard is standing there in front of her, even if she cannot see it. (115)

PA: I think this is what great painting does.

IBS: Invisible and yet tangible?

PA: Yes, the thingness of that which you can touch. Ellen is looking for a kind of transcendence in the actual. Think of the effect Vermeer can have on an attentive viewer. Everything just as ordinary as can be, a woman looking out a window—but you feel that you're in the presence of something holy and eternal. Even if I don't believe in God, I feel a divine presence when I look at Vermeer. That's what Ellen is trying to achieve in her art.

IBS: At the same time, she's recording something broken, isn't she, a kind of inner disconnection or blank?

> She is advancing now, travelling deeper and deeper into the netherworld of her own nothingness, the place in her that coincides with what she is not. (215)

PA: I think she's vanishing from herself, and in doing so she sees herself from a different perspective. We were talking about this the other day in relation to love. How it is that in giving yourself away, disappearing from yourself, you open up the connecting space between two people—*the between*. Here, it's not about two people; it's happening inside her. Ellen is a troubled person, continually on the edge of breaking down. Let's see . . .

> The sky above her is gray or blue or white, sometimes yellow or red, at times purple. The earth below her is green or brown. Her body stands at the juncture of earth and sky, and it belongs to her and no one else. Her thoughts belong to her. Her desires belong to her. Stranded in the realm of the one, she conjures up the two and three and four and five. Sometimes the six. Sometimes even the sixty. (215)

It's a statement of her disarray. She feels that she's evaporating, and she's trying to bring herself back to life. This paragraph doesn't really explicate Ellen's confusion, it embodies it, enacts the process of thinking.

IBS: There's that moment of the void, which we've talked about before.

PA: The void is where we cease to be.

IBS: It's also that fruitful moment of creativity, right? It's the place "in between" where things happen, the blank that triggers and prompts and determines. It changes from book to book, but "the place of nothingness" is a recurring figure in your writing. Basically, it's what we've been calling "white spaces," isn't it?

PA: Yes, it's a kind of metaphysical void, but it can also be in the room, inside a person, or a person out under the sky, the incomprehensible bigness. Melville's "howling infinite."

IBS: It's interesting here: "her own nothingness." You haven't said that before. Quinn in *City of Glass* seeks a "nothingness," and "he was finally nowhere" toward the end of the story. Marco also reaches a dead end in *Moon Palace* and eventually learns the importance of leaping across blank spaces.

PA: And here Morris feels

> stranded in the middle of nowhere. By late afternoon, you have begun to resign yourself to the fact that nowhere is your home now and that is where you will be spending the last years of your life. (282)

"Nowhere" here refers to the inconstant place where Morris finds himself abandoned by both his wife and son while at the same time feeling torn between them. It's a kind of exaggerated comment on the fact that, like so many characters in my books, Morris is trying to come to terms with ambiguity. Things are not going to be resolved, and he has to learn to live with it. This is what he's teaching himself.

IBS: Yes, you leave things uncertain in relation to both Willa and Miles.

PA: He refuses to abandon either one, even if Willa wants nothing to do with Miles anymore. One senses, however, that Willa will eventually come around. She really does love Morris, and I think they'll get over their problems. His near-death has changed everything, and she's going to forgive Miles. The question is whether Miles is going to forgive himself. We get a last glimpse of him traveling across the Brooklyn Bridge.

IBS: You've left several questions open, and we're uncertain about how it ends. There was now a second act of violence, which makes you think that, perhaps, the first violent act was not quite as innocent as we want to believe. Maybe there is something to it, after all, maybe he actually did push Bobby out in front of the car deliberately.

PA: I wanted it to be uncertain. Miles is in despair again. He's worked so hard for so many years *not* to be the person-who-punches, and now he's punched again. Even though it was probably justified (he was defending Alice, after all), he still feels terrible about what he's done. Objectively speaking, however, it's not the end of the world. He might be charged with assaulting a police officer, but since it's a first offense, he'll probably get off with a fine or a suspended sentence. His future is not so bleak. It just feels bleak to him at that moment.

IBS: Since *Sunset Park* came out in 2010, you've written the two autobiographical works, *Winter Journal* and *Report from the Interior*, and you told me the other day that you are now working on fiction again.

PA: Yes, I've started a new book. If I can pull it off, it may become a big book. I've been enjoying myself so far, and every day I sit at my desk and tell myself how lucky I am to be doing this. Bit by bit by bit, I think I've become better at what I do. In some way, each book has been better than the one before it. Or rather, I've kept pushing toward a greater understanding of what it is I do or what I'm trying to say. Failing better, as it were. I don't know, does this make sense?

IBS: Yes, we've talked about this before, when you said it's as if there's a rhythm of alternation between big books and small books, complex books and simple books. It makes perfect sense that the writing has become sharper, bolder, and more intricate in a simpler form. I mean, in a book like *Sunset Park* there's so much going on inside a simple frame and a reasonably ordinary cast of characters. Personally, I think *Sunset Park* is an absolute masterpiece. But, of course, it depends on what criteria you use when you talk about good books.

PA: It also depends on the mood I'm in when I say they get better.

IBS: [*Laughs.*]

COMPLETE LIST OF WORKS BY PAUL AUSTER

AUTOBIOGRAPHICAL WORKS

The Invention of Solitude, New York: SUN, 1982
Hand to Mouth: A Chronicle of Early Failure, New York: Henry Holt, 1997
The Red Notebook: True Stories, New York: New Directions, 2002
Winter Journal, New York: Henry Holt, 2012
Report from the Interior, New York: Henry Holt, 2013

NOVELS

City of Glass, Los Angeles: Sun & Moon Press, 1985
Ghosts, Los Angeles: Sun & Moon Press, 1986
The Locked Room, Los Angeles: Sun & Moon Press, 1986
The New York Trilogy, London: Faber & Faber, 1987; New York: Penguin, 1990
In the Country of Last Things, New York: Viking, 1987
Moon Palace, New York: Viking, 1989
The Music of Chance, New York: Viking, 1990
Leviathan, New York: Viking, 1992
Mr. Vertigo, New York: Viking, 1994
Timbuktu, New York: Henry Holt, 1999
The Book of Illusions, New York: Henry Holt, 2002
Oracle Night, New York: Henry Holt, 2003
The Brooklyn Follies, New York: Henry Holt, 2005
Travels in the Scriptorium, New York: Henry Holt, 2006
Man in the Dark, New York: Henry Holt, 2008
  Republished in one volume, *Day/Night: Two Novels*, New York: Picador, 2013
Invisible, New York: Henry Holt, 2009
Sunset Park, New York: Henry Holt, 2010
4 3 2 1, New York: Henry Holt, 2017

OTHER PROSE

White Spaces, Barrytown, NY: Station Hill, 1980
The Art of Hunger: Essays, Prefaces, Interviews, Los Angeles: Sun & Moon Press, 1992
Why Write?, Providence: Burning Deck, 1996

Double Game (with Sophie Calle), Violette Editions, 1999; 2007

Collected Prose: Autobiographical Writings, True Stories, Critical Essays, Prefaces, and Collaborations with Artists, London: Faber & Faber, 2003; New York: Picador, 2005

Here and Now: Letters 2008–2011 (with J. M. Coetzee), New York: Viking, 2013

Conversations with Paul Auster (ed. by James M. Hutchisson), Jackson: University Press of Mississippi, 2013

ILLUSTRATED BOOKS

City of Glass: The Graphic Novel (adaptation by Paul Karasik and David Mazzucchelli), New York: Avon Books, 1994; Picador, 2004

The Story of My Typewriter (with paintings by Sam Messer), New York: D.A.P., 2002

Auggie Wren's Christmas Story (with Isol), New York: Henry Holt, 2003

POETRY

Unearth, New York: Living Hand, 1974

Wall Writing, Berkeley: The Figures, 1976

Fragments from Cold, New York: Parenthèse, 1977

Facing the Music, New York: Station Hill, 1980

Disappearances: Selected Poems, New York: Overlook Press, 1988

Autobiography of the Eye, Portland: Beaverdam Press, 1993

Collected Poems, New York: Overlook Press, 2004

FILMS

Smoke & Blue in the Face, New York: Hyperion, 1995

Lulu on the Bridge, New York: Henry Holt, 1998

The Inner Life of Martin Frost, New York: Picador, 2007

Collected Screenplays, London: Faber & Faber, 2010

EDITOR

The Random House Book of Twentieth-Century French Poetry: With Translations by American and British Poets, New York: Random House, 1982

*I Thought My Father Was God, and Other True Tales from NPR's National
Story Project*, New York: Henry Holt, 2001
(British edition) *True Tales of American Life*, London: Faber & Faber, 2002
Samuel Beckett: The Grove Centenary Edition, New York: Grove Press, 2006

TRANSLATIONS (SELECTED)

A Little Anthology of Surrealist Poems, New York: Siamese Banana Press,
1972
Fits and Starts: Selected Poems of Jacques Dupin, Weston: Living Hand, 1973
The Uninhabited: Selected Poems of André du Bouchet, New York: Living
Hand, 1976
Life/Situations: Essays Written and Spoken, by Jean-Paul Sartre, New York:
Pantheon, 1977 (with Lydia Davis)
African Trio, by Georges Simenon (*Aboard the Aquitaine*), New York: Har-
court, 1979 (with Lydia Davis)
A Tomb for Anatole, by Stéphane Mallarmé, San Francisco: North Point
Press, 1983; New York: New Directions, 2005
The Notebooks of Joseph Joubert, San Francisco: North Point Press, 1983;
New York: New York Review Books, 2005
Vicious Circles: Two Fictions and "After the Fact," by Maurice Blanchot,
New York: Station Hill, 1985
On the High Wire, by Philippe Petit, New York: Random House, 1985
Joan Miró: Selected Writings and Interviews, Boston: G. K. Hall, 1986
Chronicle of the Guayaki Indians, by Pierre Clastres, New York: Zone
Books, 1998
Openwork: Poetry and Prose, by André du Bouchet, New Haven: Yale Uni-
versity Press, 2014 (with Hoyt Rogers)

BIBLIOGRAPHY

Alford, Steven E. "Mirrors of Madness: Paul Auster's The New York Trilogy." *Critique* 37, no. 1 (Fall 1995): 16–32.

Barone, Dennis, ed. *Beyond the Red Notebook: Essays on Paul Auster.* Philadelphia: University of Pennsylvania Press, 1995.

Bellinelli, Matteo. *Paul Auster: Le trame della scrittura.* Bellinzona, Switzerland: Casagrande, 2005.

Bewes, Timothy. "Against the Ontology of the Present: Paul Auster's Cinematographic Fictions." *Twentieth Century Literature* 53, no. 3 (Fall 2007): 273–297.

Bilton, Alan. *An Introduction to Contemporary American Fiction.* New York: New York University Press, 2003.

Bloom, Harold. *Paul Auster.* Philadelphia: Chelsea House Publishers, 2004.

Bökös, Borbála. "On Intermedial References in Paul Auster's and Wayne Wang's *Smoke* (1995)." *University of Bucharest Review*, no. 1 (2011): 20–30.

Boulter, Jonathan. *Melancholy and the Archive: Trauma, History and Memory in the Contemporary Novel.* London: Continuum, 2011.

Brown, Mark. *Paul Auster.* Manchester: Manchester University Press, 2007.

Busse, Beatrix. "'One Should Never Underestimate the Power of Books': Writing and Reading as Therapy in Paul Auster's Novels." In *Beyond Cognitive Metaphor Theory, Perspectives on Literary Metaphor,* edited by Monica Fludernik, 177–195. New York: Routledge, 2011.

Butler, Martin, and Jens Martin Gurr. "The Poetics and Politics of Metafiction: Reading Paul Auster's *Travels in the Scriptorium.*" *English Studies* 89, no. 2 (2008): 195–209.

Chénetier, Marc de. *Paul Auster as the Wizard of Odds: "Moon Palace."* Paris: Didier Erudition, 1996.

Ciocia, Stefania, and Jesús A. González. *The Invention of Illusions: International Perspectives on Paul Auster.* Newcastle upon Tyne: Cambridge Scholars, 2011.

Clark, James. *Rather Have the Blues: The Novels of Paul Auster, The Films of Jacques Demy.* Toronto: Springtime Publishers, 2008.

Contat, Michel, and Paul Auster. "The Manuscript in the Book: Conversation." *Yale French Studies* 89 (1996): 160–187.

Cortanze, Gérard de. *Paul Auster's New York*. Livre de Poche, 1997.

Conrtanze, Gérard de. *La Solitude du labyrinthe: Essai et entretiens*. Arles: Actes Sud, 1997.

Cortanze, Gérard de, and James Rudnick. *Le New York de Paul Auster*. Paris: Editions du Chêne, 1996.

Dion, Michel. *L'être et le crime: Cinq romans-phares*. Montréal: Éditions Nota bene, 2013.

Donovan, Christopher. *Postmodern Counternarratives: Irony and Audience in the Novels of Paul Auster, Don DeLillo, Charles Johnson, and Tim O'Brien*. New York: Routledge, 2005.

Duperray, Annick. *Paul Auster, Les ambiguïtés de la négation*. Paris: Editions Belin, 2003.

Duperray, Annick. *L'oeuvre de Paul Auster: Approches et lectures plurielles*. Arles: Actes Sud/Université de Provence, 1995.

Eckhard, Petra. *Chronotopes of the Uncanny: Time and Space in Postmodern New York Novels. Paul Auster's "City of Glass" and Toni Morrison's "Jazz."* Bielefeld: Transcript, 2011.

Engelmann, Jonas. *"Welches Vergessen erinnere ich?" Auschwitz im Werk von Paul Auster und Hubert Fichte*. Marburg: Tectum, 2007.

Finkelstein, Norman. "In the Realm of the Naked Eye: The Poetry of Paul Auster." In *Beyond the Red Notebook: Essays on Paul Auster*, edited by Dennis Barone, 44–60. Philadelphia: University of Pennsylvania Press, 1995.

Ford, Mark. "Inventions of Solitude: Thoreau and Auster." *Journal of American Studies* 33, no. 2 (1999): 201–219.

Gavillon, François. *Paul Auster, gravité et légèreté de l'écriture*. Rennes: Presses universitaires de Rennes, 2000.

Grandjeat, Yves-Charles. *Réussir l'épreuve de littérature, "Moon Palace," Paul Auster*. Paris: Ellipses, 1996.

Handler, Nina. *Drawn Into the Circle of Its Repetitions: Paul Auster's "New York Trilogy."* San Bernardino, CA: Borgo Press, 1996.

Herforth, Maria Felicitas. *Erläuterungen zu Paul Auster, "Moon Palace."* Hollfeld: Bange, 2009.

Herzogenrath, Bernd. *An Art of Desire: Reading Paul Auster*. Amsterdam: Rodopi, 1999.

Holzapfel, Anne M. *"The New York Trilogy": Whodunit?: Tracking the Structure of Paul Auster's Anti-Detective Novels*. Frankfurt am Main: Peter Lang, 1996.

Kammerer, Hilmar. *Paul Auster: "Moon Palace."* Freising: Stark, 2001.

Krämer, Kathrin. *Walking in Deserts, Writing out of Wounds: Jewishness and Deconstruction in Paul Auster's Literary Work.* Universitätsverlag Winter, 2008.

Kuczma, Katarzyna. *Remembering Oneself, Charting the Other: Memory as Intertextuality and Self-Reflexivity in the Works of Paul Auster.* Wissenschaftlicher Verlag Trier, 2012.

Martin, Brendan. *Paul Auster's Postmodernity.* New York: Routledge, 2008.

Nealon, Jeffrey T. "Work of the Detective, Work of the Writer: Paul Auster's City of Glass." In Detecting Texts: The Metaphysical Detective Story from Poe to Postmodernism, edited by Patricia Merivale and Elizabeth Sweeney, 117–134. Philadelphia: University of Pennsylvania Press, 1999.

O'Brien, John. *Paul Auster, Danilo Kiš.* Normal, IL: Review of Contemporary Fiction, 1994.

Patteson, Richard F. "The Teller's Tale: Text and Paratext in Paul Auster's *Oracle Night.*" *Critique* 49, no. 2 (2008): 115–128.

Peacock, James. *Understanding Paul Auster.* Columbia: University of South Carolina Press, 2010.

Peacock, Jim. "Carrying the Burden of Representation: Paul Auster's *The Book of Illusions.*" *Journal of American Studies* 40, no. 1 (April 2006): 53–69.

Pesso-Miquel, Catherine. *Toiles trouées et déserts lunaires dans "Moon Palace" de Paul Auster.* Paris: Presses de la Sorbonne nouvelle, 1996.

Rowen, Norma. "The Detective in Search of the Lost Tongue of Adam: Paul Auster's City of Glass." *Critique* 32, no. 4 (1991): 224–234.

Rubin, Derek. "'The Hunger Must Be Preserved at All Costs': A Reading of *The Invention of Solitude.*" In *Beyond the Red Notebook: Essays on Paul Auster*, edited by Dennis Barone, 60–71. Philadelphia: University of Pennsylvania Press, 1995.

Russell, Alison. "Deconstructing The New York Trilogy: Paul Auster's Anti-Detective Fiction." *Critique* 31, no. 2 (Winter 1990): 71–84.

Saed, Ivonne. *Sobre Paul Auster: Autoría, Distopía y Textualidad.* Mexico City: Lectorum, 2009.

Salmela, Markku. *Paul Auster's Spatial Imagination.* Tampere University Press, 2006.

Sarmento, Clara. *As Palavras, a Página e o Livro: A Construção literária na obra de Paul Auster.* Lisbon: Ulmeiro, 2001.

Sauer-Kretschmer, Simone, and Christian A. Bachmann, eds. *Paul Auster: Beiträge zu Werk und Poetik.* Essen: Bachmann, 2012.

Scardino, Rafaela. *Movimentos de Demolição: Deslocamentos, identidades e Literatura*. Vitória, Brazil: Edufes, 2011.

Shiloh, Ilana. "A Place Both Imaginary and Realistic: Paul Auster's *The Music of Chance*." *Contemporary Literature* 43, no. 3 (Autumn 2002): 488–517.

Shiloh, Ilana. *Paul Auster and Postmodern Quest: On the Road to Nowhere*. New York: Peter Lang, 2012.

Simon, Anke. *Paul Auster, "Moon Palace."* Paderborn: Schöningh, 2007.

Slethaug, G. "From Auster to Wang: Postmodern Indeterminacy, 'Auggie Wren's Christmas Story,' and *Smoke*." *Literature and Aesthetics*, no. 10 (2000): 127–146.

Soucy, Pierre-Yves. *L'oeil et le mur: sur la poésie de Paul Auster*. Bruxelles: La Lettre Volée, 2003.

Springer, Carsten. *Crises: The Works of Paul Auster*. Frankfurt: Peter Lang, 2001.

Springer, Carsten. *A Paul Auster Sourcebook*. Frankfurt: Peter Lang, 2001.

Süßenguth, Martina. *"A Poet of the Eye"—the Role of Art in Paul Auster's Works*. Marburg: Tectum Verlag, 2014.

Theobald, Tom. *Existentialism and Baseball: The French Philosophical Roots of Paul Auster*. Lambert Academic Publishing, 2010.

Trofimova, Evija. *Paul Auster's Writing Machine: A Thing to Write With*. New York: Bloomsbury Academic, 2014.

Tulinius, Torfi H. *Bjartur og frú Emilía* no. 1 (1997).

Vanskike, Elliott Lee. "Reading Masochistically: The Workings of Frustration in the Fiction of Gertrude Stein, Alain Robbe-Grillet, Paul Auster, Kathy Acker, and J.G. Ballard" (PhD thesis, University of Iowa, 2000).

Varvogli, Aliki. *The World That Is the Book: Paul Auster's Fiction*. Liverpool: Liverpool University Press, 2001.

Vidal, Jean-Pierre. *Babel et après: Paul Auster*. Tangence, Rimouski, 1994.

INDEX

PAUL AUSTER is one of the very few giants of English-language literature who has successfully made the leap from the twentieth to the twenty-first century. A poet and translator before he achieved international prominence as a memoirist and novelist, Auster continues to challenge and dazzle his readers in America and around the world. His most recent novel is *4 3 2 1*.

I. B. SIEGUMFELDT is an associate professor of English, Germanic, and Romance Studies at the University of Copenhagen in Denmark, and the driving force behind the university's forthcoming Center for Paul Auster Studies.